Parent Education as Early Childhood Intervention: Emerging Directions in Theory, Research and Practice

ANNUAL ADVANCES IN APPLIED DEVELOPMENTAL PSYCHOLOGY VOLUME 3

VOLUME EDITOR:

Douglas R. Powell
Purdue University

SERIES EDITOR:

Irving E. Sigel
Educational Testing Service

ABLEX PUBLISHING CORPORATION
NORWOOD, NEW JERSEY

ISBN: 0-89391-502-5   ISSN: 0748-8572

Ablex Publishing Corporation
355 Chestnut Street
Norwood, New Jersey 07648

Contents

List of Contributors

Douglas R. Powell (Editor)
Department of Child Development
 and Family Studies
Purdue University
West Lafayette, IN 47907

Irving Sigel (Series Editor)
Educational Testing Service
Princeton, NJ 08541

Linda Barbera-Stein
National Committee for Prevention of
 Child Abuse
332 South Michigan Ave.
Suite 950
Chicago, IL 60604

Moncrieff Cochran
Department of Human Development
 and Family Studies
Cornell University
Ithaca, NY 14853

Carl J. Dunst
Family, Infant and Preschool
 Program
Human Development Research and
 Training Institute
Western Carolina Center
Morganton, NC 28655

Robert Halpern
Erikson Institute
25 West Chicago Avenue
Chicago, IL 60610

Alice Sterling Honig
Department of Child, Family, and
 Community Studies
Syracuse University
Syracuse, NY 13210

J. Ronald Lally
Far West Laboratory for Educational
 Research and Development
1855 Folsom Street
San Francisco, Ca 94103

Mary Larner
High/Scope Educational Research
 Foundation
600 North River Street
Ypsilanti, MI 48197

Peter L. Mangione
Far West Laboratory for Educational
 Research and Development
1855 Folsom Street
San Francisco, CA 94103

Burton Mindick
Department of Sociology
Cornell University
Ithaca, NY 14853

Judith Musick
Ounce of Prevention Fund
188 West Randolph
Suite 2200
Chicago, IL 60601

Carol Trivette
Family, Infant and Preschool
   Program
Human Development Research and
   Training Institute
Western Carolina Center
Morganton, NC 28655

Donald G. Unger
Department of Individual and Family
   Studies
University of Delaware
Newark, DE 19711

Lois Pall Wandersman
Department of Preventive Medicine
   and Community Health
School of Medicine
University of South Carolina
Columbia, SC 19716

Preface for Volume 3
Advances in Applied Developmental Psychology

Irving E. Sigel
Educational Testing Service

This is the third volume in the *Advances in Applied Developmental Psychology* series. The mission of the series is to present research reports or concept papers which deal with applied developmental issues.

The field of Applied Developmental Psychology is becoming an area of interest to many researchers and practitioners, those individuals who see the relevance of Developmental Psychology for dealing with real-life problems. The challenge is to link what has been learned from basic research in developmental psychology to the everyday problems facing educators, clinicians, policy makers and social activists. Applied developmental psychology not only involves the application of basic research findings, but also the generating of new information obtained in a practical setting. One way is to engage in research evaluating intervention programs in areas involving developmental concerns and in this way identifying the specific experimental treatment effects; in other words, the effectiveness of a particular program.

What area is closer to the basic questions of human development than research with families? Considerable research has been done by developmental psychologists studying how parents influence the course of children's development. Much has been learned about the positive and negative aspects inherent in childrearing. The research so obtained has mostly been done in laboratory-type settings with little or no attention paid to the social implications of the research. What is to be done with the findings from these basic research studies? Well, one of the outcomes would be to establish intervention programs using the research from psychology and related disciplines to alter the way parents interact with their children.

This volume, organized and edited by Douglas R. Powell, is just that. The writers in this volume, all experienced investigators, have directed considerable thought and energy to the questions regarding influencing parents by creating programs which would be of benefit to them. Evaluations of these programs tell us much about program effectiveness: what works and what does not work. Intervention programs also teach us much about the way parents and children think, relate and develop. Evaluation of intervention programs can be useful in two ways, one to test effectiveness of a program and the other to generate new knowledge about human functioning, social contexts in particular.

This is what this volume is all about. Its mission is consistent with the program of the *Advances in Applied Developmental Psychology* series. It demonstrates how developmental psychology contributes in a socially useful way to further the psychological health of our citizens. In addition, these studies have much to teach us about how to do research with families in action-based programs. The assessment problems are complex since methods do not have the purity of design and measurement typical of controlled studies. The environment is often not under the control of the investigators, and the usual experimental design controls which are usually manageable in laboratories have to be modified if the work is to be done. Since there is general agreement that program evaluation is critical to justify program continuation, then it behooves investigators to develop methods which are reliable and valid. This volume addresses issues of that type.

Dr. Powell and his colleagues are to be commended for producing a thoughtful set of chapters which in their totality express the issues and findings and identify problems to be solved in the field of parent education. The link between research and practice is well documented in this volume. The chapters will demonstrate to developmental psychologists that the theoretical and empirical results of their work and the world of practical living intersect—each feeding the other—thereby contributing to the social good.

Chapter 1
Emerging Directions in Parent–Child Early Intervention

Douglas R. Powell
Purdue University

Since the late 1960s, parent education has been widely and eagerly pursued as an intervention strategy for improving the cognitive and social functioning of children considered at developmental risk due to the low-income status of their family, the young age of their parent, or a handicapping condition. The enthusiasm for working with parents has far surpassed the level of available knowledge about ways to provide parent education to families living in high-risk circumstances. Parent education has been primarily a white, middle-class enterprise. Throughout the field's long history, only periodic and scattered attempts have been made to work with low-income and ethnic populations (see Schlossman, 1976). In the 1960s there was limited program experience and an exceptionally meager research base to inform the design and implementation of the many parent-focused early intervention programs established. It did not take long for questions to arise regarding the feasibility and effectiveness of traditional parent education content and methods, deeply rooted in middle-class values, for parents facing stressful situations.

Significant diversity in program approaches has resulted from more than two decades of experimentation with programs for families of at-risk children. More importantly, a concomitant set of changes is emerging in: (a) the field's interest in matching program design to population characteristics, (b) the roles of staff and parents in programs, and (c) the programmatic consideration of contextual determinants of parenting. These directions forecast a major paradigm shift in the field of parent education. Yet, if the current substantive ferment is to yield useful guidelines for the theory and practice of interventions with parents, research data and program analyses must be marshalled for a careful assessment of the problems and benefits of the strategy in general and the emergent trends in particular.

The purpose of this volume is to extend our understanding of the use of parent education in early childhood intervention programs, especially in view of the evolving directions noted above. To do so, we opt for depth over breadth. The volume draws upon the experiences of six prominent parent–child intervention programs to examine research and theoretical frameworks of parent-focused interventions; to report research on program effects and variations in program utili-

1

zation; and to identify and analyze issues in the development and implementation of parent programs. Collectively, the chapters provide a theoretical and empirical basis for clarifying the issues and pointing to needed directions in the scope, design, and evaluation of early intervention aimed at parents of at-risk children.

The developments giving rise to the substance of this volume may be summarized as follows. Since the late 1960s, there has been growing interest in the use of parent education as a form or a major component of early childhood intervention. Consequently, a field with white, middle-class roots has been called upon to serve populations and circumstances not addressed in a systematic or extensive fashion prior to the late 1960s. The resulting program experiences, combined with profound social and demographic changes in American society, have triggered the evolution of new directions in the methods and content of programs aimed at parents of young children deemed to be developmentally at risk. These emerging directions hold the potential for major advances in the design, implementation, and evaluation of educational and support programs for parents. For such advances to occur, however, there must be thoughtful examinations of intervention rationales, processes, and effects. The emerging directions pose new challenges and questions that require research data and critical program analyses if the trends are to result in advances in the field. It is toward this end that the present volume has been formulated.

In this introductory chapter I provide a context for the volume by, first, describing briefly the factors influencing the growth of parent education in early childhood intervention programs in the past 20 years; and, second, by examining the nature and antecedents of the three emerging directions in the field. I conclude with an introduction to each chapter in the volume.

PARENT EDUCATION AND THE AT-RISK CHILD

In the 1960s the interest in educational programs for parents of at-risk children was propelled by a core assumption of the early childhood intervention movement regarding the family. Deficient home environments were thought to contribute to low skill levels of "disadvantaged" children at school entry (see Laosa, 1984; Cooke, 1979; Gallagher, Haskins, & Farran, 1979). Parents were seen as a likely entry point for intervention in breaking the cycle of poverty. By giving parents information and skills in rearing the young child, it was assumed children from low-income homes would fare better in school, secure employable skills, and eventually find work that paid above poverty wages. A variety of parental attributes was seen as deficient, including achievement attitudes, verbal interactions with the child, and the organization and predictability of the home environment. This prevailing assumption about the family became known as the deficit model and, as discussed later in this chapter, increasingly was criticized as an inappropriate premise of early intervention.

The focus on parents as a target of change in early intervention programs was not surprising. The educational establishment has long viewed the home (i.e., mothers) as a major determinant of child functioning. Years ago, Johann Pestalozzi (1747-1827) argued that, for children, "the teaching of their parents will always be the core"; the role of the school teacher is to provide a "decent shell" around the core (Pestalozzi, 1951, p. 26). Research studies in the 1960s and 1970s fueled this belief by concluding that such child background characteristics as family socioeconomic status were more powerful than schools in predicting a child's academic performance (Coleman et al., 1966; Jencks et al., 1972). Moreover, all theories of child development have suggested that lay persons need expert guidance in the rearing of young children (Kessen, 1979). It has been popular to argue that children need and deserve a trained parent (Bell, 1975; Rheingold, 1973).

The 1960s certainly were not the first time parent education was employed as an instrument of social reform. In the Progressive Era, for instance, members of the Parent–Teacher Association (then known as the National Congress of Mothers) functioned as "moral and scientific missionaries" to the poor, offering guidance in child rearing and domestic management (Schlossman, 1976, p. 450). Parent education also was a central component of settlement house services to immigrant families with young children. Prior to the 1960s, programs for low-income and ethnic parents represented a minor deviation from the middle-class mainstay of parent education programs. Earlier efforts aimed at the poor largely were charitable acts sponsored by philanthropic organizations. This is in marked contrast with the current wave of parent programs, which is embedded in a substantial public commitment to the provision of educational opportunity to disenfranchised populations. Yet the premises and practices of earlier forms of parent education for the poor are strikingly similar to the parameters of many programs established in the 1960s' early intervention movement.

The early childhood intervention movement of the 1960s reinforced the notion that low-income parents need training to a greater extent than parents of other economic strata. The federal government's huge commitment to early intervention continued the public policy practice of defining the needs of children largely on the basis of the socioeconomic status of their families (Laosa, 1984). The "at-risk" or "disadvantaged" child designation referred to assumptions about the adequacy of the child's environment and not the child per se. The early intervention movement perpetuated a tradition, evident in such earlier causes as the settlement house movement (Levine & Levine, 1970), where the presumed superior character and world view of mainstream society was to be passed on to less advantaged people.

In the 1970s, the use of parent education in early intervention gained momentum with the growth of societal concern about the quality of American family life. Teenage pregnancy rates, increases in divorce, the rise in numbers of single-parent households, public awareness of child abuse and neglect, the escalation of maternal employment, and concern about the effects of unemployment and economic instability on children were in the forefront of American public policy considerations. President Jimmy Carter's administration created an Office for Families, and changed the name of the Office of Child Development to the Administration for Children, Youth and Families. Public interest in the welfare of children was embedded within concerns about the ability of the family to function as a nurturing child-rearing system. These societal preoccupations strengthened the commitment to parent education as an early intervention approach, and contributed to the development of an emphasis on family functioning in parent programs (see subsequent discussion in this chapter). What is more, a 1974 report on the effects of early intervention concluded that programs involving both parent and child were more effective than programs focused primarily or exclusively on the child (Bronfenbrenner, 1974). This analysis was influential in the intervention field and public policy decisions by providing an empirical rationale for a concept American society had long valued.

Thus, programs launched as part of the early childhood intervention movement, beginning in the mid-1960s, reflected the shift from an almost exclusive focus on children to an interest in the roles of parents, and eventually a move to an ecological systems perspective emphasizing family and community influences on child development (Powell, 1982). The evolution of Head Start, the federal government's largest and most comprehensive early childhood program, is exemplary of the change. In contrast to its 1965 beginnings as a summer program for children from low-income families, Head Start now mandates parent involvement and in the early 1970s developed several program models that approached parents as the primary recipient of services. These programs included Home Start, the Parent Child Centers, and the Child and Family Resource Program. Each emphasized the parents' understanding and use of educational, health, and social services in the community; the Child and Family Resource Program was the most comprehensive demonstration model in terms of the emphasis on families.

Pragmatic considerations also affected the emphasis on parent education. The renewed interest in environmental influences on the child and the presumed malleability of children, prompted largely by Hunt's (1961) work, led to the notion that the family is in a much better position than a preschool program to provide long-term stimulation and support for the child. Work with parents in the preschool years was viewed as far more economical than the continuation of costly child-oriented interventions throughout a child's schooling. This idea secured additional support in the 1970s, when it became clear the inoculation approach to early intervention was not effective. Continuous intervention, as opposed to a single dose in the early years, was seen as necessary, and the family was considered a logical system for providing an ongoing form of educational support for the child (Zigler & Berman, 1983).

In addition, changes in parents were expected to have impact on other children in the family, thereby maximizing the return on the economic investment in early childhood intervention. One of the first well-designed studies of an early intervention program lent support to this possibility with the finding of IQ gains for the target children's younger siblings (Gray & Klaus, 1970). The investigators speculated that the intervention's focus on maternal interactions with the target child transferred to other children in the family.

The focus on parents in early intervention, then, extended and reflected some long-standing beliefs about the primacy of the family unit as a primary socialization agent and a cornerstone of American society. The intensity of the commitment to these principles rose to new levels in the 1960s with the excitement and high expectations surrounding the War on Poverty programs. Like early childhood education, parent education was called upon to serve purposes (i.e., eradicate poverty) and populations (i.e., low-income ethnic groups) historically peripheral to its purview. An educational practice with dubious effects on middle-class parents (see Harman & Brim, 1980) was suddenly center stage in an uncharted but closely monitored arena of massive publicly supported programs for low-income populations.

EMERGING DIRECTIONS AND THEIR DETERMINANTS

American society's interest in educational programs for parents of at-risk children is no less intense today than it was in the initial years of the early childhood intervention movement. Major changes are underway in the ideological framework, content, and procedures of programs targeted for parents deemed to be in a vulnerable position for providing an optimal child-rearing environment. The three directions can be summarized as follows:

1. Individual differences in parents' needs, characteristics, and program participation patterns are of growing interest. The notion that a particular program model can work with *any* parent has given way to questions about matching parents to different types of programs, and to programs that individualize services to families.
2. There is movement toward a realignment of the traditional balance of power between program staff and participants. Parents are to contribute to decisions about the scope and content of services received; the program worker is to function as a facilitator and collaborator, not an expert who engages in diagnosis and prescription. The concept of parental empowerment reflects this shift.
3. The social context of parent functioning is increasingly a focus of programs. Interventions are designed to strengthen parents' social networks, social support, and community ties as a buffer against stressful situations.

The nature and antecedents of the above directions are discussed in this section of the chapter. My treatment of each direction is organized as follows: a brief description of the substantive parameters of the trend; an identification and examination of the roots of the emerging direction; and an indication of critical unanswered questions and issues related to the trend that are addressed by chapters in this volume. The three emerging directions are discussed again in the final chapter of the volume (Chapter 10) in light of the insights and data provided by chapters in this volume.

Matching Programs and Parents

Parameters. The idea of matching program content and methods to the needs and characteristics of parents has gained considerable currency in the parent education field. The concept is a straightforward one: Different types of parents and communities need different strategies of parent education. There are several indications of the field's current interest in the matchmaking idea. One is the shift from standardized to individualized programs. Increasingly programs aimed at low-income and high-risk populations attempt to tailor the services and methods to the perceived and expressed needs of participants. Another indication of interest in program–participant congruence is the field's ongoing debate about the conditions under which home-based versus group-based delivery systems are appropriate. Interest in matching programs to parents also is evident in current efforts to develop programs that are responsive to cultural characteristics and values of ethnic populations. In terms of program development work, the field has moved beyond the notion that, to serve low-income ethnic populations, the primary task is to make existing programs *accessible* to members of ethnic minorities. As in the mental health field (Rogler, Malgady, Costantino, & Blumenthal, 1987), there is recognition that programs also need to be culturally *responsive.* At present the interest in this issue is focused most heavily on the development of programs for Hispanic populations (e.g., see special issue of *Family Resource Coalition Report* on programs for Hispanic families, vol. 6, no. 2, 1987).

The shift toward the concept of matching parents and program has not come easily. Similarly to other domains of educational, social, and therapeutic intervention, the parent education field is characterized by a "true believer" syndrome, whereby certain practices or theoretical orientations are highly revered regardless of limited or contrary research evidence. A prime example is the field's commitment to the group discussion mode. Adult education principles long have held peer group discussion to be an "indispensable method" for facilitating change in adults (Brookfield, 1986), and many parent educators are no less adamant in their designation of peer discussion as a superior form of practice. It has been difficult for the field, in general and model programs in particular, to acknowledge that certain methods may be inappropriate or ineffective with particular populations.

Antecedents.   Four related lessons from experiences with early intervention programs in the 1960s and 1970s seem responsible for the increased interest in program-parent congruence. The lessons pertain to: problems in the use of group discussion methods with low-income populations; the role of culture in programs for ethnic minorities; individual differences in parents' characteristics and responses to the content and structure of intervention programs; and the influence of local community factors on the design, implementation, and effects of intervention programs.

One of the earliest signs that parent education methods frequently used with middle-class populations might not readily transfer to low-income parents was the *presumed* failure of group discussion with parents in early intervention programs. Chilman's (1973) review of the research literature on parent intervention programs offered numerous examples of unsuccessful attempts to use a group discussion format. The initiatives were unable to attract a sufficient number of parents, experienced a high early attrition rate that led to the group's termination, or had no measurable impact on parents. Chilman argued that environmental "reality factors" such as marital disruption, financial instability, and inadequate housing worked against effective use of group methods with low-income parents, unless the group was supplemented by other services to parents. Conclusions of this nature contributed to the development of the widespread belief in the field that group-based approaches to parent education were unlikely to succeed in low-income communities. My use of the phrase "presumed failure" is intentional here, since other critical elements of a group-based approach (e.g., race of leader; content appropriateness) could account for problems independent of the group format. Indeed, there is evidence to suggest long-term group work can be effective with low-income ethnic populations (Slaughter, 1983). Nevertheless, problems in the use of group methods with low-income parents typically were attributed to the group approach, resulting in heightened interest in the match between program design and population characteristics.

With regard to the second lesson, attempts to provide educational and human services to low-income ethnic populations led to interest in the role of the participants' culture in service delivery. The lack of cultural responsivity in program services was seen as the main problem in providing early intervention (Baratz & Baratz, 1970) and mental health services (Special Populations Task Force, 1978) to ethnic minorities. The crux of most proposals to remedy the situation rested with the process of match: Program services should fit or match the cultural backgrounds and experiences of participants (Sue & Zane, 1987). Recommendations along these lines were advanced for early childhood programs (e.g., Cardenas & Zamora, 1980) as well as mental health services (e.g., S. Sue, 1977; D. W. Sue, 1981).

The third lesson contributing to the field's interest in program–parent match pertains to individual differences in parents' characteristics and responses to intervention programs. Programmatic acknowledgment of individual differences appears to have moved through three phases since the 1960s. In the 1960s, recognition of variations in the characteristics and program experiences of participants occurred primarily at the level of program implementation, not at the program design or evaluation level. For instance, the Ypsilanti-Carnegie Infant Education program, established in 1968, recognized that mothers varied considerably in the types of parent–child interactions they thought were beneficial to child development and in their expectations of child accomplishments by certain ages. Qualitative differences in the interpersonal relationship between teachers and mothers, including disagreements about child development philosophies, also were acknowledged (Lambie, Bond, & Weikart, 1974). In the Ypsilanti-Carnegie project and other interventions in the late 1960s, the usual program accommodation of participant individual differences was to provide staff with a high degree of autonomy in carrying out a program model. This stance reflects a premise operating in the larger human service arena that workers in people-changing enterprises need discretionary power in working with clients and their situational factors (see Hasenfeld & English, 1974). In the late 1960s and very early 1970s, program recognition of individual differences was not evident in the design and evaluation of most intervention programs, however. The evaluation of the Ypsilanti-Carnegie program, for example, disregarded the aforementioned variations by comparing treatment and control mothers on outcome indices. At this point in the early childhood intervention movement, the field was attempting to develop and test models that could be precisely specified and replicated in different sites. Variations in the delivery and receipt of a program typically were viewed as irritating violations of the experimental paradigm.

A second phase in the evolution of the field's response to individual differences among parents was marked by the establishment of Head Start's Child and Family Resource Program (CFRP) in 1973. This program carried the staff discretionary power concept to the level of program design by individualizing the service goals and methods for each family through a Family Action Plan developed jointly by each family and program worker. The flexibility in the determination of the treatment plans in CFRP and other parent interventions is in stark contrast with the standardized approach to predetermined services usually deemed necessary for evaluation and replication purposes. By the late 1970s and early 1980s, the third and current phase can be seen with calls for program evaluations that consider variations in participants' program experiences and effects. The report of the Panel on Outcome Measurement in Early Childhood Demonstration Programs, organized by the National Research Council, is a case in point (Travers & Light, 1982). It called for research that would improve our understanding of *why* programs work or fail to work, including evaluations that consider differences in the treatment variable. These developments present enormous challenges to evaluation researchers. Some investigators have taken steps to move beyond treatment–control comparisons in intervention programs by examining predictors and/or effects of variations in program participation (Cochran, Chapter 2; Lally, Mangione, & Honig, Chapter 5; Unger & Wandersman, Chapter 6; Travers, Irwin, & Nauta, 1982; Powell, 1983, 1984; Eisenstadt & Powell, 1987). As discussed in Chapter 10, major conceptual and methodological problems exist in the systematic investigation of interactions among participant attributes, program participation, and program outcomes. While it is not clear whether or how these problems might be resolved, currently the field has a strong interest in better understanding and programmatically responding to individual differences among parents.

The fourth lesson responsible for the field's current interest in matching program design to population characteristics stems from large-scale efforts to replicate intervention programs in diverse communities. The planned variation studies involving Head Start and Follow Through models demonstrated the impossibility of exact duplication of a program model in different communities, and suggested that the effects of model programs depend largely on a program's interactions with local circumstances (House, Glass, McLean & Walker, 1978; Anderson, St. Pierre, Proper, & Stebbins 1978; Rivlin & Timpane, 1975). A subsequent program replication project involving the Parent Child Development Center experiment showed sensitivity to the tension between replication and adaptation to local settings by establishing a separate, external entity (replication management organization) to play a major role in negotiating locally initiated changes in the model (Dokecki, Hargrove, & Sandler, 1983). The influence of host community factors on program design also was highlighted in the establishment of the CFRP, discussed above. In an ethnographic study of the implementation of this comprehensive intervention, researchers discovered that the program was "reinvented 11 times in 11 different sites" (Travers et al. 1981). For the parent education field, the cumulative effect of these experiences with different research and demonstration intervention projects is significantly increased awareness of the need to design and implement parent programs that are responsive to characteristics and needs of the local community and population to be served.

In sum, the presumed failures of group discussion methods with low-income populations, cultural insensitivity of programs for ethnic minorities, acknowledgement of individual differences in parents, and recognition of local community influences on program design and implementation have stimulated the field's interest in matching programs and parent populations. While there is endorsement of the matchmaking concept in principle, the field is seriously hampered in efforts to systematically operationalize the concept. There is a limited knowledge base to guide decisions about the "goodness of fit" between parent characteristics and program design. What types of parent characteristics relate to what dimensions of program utilization and effects? What mechanisms might programs use to gather information about and adapt to differences in parent needs and characteristics? To date, many discussions of program responsiveness to local conditions have been vague or lacking in the identification of factors at the community level that impinge on program design and implementation. What variables influence local adaptation or the design of a community-based intervention program?

Realignment of Parent–Professional Relations

Parameters.   A topic of great interest in the field today surrounds the roles assumed by professionals in parent-focused early intervention programs (Powell, 1984). The program literature suggests a trend toward collaborative, coequal relations between parents and program staff wherein the flow of influence is reciprocal. Reviews of program descriptions reveal frequent use of the term *empowerment*, and indications of staff serving as facilitators of goals and activities determined jointly by parents and staff. In one variant of this trend, parents are viewed as consumers of child development information; the program role is to provide information on a range of options so parents can make informed decisions about child-rearing approaches. The terms *client* and *expert* have come to represent an outdated program paradigm of professional dominance and parental passivity as participants.

Antecedents.   Antecedents of the ongoing realignment of parent–professional relations largely are found in the social and political currents of the civil rights movement and Great Society programs of the 1960s. Specifically, four sources of influence can be discerned: (a) criticisms of the deficit model inherent in early intervention programs; (b) provisions for parent participation in social and educational program legislation; (c) societal concerns about professional involvement in the private matters of family child rearing; and (d) views of how to affect change in adults. Each source is discussed below.

The assumptions of the deficit model, discussed earlier in this chapter, came under strong attack in the 1970s. Arguments were advanced that child-rearing practices of low-income homes represented differences, not inadequacies, in relation to middle-class homes (Yando, Seitz, & Zigler, 1979; Bronfenbrenner & Weiss, 1983). The deficit perspective undergirding intervention programs was viewed as a case of "blaming the victim" rather than the conditions associated with victimization (Ryan, 1971). Critics pointed to the imposition of white middle-class values on low-income and ethnic populations in parent education programs (Laosa, 1983), and to the fallacy of social service policies that require individuals to claim themselves deficient in order to receive services (Cochran & Woolever, 1983; Hobbs, Dokecki, Hoover-Dempsey, Moroney, Shayne, & Weeks, 1984). Parental input into program service decisions, and the use of paraprofessionals indigenous to the host community, were program structural mechanisms for helping interventions be sensitive and responsive to the needs and cultural norms of the population being served. Certainly the ideology and/or practices of many parent programs continue to represent the deficit model in their assumptions about parent functioning. In some instances the terms *collaboration* and *empowerment* may be nothing more than a public relations veneer for program operations where staff assert superiority by prescribing child-rearing practices. Nevertheless, criticism of the deficit perspective has led to a rhetorical if not substantive change in the ways practitioners approach relations with program participants.

The balance of power between parents and social institutions entered a new era with the Economic Opportunity Act of 1964. This legislation called for "maximum feasible participation" of individuals served by community action programs, and functioned as an impetus for Head Start's decisions on how to operationalize the principle of parent participation (Fein, 1980; Valentine & Stark, 1979). The vagueness of the "maximum feasible participation" legislation provided ample room for theoretically diverse interpretations (see Moynihan, 1968). Two basic strategies emerged, one focused on *individual* change through education and another dealing with *institutional* change achieved by parental involvement in organizational decision-making structures. The latter approach influenced the trend of professionals doing things *with* rather than *to* parents in early intervention programs. The placement of parents in program decision-making roles in Head Start (primarily via the local Policy Council) reflected the spirit of citizen involvement in democratic processes, and the rationale that participation at the early preschool level could be the first political step in a grassroots movement to change the schools and other social institutions serving people living in poverty. At both conceptual and operational levels, this strategy served to remind professionals and parents that parents can and should have a clear voice in the determination of program content and structure. While the strategy is controversial and has lost prominence in Head Start in recent years, its impact on the current realignment of parent–professional relations in parent programs has been significant and long lasting. Another legislative reminder of parental rights came in 1975 with the passage of the Education of All Handicapped Children Act (Public Law 94-142). The law includes provision for parental rights in decisions about a child's educational placement and treatment plan.

The rethinking of parent–professional relations also is a response to concerns about the dominance and expertise of the helping professions. With tremendous fervor, Americans value individual self-sufficiency and independence, and hence the growth in parent intervention programs prompted the concern that parents might become dependent upon programs. Serious questions were raised about rapidly increasing professional involvement in functions and decisions historically handled by the family (Lasch, 1977), and whether the scientific base of child development knowledge was sufficiently rigorous and definitive to warrant professional edicts about how to rear young children (Cochran & Woolever, 1983). The convergence of these forces contributed to the development of program practices that emphasized parents as experts about their own child, and the role of lay peers (instead of or in addition to professionals) as sources of child-rearing information and support. Collaborative and mutual exchange between professionals and clients resolves the basic incongruity between relationships that involve professionals as experts and clients as dependent, and the goal of using the relationship to foster the clients' independence (Tyler, Pargament, & Gatz, 1983).

The idea that parents should assume active roles in intervention programs was inspired in part by a theoretical view of adult change processes that suggested participation in democratic deliberations—formulating problems and negotiating solutions—would influence relations with the child. Experiences in developing and implementing plans were expected to enhance the confidence and ability of parents, with a transfer of these skills to the home and children (Fein, 1980). Control over one's destiny in a program was seen as a mechanism for helping individuals to improve their feeling of competence (Zigler & Berman, 1983) and to pursue productive, contributing roles in the larger society (Valentine & Stark, 1979). Children were expected to benefit from this change in parental behavior and attitudes. Existing research in the late 1960s lent some support to this approach by indicating, for example, that low-income black mothers who interacted with institutions of the community were more likely to engage the child effectively and to be more optimistic about their chances to improve their lives (Hess, Shipman, Brophy, & Bear, 1968).

In sum, four developments—criticism of the deficit model, parent participation legislation, concerns about professional involvement in family matters, and views of adult change strategies—are the primary precursors of an evolving realignment of relations between parents and staff in parent-oriented early intervention programs. While these antecedents set the stage for change in staff roles, they do not provide answers to some basic questions about the nature and implications of reciprocal exchanges between programs and their participants. Arguments and rationales for reciprocal parent–professional relations are abundant, but there are few reports of the experiences and effects of programs employing a collaborative model of working with parents. What is meant by parental empowerment, and what is the process by which parents come to feel and act empowered? What types of staff roles and practices enable parents to assume a sense of control over the nature of their program participation? How do programs respond to parents who have been socialized to expect program staff to function as expert helpers and participants as passive helpees? What are the effects of programs adhering to the collaborative mode of working with parents?

Social Context of Parenthood

Parameters.   I now turn to the third evolving direction in parent–child intervention programs. Socioecological influences on human development have commanded a good deal of attention in the parent education field since the late 1970s. The interest is responsible for use of the term *parent support* in lieu of or in addition to the more conventional *parent education* label to describe programs for parents. The name change reflects a substantive shift in program assumptions about the determinants of parent functioning. Whereas traditional parent education programs assume the dissemination of information to parents will affect behaviors and attitudes, the parent support notion assumes the provision of social support will have a positive influence on parent functioning. Knowledge is a key ingredient in the educational approach, while interpersonal relationships are central to the social support strategy (for further discussion of this distinction, see Powell, in press). There is variation across programs in the amount of emphasis given to education versus support; some interventions attempt to combine the two.

Currently, interest in the development and expansion of programs for enhancing the social context of parenthood is manifest primarily in what has become known as the family resource movement (see Kagan, Powell, Weissbourd, & Zigler, 1987; Weissbourd, 1983). Programs within this rubric attempt to support the family in its child-rearing role through such means as drop-in centers, parent advocacy, self-help groups, and home visitors. Parent education is one component of an array of services to the family, and in some programs may exist only in the most informal sense of parents exchanging reports of their child-rearing experiences. A dominant theme of programs espousing the family support strategy is that close interpersonal ties with peers promote the well-being of individual and family.

Conceptually, two variants of the parent/family support approach seem to be in operation. In one strand, it is assumed the provision of support is sufficient in and of itself for enhancing parent behavior and attitudes. One of the prevailing notions in this strand is that parents lack confidence in their own child-rearing beliefs and practices. The program's role is to provide reassurances and affirmations regarding the parent's competence. The program does not attempt to move the parent toward a predetermined image of what the ideal parent should do with children; rather the intent is to offer support for the parent's existing beliefs and behaviors. The program attempts to approximate elements of informal support systems traditionally available through family and friend networks. In the other strand, the existence of support is viewed as a requisite condition for the parent's receptivity to expert information and advice. That is, it is assumed that needs in the family's environment (e.g., no nearby extended family and friends; inadequate food and housing) create stresses that preempt parents from attending to the information and pedagogical demands of the parent education program. Illustrations of this latter strand are evident in Chilman's (1973) previously discussed interpretation of why group discussion formats failed with low-income parents, and more recently in Halpern's (1984) suggestion that fairly healthy, adaptive family functioning may be necessary for parents to profit from a program.

In addition to these variants, programs differ in whether the provision of support emphasizes informal, naturally occurring interpersonal ties and/or formal agency services. The former is particularly appealing to cost-conscious policymakers since informal helping systems are thought to be a suitable alternative to expensive professional services.

The parent education field is not unique in its growing interest in the social contexts of individual and family functioning. Since 1974 there has been burgeoning growth in studies and interventions focused on support and well-being. In the fields of medicine and public health, numerous social support researches and interventions have been inspired by Cassel's (1974) hypothesis that the disruption of social ties under stressful environmental conditions increases susceptibility to illness. In the mental health field, Caplan's (1974) argument that social support is a protection against pathology has been a conceptual basis for considerable theoretical, empirical, and intervention work (see Gottlieb, 1981). The emphasis on social support in parent programs is not unlike a social network intervention for the elderly (Chapman & Pancoast, 1985), or a peer self-help group for individuals with scoliosis (Hinrichsen, Revenson, & Shinn, 1985), for instance, in terms of assumptions about the influence of support on individuals. A major foundation for current social support theory and research was Durkheim's (1951) work on the role of close social ties in suicides, and research by the Chicago school of sociologists (McKenzie, 1926; Park & Burgess, 1926) interested in the effects of the disruption of social networks (see Brownell & Shumaker, 1984).

Antecedents.   Several factors have stimulated the parent education field's increased focus on the conditions of parenthood. One is public policy analyses and research on the contexts of parenting. The policy report of the Carnegie Council on Children (Keniston & the Carnegie Council on Children, 1977) pointed to the economic and social stresses on families, and questioned the American propensity to view the nuclear family as a protected and isolated unit in relation to the larger social environment. Research on the determinants of parenting has underscored the influence of stress and support on parents (for a review, see Belsky, 1984), including the abuse and neglect of children (Garbarino, 1987). Social support in particular has been identified in studies as a predictor of the quality of parental behavior (e.g., Colletta, 1979; Crnic, Greenberg, Ragozin, Robinson, & Basham, 1983). The theoretical and empirical work of Urie Bronfenbrenner has had a singularly powerful influence on the field's interest in the social context of child rearing. Of particular impact was Bronfenbrenner's (1974) report on the effects of early childhood intervention in which he argued that what parents need is ecological intervention in the form of family support systems. Four years later, this analysis was followed by the notion that the persons in greatest need of parent education were policymakers in charge of work settings and service institutions upon which families are dependent (Bronfenbrenner, 1978). Also influential was Bronfenbrenner's (1979) theoretical propositions about the ecology of human development.

In addition to policy and research reports, the field's interest in the social context of parenting has been prompted by residue of criticism of the deficit model discussed earlier. If individuals are not to be held responsible for their difficult life circumstances, then the environment is a logical target of blame. Failures of the social environment, and not personal deficiencies, are the cause of deprivation or suffering. This ideological perspective is embodied in what has been called the compensatory model of helping. Within this model, individuals are not responsible for their situation but they are responsible for solutions by taking action to compel an unwilling social environment to yield necessary resources. Energies are directed outward, toward a transformation of the environment (see Brickman et al., 1982). Parent programs representative of this view of empowerment are included in the present volume.

Lastly, demographic changes have been cited as reasons for the emphasis on support in parent programs. Geographic mobility has reduced the availability of extended family members, leading to the possibility of social isolation and its consequences. It is not uncommon for proponents of parent programs to argue that their initiatives are a substitute for the extended family as a role model and social support system (e.g., Weissbourd, 1987).

In sum, policy analyses and research on parenting, alternatives to the deficit model of parent functioning, and demographic changes have prompted the parent education field to consider seriously the conditions of parenthood in designing and evaluating programs. The growing programmatic focus on parents' social contexts broadens the conventional boundaries of parent education content and raises a host of questions about procedures and their effects. Questions addressed in the present volume include the following: What dimensions of social support are related to what aspects of child and parent functioning? What intervention principles and methods can be derived from research on the effects of social support on parents conducted within a nonintervention context? What methods might be used to strengthen parents' relations with the social environment, and what are the effects on parents and children? In what ways does the social context of parent functioning (e.g., existing sources of support) relate to participation in a program?

INTRODUCTION TO THE CHAPTERS

Each of the chapters in this volume pertains to one or more of the emerging directions examined above. The parent programs represented in the volume were aimed at populations typically targeted for early childhood intervention: low-income parents; adolescent parents; and parents of handicapped or developmentally at-risk children. The chapters contain research data and program analyses that extend and refine the scientific literature on the design and evaluation of intervention programs for parents of children considered to be at risk.

A detailed and critical examination of a parental empowerment program carried out in diverse Syracuse, New York, neighborhoods is contained in Chapters 2, 3, and 4. The Family Matters intervention was an integral part of the Comparative Ecology of Human Development project initiated by Urie Bronfenbrenner, William Cross, Jr., and Moncrieff Cochran in 1977. The program design placed Family Matters in the forefront of two major trends in the field today. The intervention represented an effort to move beyond the deficit model of human service delivery by not limiting participation to low-income populations, and by placing program workers in facilitator roles to emphasize and disseminate parents' (not professionals') expertise in child development. Family Matters was theoretically driven by an ecological framework that called for parents to act upon and feel in control of a key aspect of their social environment, the public school.

In view of the field's need for guidance in the major trends set forth in this chapter, the Family Matters experiment is a rich case study in the design, implementation, and study of a parental empowerment program. Moreover, research on the program considered variations in program effects by race and family structure, and attempted to identify the process by which the intervention may have influenced parents. Thus, the program offers a perspective on a number of program design and evaluation questions pertaining to most parent programs: What does it mean to empower parents? What are elements of the empowerment process? What are the roles and requisite skills of program workers? How much and what type of information is needed prior to the launching of an intervention program? How are equivocal program evaluation results to be interpreted?

This volume's examination of Family Matters appears in the form of description and debate. In Chapter 2, Cochran describes the program's rationale, operational plan, and major evaluation findings. He also responds to a critical assessment of the intervention by Burton Mindick (1986), who conducted a process study of the Family Matters implementation. Mindick's investigation suggested that Family Matters was characterized by major implementation problems, and that the program effects were small and limited, contrary to Cochran's conclusions. In Chapter 3, Mindick responds to Cochran's Chapter 2 critique of the Mindick assessment, claiming that, in implementation, Family Matters was far less novel than the program designers thought; inadequate attempts were made to secure information about families prior to the program launching; original program designs were prematurely abandoned; and implementation problems led to "non-significant effects, non-effects, and perhaps . . . negative or reverse effects." Cochran's rejoinder to Mindick, found in Chapter 4, is organized around five generic issues facing those interested in parent education and support programs: distinctions between basic research and program evaluation; key principles of the ecological perspective; conceptions of empowerment; the use of program workers for information about project families; and relationships between program outcomes and participation rates.

Results of a 10-year follow-up of children and parents involved in the Family Development Research Program at Syracuse University are reported in Chapter 5 by J. Ronald Lally, Peter Mangione, and Alice S. Honig. The Family Development Research Program was one of the early parent–child intervention programs to utilize a comprehensive family support approach, and was a pioneer in embracing the concept of empowerment in parent programs. In the program, very low-income families with children under 5 years of age received child care and weekly home visits. Lally, Mangione, and Honig describe the program's theoretical bases and operational details, with attention to such important elements as the roles of program workers and the curriculum of the early education component. The follow-up study reported in Chapter 5 included assessments of 51 program families and 42 control families on a variety of outcome measures. The data indicate positive intervention effects on: the school functioning of girls; parental reports of family unity, prosocial attitudes and behaviors among children, and parental encouragement of child achievement; children's positive feelings toward self; and a reduced level of program children's involvement in juvenile delinquency.

In Chapter 6, Donald G. Unger and Lois Pall Wandersman examine an important process research question related to the field's interest in matching parents and programs: What are the antecedents of active and inactive status in a parent support program? Their research is based on a home-based program for rural teenage mothers, known as the Resource Mother Program. The chapter describes the program rationale and design, including the use of paraprofessionals as primary program workers, and reports findings of research on the role of personal network ties and the timing of entry into the intervention program as predictors of participation level. A main finding was that teen mothers who actively participated in the program were living with their families, felt they could rely on their families for financial assistance and instrumental support, and were not very involved with the baby's father. In discussing the implications of the findings for program development, Unger and Wandersman address the need to deal with the teen within the context of her family; problems and prospects of working with the baby's father; heterogeneity among teenage mothers; and the timing of intervention programs.

The theoretical and research bases of a program model of family support for handicapped and developmentally at-risk children are described in detail in Chapter 7 by Carl Dunst and Carol Trivette. The material pertains directly to two evolving directions in the field: the realignment of parent–professional relations, and the programmatic focus on the social context of parenting. The chapter summarizes the results of eight studies on the effects of different forms of social support on child, parent, and family functioning. The patterns in the data suggest that social support affects well-being, which in turn affects parent interactional styles, which in turn influence child behavior. The data also suggest the importance of a congruence between the type of support needed and the type of support offered, and point to the effects of the manner in which support is offered. The chapter offers examples of how the Family, Infant, and Preschool Program interventions bridge theory, research, and practice through the use of empowerment strategies and helping relationships that emphasize a proactive rather than a deficit approach. The chapter concludes with a brief delineation of unanswered questions and unresolved issues in parent-focused early intervention research and practice.

Processes of designing and implementing community-based programs that are sensitive to the needs and characteristics of high-risk populations are examined in Chapters 8 and 9. The chapters contribute to the field's growing interest in the match between program design and population characteristics.

In Chapter 8, Robert Halpern and Mary Larner discuss ways in which parent programs serving disenfranchised populations are shaped by factors at the local level. Their thesis is that the specific form and content of parent support programs are determined through interactions among program administrators, staff, and target families, all of whom hold competing views of family needs and desired program strategies. Projects serving communities in the Ford Foundation's Child Survival/Fair Start initiative serve as case study material in this chapter. Halpern and Larner examine program development and change in relation to characteristics and roles of lay home visitors, the cultural traditions and minority status of populations served, and attributes of the sponsoring agency. The chapter includes a description of how a program for rural black teenage mothers shifted from a didactic, instructional mode to an emphasis on supportive, personal relationships between program workers and participants. Halpern and Larner conclude that the key task of a program sensitive to its context is to "provide new sources of support to families without supplanting or tearing down existing ones."

In Chapter 9, Judith Musick and Linda Barbera-Stein examine the role of research in initiating and developing programs that are responsive to parents living in high-risk circumstances. The research and program development experiences of the Ounce of Prevention Fund (OPF) in Illinois are described regarding the uses and nonuses of research in determining and refining program initiatives. While research had no direct influence on the establishment of the OPF, an interactive relationship between research and program development now operates at the OPF: programs inspire new research and research leads to program development. Musick and Barbera-Stein describe briefly the types of research and program evaluation undertaken with OPF programs aimed at adolescent parents (e.g., view of child adoption; child care arrangements; prevalence of sexual abuse), and the ways in which findings have influenced program design and staff training. For instance, OPF data have contributed to interest in the reluctance of service providers to raise the topic of adoption with pregnant adolescents, the lack of focus on the child and parenting issues in family support programs, and the limitations of paraprofessional staff. The chapter offers a case study of how research can be used to generate new programs and to fine tune or alter the course of ongoing services.

In Chapter 10, I draw upon the preceding chapters to identify critical challenges in the design and evaluation of parent programs. The three emerging directions described earlier in this chapter provide an organizational framework for considering unanswered and unresolved issues in the field. The chapter is intended as a point of departure for future program development and research regarding parent–child interventions.

REFERENCES

Anderson, R. B., St. Pierre, R. G., Proper, E. C., & Stebbins, L. B. (1978). Pardon us, but what was that question again? A response to the critique of the follow through evaluation. *Harvard Educational Review, 48,* 161-170.

Baratz, S. S., & Baratz, J. C. (1970). Early childhood intervention: The social science base of institutional racism. *Harvard Educational Review, 40,* 29-50.

Bell, T. (1975). The child's right to have a trained parent. *Elementary School Guidance and Counseling, 9,* 271.

Belsky, J. (1984). The determinants of parenting: A process model. *Child Development, 55,* 83-86.

Brickman, P., Rabinowitz, V.C., Karuza, J., Coates, D., Cohn, E., & Kidder, L. (1982), Models of helping and coping. *American Psychologist, 37,* 368-384.

Bronfenbrenner, U. (1974). *Is early intervention effective? A report on longitudinal evaluations of preschool programs.* (Vol. 2). Washington, DC: Office of Child Development, Department of Health, Education and Welfare.

Bronfenbrenner, U. (1978). Who needs parent education? *Teachers College Recrd, 79,* 767-787.

Bronfenbrenner, U. (1979). *The ecology of human development: Experiments by design and nature.* Cambridge, MA: Harvard University Press.

Bronfenbrenner, U., & Weiss, H. (1983). Beyond policies without people: An ecological perspective on child and family policy. In E. Zigler, S. Kagan, & E. Klugman (Eds.), *Children, families and government: Perspectives on American social policy* (pp. 393-414). Cambridge, England: Cambridge University Press.

Brookfield, S. (1986). *Understanding and facilitating adult learning.* San Francisco, CA: Jossey-Bass.

Brownell, A., & Shumaker, S. A. (1985). Social support: An introduction to a complex phenomenon. *Journal of Social Issues, 40,* 1-9.

Caplan, G. (1974). *Support systems and community mental health.* New York: Behavioral Publications.

Cardenas, J. A., & Zamora, G. (1980). The early education of minority children. In M. D. Fantini & R. Cardenas (Eds.), *Parenting in a multicultural society.* New York: Longman.

Cassel, J. (1974). An epidemiological perspective of psychosocial factors in disease etiology. *American Journal of Public Health, 64,* 1040-1043.

Chapman, N. J., & Pancoast, D. L. (1985). Working with the informal helping networks of the elderly: The experience of three programs. *Journal of Social Issues, 41,* 47-63.

Chilman, C. S. (1973). Programs for disadvantaged parents. In B. M. Caldwell & H. N. Ricciuti (Eds.), *Review of child development research (Vol. 3),* (pp. 403-465). Chicago, IL: University of Chicago Press.

Cochran, M., & Woolever, F. (1983). Beyond the deficit model: The empowerment of parents with information and informal supports. In I. Sigel & L. Laosa (Eds.), *Changing families* (pp. 225-245). New York: Plenum.

Coleman, J. S., Campbell, E. Q., Hobson, C. J., McPartland, J., Mood, A. M., Weinfeld, F. D., & York, R. L. (1966). *Equality of educational opportunity.* Washington, DC: Government Printing Office.

Colletta, N. (1979). Support systems after divorce: Incidence and impact. *Journal of Marriage and the Family, 41,* 837-846.

Cooke, R. E. (1979). Introduction. In E. Zigler & J. Valentine (Eds.), *Project Head Start: A legacy of the War on Poverty* (pp. xxiii-xxvi). New York: Free Press.

Crnic, K., Greenburg, M., Ragozin, A., Robinson, N., & Basham, R. (1983). Effects of stress and social support on mothers and premature and full-term infants. *Child Development, 54,* 209-217.

Dokecki, P. R., Hargrove, E. C., & Sandler, H. M. (1983). An overview of the Parent Child Development Center social experiment. In R. Haskins & D. Adams (Eds.), *Parent education and public policy* (pp. 80-111). Norwood, NJ: Ablex Publishing Corp.

Durkheim, E. (1951). *Suicide: A study in sociology.* (G. Simpson, Ed.). Glencoe, IL: The Free Press. (Original work published in 1897.)

Eisenstadt, J. W., & Powell, D. R. (1987). Processes of participation in a mother-infant program as modified by stress and impulse control. *Journal of Applied Developmental Psychology, 8,* 17-37.

Fein, G. (1980). The informed parent. In S. Kilmer (Ed.), *Advances in early education and day care, Vol. 1* (pp. 155-185). Greenwich, CT: JAI Press.

Gallagher, J. J., Haskins, R., & Farran, D. C. (1979). Poverty and public policy for children. In T. B. Brazelton & V. C. Vaughn III (Eds.), *The family: Setting priorities.* New York: Science & Medicine.

Garbarino, J. (1987). Family support and the prevention of child abuse. In L. Kagan, D. Powell, B. Weissbourd, & E. Zigler (Eds.) *America's family support programs: Perspectives and prospects* (pp. 99-114). New Haven, CT: Yale University Press.

Gottlieb, B. (1981). Preventive interventions involving social networks and social support. In B. Gottlieb (Ed.), *Social networks and social support* (pp. 201-232). Beverly Hills, CA: Sage.

Gray, S. W., & Klaus, R. A. (1970). The early training project: A seventh-year report. *Child Development, 41,* 909-924.

Halpern, R. (1984). Lack of effects for home-based early intervention? Some possible explanations. *American Journal of Orthopsychiatry, 54,* 33-42.

Harman, D., & Brim, O. (1980). *Learning to be parents.* Beverly Hills, CA: Sage.

Hasenfeld, Y., & English, R. (Eds.) (1974). *Human service organizations.* Ann Arbor, MI: University of Michigan Press.

Hess, R. D., Shipman, V. C., Brophy, J. E., & Bear, R. M. (1968). *The cognitive environments of urban preschool children.* Chicago, IL: Graduate School of Education, The University of Chicago.

Hinrichsen, G. A., Revenson, T. A., & Shinn, M. (1985). Does self-help help? An empirical investigation of scoliosis peer support groups. *Journal of Social Issues, 41,* 65-87.

Hobbs, N., Dokecki, P. R., Hoover-Dempsey, K. V., Moroney, R. M., Shayne, M. W., & Weeks, K. H. (Eds.). (1984). *Strengthening families.* San Francisco, CA: Jossey-Bass.

House, E. R., Glass, G. V., McLean, T. D., & Walker, D. F. (1978). No simple answer: Critique of the Follow Through evaluation. *Harvard Educational Review, 48,* 128-160.

Hunt, J. M. (1961). *Intelligence and experience.* New York: Ronald Press.

Jencks, C., et al. (1972). *Inequality: A reassessment of the effect of family and schooling in America.* New York: Harper & Row.

Kagan, L., Powell, D., Weissbourd, B., & Zigler, E. (Eds.) (1987). *America's family support programs: Perspectives and prospects.* New Haven, CT: Yale University Press.

Keniston, K., & Carnegie Council on Children (1977). *All our children: The American family under pressure.* New York: Harcourt Brace Jovanovich.

Kessen, W. The American child and other cultural inventions. *American Psychologist, 34,* 815-820.

Lambie, D. Z., Bond, J. T., & Weikart, D. P. (1974). Home teaching with mothers and infants. *Monographs of the High/Scope Educational Research Foundation* (Number 2). Ypsilanti, MI: High/Scope Press.

Laosa, L. (1983). Parent education, cultural pluralism and public policy: The uncertain connection. In R. Haskins & D. Adams (Eds.), *Parent education and public policy*. Norwood, NJ: Ablex Publishing Corp.

Laosa, L. (1984). Social policies toward children of diverse ethnic, racial, and language groups in the United States. In H. W. Stevenson & A. E. Siegel (Eds.), *Child development research and social policy* (pp. 1-109). Chicago, IL: University of Chicago Press.

Lasch, C. (1977). *Haven in a heartless world: The family beseiged*. New York: Basic Books.

Levine, M., & Levine, A. (1970). *A social history of helping services: Clinic, court, school, and community*. New York: Appleton-Century-Crofts.

McKenzie, R. (1926). The ecological approach to the study of the human community. In R. Park & E. Burgess (Eds.), *The city*. Chicago, IL: University of Chicago Press.

Mindick, B. (1986). *Social engineering in family matters*. New York: Praeger.

Moynihan, D. P. (1968). The crisis in welfare. *The Public Interest, 10*, 3-29.

Park, R., & Burgess, E. (Eds.) (1926). *The city*. Chicago, IL: University of Chicago Press.

Pestalozzi, F. J. (1951). *The education of man*. New York: Philosophical Library.

Powell, D. R. (1982). From child to parent: Changing conceptions of early childhood intervention. *Annals of the American Academy of Political and Social Science, 416*, 135-144.

Powell, D. R. (1983). Individual differences in participation in a parent-child support program. In I. Sigel & L. Laosa (Eds.), *Changing families* (pp. 203-224). New York: Plenum.

Powell, D. R. (1984). Social network and demographic predictors of length of participation in a parent education program. *Journal of Community Psychology, 12*, 13-20.

Powell, D. R. (1984). Enhancing the effectiveness of parent education: An analysis of program assumptions. In L. Katz (Ed.), *Current topics in early childhood education*, Vol. V (pp. 121-139). Norwood, NJ: Ablex Publishing Corp.

Powell, D. R. (in press). Support groups for low-income mothers: Design and participation considerations. In B. Gottlieb (Ed.), *Marshaling social support: Formats, processes, and effects*. Beverly Hills, CA: Sage.

Rheingold, H. (1973). To rear a child. *American Psychologist, 28*, 42-46.

Rivlin, A. M., & Timpane, P. M. (1975). Planned variation in education: An assessment. In A. M. Rivlin & P. M. Timpane (Eds.), *Planned variation in education: Should we give up or try harder?* (pp. 1-21). Washington, DC: Brookings Institution.

Rogler, L. H., Malgady, R. G., Costantino, G., & Blumenthal, R. (1987). What do culturally sensitive mental health services mean? The case of Hispanics. *American Psychologist, 42*, 565-570.

Ryan, W. (1971). *Blaming the victim*. New York: Pantheon Books.

Schlossman, S. (1976). Before Home Start: Notes toward a history of parent education in America, 1897-1929. *Harvard Educational Review, 46*, 436-467.

Slaughter, D. T. (1983). Early intervention and its effects on maternal and child development. *Monographs of the Society for Research in Child Development, 48*, (4, Serial No. 202).

Special Populations Task Force of the President's Commission on Mental Health (1978). *Task panel reports submitted to the President's Commission on Mental Health: Vol. 3*. Washington, DC: U.S. Government Printing Office.

Sue, D. W. (1981). *Counseling the culturally different: Theory and practice*. New York: Wiley.

Sue, S. (1977). Community mental health services to minority groups: Some optimism, some pessimism. *American Psychologist, 32*, 616-624.

Sue, S., & Zane, N. (1987). The role of culture and cultural techniques in psychotherapy: A critique and reformulation. *American Psychologist, 42*, 37-45.

Travers, J., & Light, R. (Eds.) (1982). *Learning from experience: Evaluating early childhood demonstration programs*. Washington, DC: National Academy Press.

Travers, J., Irwin, N., & Nauta, M. (1981). *The culture of a social program: An ethnographic study of the Child and Family Resource Program.* Report prepared for the Administration for Children, Youth and Families. Cambridge, MA: Abt Associates.

Travers, J., Nauta, M., & Irwin, N. (1982). *The effects of a social program: Final report of the Child and Family Resource Program's infant-toddler component.* Cambridge, MA: Abt Associates.

Tyler, F. B., Pargament, K. I., & Gatz, M. (1983). The resource collaborator role: A model for interactions involving psychologists. *American Psychologist, 38,* 388-398.

Weissbourd, B. (1983). The family support movement: Greater than the sum of its parts. *Zero to Three, 4,* 8-10.

Weissbourd, B. (1987). A brief history of family support programs. In L. Kagan, D. Powell, B. Weissbourd, & E. Zigler (Eds.), *America's family support programs: Perspectives and prospects* (pp. 38-56). New Haven, CT: Yale University Press.

Valentine, J., & Stark, E. (1979). The social context of parent involvement in Head Start. In E. Zigler & J. Valentine (Eds.), *Project Head Start: A legacy of the War on Poverty* (pp. 291-313). New York: Free Press.

Yando, R., Seitz, V., & Zigler, E. (1979). *Intellectual and personality characteristics of children: Social-class and ethnic group differences.* Hillsdale, NJ: Erlbaum.

Zigler, E., & Berman, W. (1983). Discerning the future of early childhood intervention. *American Psychologist, 38,* 894-906.

Chapter 2
Parental Empowerment in Family Matters: Lessons Learned from a Research Program*

Moncrieff Cochran
Cornell University

Ten years ago Urie Bronfenbrenner, William Cross, Jr., and I initiated a program of research, called the Comparative Ecology of Human Development, aimed at learning more about the stresses and supports experienced by American families in the urban context.[1] In that research program we included a family support intervention, known as Family Matters. This intervention was deemed important, first, because we were interested in the ecological systems encompassing the child and the nuclear family, and believed that, in order to understand those systems, you needed to "nudge" them to see how their constituent parts responded. Second, the intervention was itself an experiment. Our goal was to provide support to families with young children in a manner calculated to avoid what we viewed as the most debilitating aspect of most American "family assistance" programs, the focus on deficit as a basis for the formulation of "helping" strategies. We wished to develop a strategy based upon the identification and reinforcement of family strengths, and so offered the program to a cross-section of urban families, regardless of income level, ethnic background, or family structure. This research effort was launched in the field in 1978, the intervention was carried out for about 2 years, and follow-up data collection was initiated in 1981. Two hundred and twenty-five families, each with a 3-year-old at the time of entry into the project, participated in the entire research program.[2]

The conceptual framework underlying our research was unusual in its reliance upon an ecological framework emphasizing the importance of a set of environmental structures, each distinguished from the others and all interacting to provide the overall developmental context.[3] The structure most directly involved with the developing child, and so at the center of our intervention, was the nu-

---

* Special appreciation is expressed to the W. K. Kellogg Foundation and Extension, U.S.D.A., for support of Family Matters program activities, and to the National Institute of Education and the W. T. Grant Foundation for funds covering the costs of data analysis.

[1] For details of the original proposal, see Bronfenbrenner and Cochran (1976).

[2] For a detailed report of the entire research effort, see Cochran and Henderson (1986).

[3] For elaboration of these ecological systems, see Bronfenbrenner (1979) and Cochran and Brassard (1979).

clear family. Embracing the immediate family in both supportive and stressful ways was thought to be an informal social system made up of the parents' relatives, friends, neighbors, and co-workers—their personal social networks. A third system, still more distant from the child but influential via its impact on the parents, was made up of major economic and cultural institutions: the workplace, the schools, the church, public services. This framework provided a unique vantage point from which to examine the *processes* through which the Family Matters program achieved its impacts upon particular groups of parents and children. Ecologically related processes of special interest were located in the nuclear family and in the personal networks, parent–child activities and changes in mothers' involvement with relatives and friends. Also important to the empowerment perspective were the parents' perceptions of themselves as parents. These three elements—perception of self as parent, parent–child activities, and network-based mutual support—all emerged as central to the intervention strategy undertaken by Family Matters.

When designing the overall project we were also fortunate to be able to include as an independent undertaking a study of program implementation conceived to provide "the systematic examination of . . . those factors associated with program success or failure" (Bronfenbrenner & Cochran, 1977, p. 2). The idea was to monitor all aspects of the family support program, from conception through implementation, to insure that the programmatic processes involved in producing any impacts—positive or negative—be carefully documented and available to provide insight into *the means by which* such outcomes were achieved. Thus the emphasis in the implementation study was not on the *ecological processes* operating in the natural environment, but on the *processes of intervention* engaged in by those of us undertaking the Family Matters Program. This implementation study began in 1978 and continued in parallel with the entire course of the program. Dr. Burton Mindick became its director in 1979. His book describing the findings of the study, entitled *Social Engineering in Family Matters*, was published in 1986.

Since 1982, I and my colleagues have been assessing what we learned from the families participating in the Family Matters Program about the evolution of an approach to family support built upon the strengths rather than the deficits of families. This new approach, which we believe is *fundamentally different* from the orientation characterizing family assistance programs in the U.S. since World War II, has now been articulated and discussed by us in print (Cochran & Woolever, 1983; Cochran, 1985). An overview of its basic premises and dimensions is provided later in the chapter. More recently, Charles R. Henderson, Jr. and I have published the results of quantitative, longitudinal analyses documenting the effects of this empowerment process upon *both* child performance in school *and* the processes we believe are involved in empowerment: positive self-regard, parent–child activities, social network supports, and parent involvement with the child's school (Cochran & Henderson, 1986). These findings indicate that involvement with the empowerment program had *significantly positive effects* upon the child-rearing capacities of families, and enhanced the school performance of those children with less educated parents. The knowledge gained about the empowerment process, and the findings documenting the positive effects of that process, have convinced us that the overall Comparative Ecology of Human Development research program was a good investment.

Burton Mindick, writing from the perspective provided by the ethnographic implementation study monitoring delivery of the Family Matters Program, *comes to different conclusions about the value of the undertaking.* Using Family Matters as a case study, he concludes that inadequacies in service delivery, in the face of deeply rooted social problems, led to the kinds of disappointing results typically produced by the Great Society programs. Addressing the "magnitude of effects problem," Mindick says:

> Furthermore, by comparison with the grandeur generally promised by many program designers (cf. Nicol, 1976)—the exaggerated promises of I.Q. change to be achieved by Head Start, and the superpotent intervention that was the object of Bronfenbrenner's search—the gradualism, the very modest cognitive gains, and the only episodically potent interventions that have resulted are by no means heartening. (p. 177)

My central thesis in this chapter is that the Family Matters Project has contributed substantially to the body of knowledge about how best to provide community support for family life. While I acknowledge the shortcomings in service delivery documented so usefully by Mindick and his research team, I argue that many of the problems of service delivery encountered in our Syracuse experiment have been overcome, and present evidence demonstrating that our empowerment approach and methodology have been widely adopted. Regarding the Mindick critique, I conclude that it is deeply flawed by the mistaken belief that Family Matters was a public policy, when in fact it was a research program.

Material bearing upon this presentation is arranged in four sections. First comes a brief description of the *evolution* of our Syracuse family support program. This is followed by an outline of findings regarding the effects of the program on both family ecologies and child outcomes, and the linking of those findings to the empowerment process. The third part of the chapter is used to describe the steps we have taken since the Syracuse effort to sharpen the focus of the empowerment approach, and train professionals in the use of it. Finally, I outline the details of the Mindick argument, and weigh his effort to dismiss Family Matters as another of those "big ideas" that "seem to have become caricatures of themselves the moment they ceased to be ideas and began to be translated into action" (p. 186).[4]

---

[4] Mindick uses this quote from Elmore (1978) on page 7 of his book to characterize the record of social programs over the past three decades.

EVOLUTION OF THE FAMILY MATTERS PROGRAM

The Family Matters program was formulated with two overlapping purposes. Our primary interest was in the program as a way of nudging the social and psychological adaptations made by parents to their particular life circumstances, in the hope that responses to such a stimulus might cast in sharper relief the key features of family ecologies and contribute to our scientific understanding of family life. The other objective was to develop and implement a program of family supports for parents and their young children based upon the assumption of strengths rather than deficits, which would give positive recognition to the parenting role; encourage the exchange of information with and among parents about children, neighborhood, and community; reinforce and encourage parent–child activities; encourage mobilization of informal social supports; and facilitate concerted action by program participants on behalf of their children.

The Family Matters program was designed with explicit reference to an ecological perspective. This perspective was manifested in a number of interlocking ways. First, the program paid particular attention to systems outside an individual's psychic processes, in particular the parent–child microsystem, and two systems operating at the meso-level—the parents' personal social networks, and communication linkages between home and school (Bronfenbrenner, 1979; Cochran & Brassard, 1979). Of special concern were the roles played by parents in mediating the influences of larger systems (network, neighborhood, school, workplace) on their child's development. Second, the program was delivered to a variety of kinds of families, and made flexible enough to accommodate various expectations and needs, because of our particular interest in comparing the differing environmental characteristics of the ecological niches occupied by different groups of American families. Third, we had a particular concern in programming for the parents' definitions of appropriate subject matter and developmental goals, which stemmed from the phenomenological orientation underlying much of the past and present thinking associated with the ecology of human development and family life (Mead, 1934; Bateson, 1972; Bronfenbrenner, 1979).

These theoretical starting points both reflected and influenced the assumptions underlying the family supportive process that came to be known (largely in retrospect) as the parental empowerment process. We assumed from the beginning that *all* families have strengths, and that much of the most valid and useful knowledge about the rearing of children can be found in the community itself— across generations, in networks, and in ethnic and cultural traditions—rather than in the heads or books of college professors or other "experts" (Berger & Neuhaus, 1977; Ehrenreich & English, 1979). We also recognized the legitimacy of a variety of family forms, the important contributions made by fathers to the parenting process, and the special value in cultural differences. The details of the parental empowerment program have been presented in detail elsewhere (Cochran, 1985; Cochran & Woolever, 1983; B0, 1979; Mindick & Boyd,

1982[fj Mindick, 1980). Here I will simply review the basic goals underlying the program, and outline the processes engaged in to achieve those goals.

Program Goals

The goals of the program were all related broadly to the parenting role, and ranged, on a parent-involvement continuum, from simple engagement and awareness to more active initiation and follow-through. In the first instance, the aim was to find ways to recognize parents as experts, based upon our assumption that parents brought strengths and special expertise to child-rearing and our awareness of the systematic ways in which such recognition is provided to parents in other cultures (Kamerman & Kahn, 1981). Another goal was to exchange information with family members about children, the neighborhood, community services, schools, and work. Here we were responding to the body of literature (Caplan, 1974; Sarason, Carroll, Maton, Cohen & Lorentz, 1977) identifying resource exchange as a key to the maintenance of mentally healthy communities. Reinforcement of, and encouragement for, parent–child activities was a third goal of the program, and this priority stemmed from the recommendations of those reviewing the early education programs of the 1960s and early '70s who concluded that active involvement of parents in the learning of children was a key to success (Bronfenbrenner, 1974; Florin & Dokecki, 1983).

A fourth goal involved social exchange beyond, rather than within, the immediate family: the exchange of informal resources like babysitting, child-rearing advice, and emotional support with neighbors and other friends. This informal exchange process was distinguished from the information and referral process more commonly associated with formal agencies and community organizations (Stack, 1974; Tolsdorf, 1976; Collins & Pancoast, 1976; Killilea, 1976; Cochran & Brassard, 1979; Gourash, 1978). Finally, we wished to facilitate concerted action by program participants on behalf of their children, where those parents deemed such action appropriate. A neighborhood-based community development process was envisioned, in which needs assessments carried out by the parents of young children would lead to the identification of issues of common concern and to' a change in efforts related to those issues.

Implementation Strategies

The program was offered to 160 families, each containing a 3-year-old child, in 10 different Syracuse neighborhoods. Initially, two separate mechanisms were used to involve families in activities related to their children. One, a home-visiting approach aimed at individual families, was made available to all participants in half of the program neighborhoods. Initial emphasis during home visits was on exchange of information about developmentally valuable parent–child activities. Parents described activities already under way that they deemed useful, and these ideas were shared among program families. Later on, home visitors began sharing a smorgasbord of activity possibilities with families and providing necessary materials or equipment if parents or children made a selection. Equally important in many home visits were several other kinds of content: emotional support/listening, and general information and referral related to health care, housing, legal assistance, budgeting, job-seeking, further schooling, day care, and child-rearing tips. A great deal of emphasis was paid in home-visiting to finding ways of providing positive recognition to parents for their contributions in the parenting role. This building of self-esteem often led to needs assessments initiated by the parents themselves, and thereby to a broadened facilitator role for the home visitor (Cochran, 1985).

Families in the other five neighborhoods were asked to become involved in group activities with clusters of other Family Matters families in their own neighborhoods, in an effort to emphasize mutual support and cooperative action, with family dynamics and the parent–child dyad as a secondary (although still explicitly acknowledged) focus. Child care was provided at all cluster-group gatherings, and the content of the sessions included socializing as well as group activities aimed at finding solutions to neighborhood problems of common concern.

We had predicted in our original grant proposal (Bronfenbrenner & Cochran, 1976) that a combination of home visits and clusters would be more attractive to parents than either approach alone. Two early findings seemed to confirm that hypothesis. On the one hand, once certain families became comfortable with home visiting, they began to express an interest in meeting neighbors involved with the program, forcing workers into the difficult position of having to resist the constructive initiatives of parents in order to prevent contamination with the cluster-building approach. On the other hand, only about half of the invited families in the cluster-building neighborhoods could be coaxed out of their homes into group activities.

Based on these two sources of programmatic tension, we decided after 9 months to merge the two approaches. Workers in the group-oriented neighborhoods began to make themselves available as often as every 2 weeks for home visits focused initially upon parent–child activities, and those who had been doing only home visits started to facilitate the formation of neighborhood groups and clusters. One consequence of access to both components of the newly integrated program was an increase in overall program participation. Initially this took the form of more parent–child activity home visits, primarily to families who previously had been offered only the neighborhood linking alternative. With more time came involvement by more families in clusters and groups, and some who participated simultaneously in both home-visiting and neighborhood-based group activities.

As the children associated with the program grew older and approached the age of entry into kindergarten and first grade, we placed increased emphasis on programming related to the transition from home to school. These activities, prepared for delivery in both home-visiting and cluster-grouping formats, focused on topics like the value of home and school, evaluating kindergarten and first grade classrooms, preparing for a parent–teacher conference, understanding the child's report card, and parent–child activities for school readiness. The emphasis in each of the activities was always on the parent as the most important adult in the life of the developing child.

Families were involved with program activities for an average of 24 months, and the program itself came to a close early in the summer prior to first-grade entry for most of the target children included in the study.

THE EFFECTS OF FAMILY MATTERS

Home visitors and neighborhood workers were in regular contact with 160 families, helping parents identify their strengths and their needs, and work toward improvements in their life circumstances. What had started primarily as an effort to better understand parental stresses and supports by nudging the ecologies surrounding families was becoming increasingly interesting in its own right. We had begun to refer by then to a concept called *parental empowerment*. Two aspects of the concept were of particular significance to us at that juncture. First, there was the sense that empowerment was a process rather than an end state. Parents didn't "achieve empowerment"; rather, they changed over time in what appeared to be systematic ways. Second, there was anecdotal evidence coming from program workers of what seemed to be phases or stages in this change process. The initial change appeared to involve parents' perceptions of themselves. Some of the mothers who viewed themselves quite negatively early in the life of the program showed signs, over time, of beginning to believe in and look after themselves in new ways. Another phase seemed to involve relations with others—new efforts to reach out to spouse and child, and also to relatives, neighbors and friends outside the family. A later change involved action on behalf of the child. A number of neighborhood cluster groups were organized around plans for neighborhood improvement, and some parents became involved with the schools their children were attending.

When the time came to assess the effects of the program, the evaluation was carried out with this emergent process in mind. Figure 1 provides an overview of the hypothesized relations among the major classes of variables. Home–school communication, and the child's performance in school, although conceptually distinct, are shown in a single box, to minimize the number of connecting arrows. The same is true for sociodemographic variables and the program.

Sample Design

We employed a stratified random sampling procedure at both the level of neighborhoods and of families. First, 29 city and 28 suburban neighborhoods in the Syracuse, New York, area were identified. The neighborhoods were then further

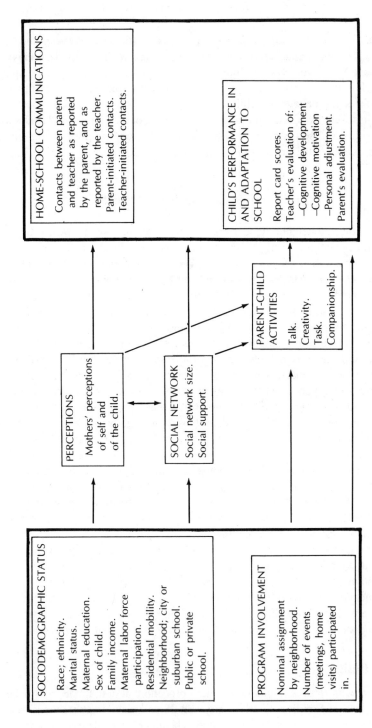

Figure 1. Conceptual Schema for Program Evaluation: Hypothesized Interrelations Among Domains

classified by income level and by ethnic/racial composition. We then randomly selected 10 program and 8 control neighborhoods, stratified by race and income. Once study neighborhoods had been specified, we began the process of identifying all the families with a 3-year-old child in each neighborhood. Race (Black vs. non-Black), family structure (married vs. single), and sex of target child were factors of primary interest. A stratified random sampling method within each neighborhood was then employed, choosing families within each of the eight subgroups defined by family race, family structure, and sex of child, and oversampling for Afro-American and single parent families. This method of sampling resulted in a higher proportion of Black and single-parent families than in the Syracuse area as a whole.[5] Table 1 shows the racial and marital status characteristics of the families that participated in the entire research program (82% of the baseline sample).[6]

The possibility of differential patterns of attrition in the treatment and control groups from Time 1 to Time 2 was considered in some detail (Cochran & Henderson, 1985). Analyses indicated no attrition differences by program assignment or other factors.

Assessment Measures

Of particular interest for this discussion are the measures of processes hypothesized to be affected by the empowerment approach to family support. In the case of *mothers' perceptions of themselves as parents* the variable consisted of the mother's rating of her performance on a 25-item checklist, with each item consisting of a seven-point scale. The four *mother–child activity* variables—talk, creativity, tasks, and companionship—were derived from a set of 55 checklist questions completed by the mother, each of which was presented as a four-point scale. The *social network* variables were concentrated in the primary network.

Table 1.   Number of Families by Program, Race, and Marital Status

		Control	Program	Total
Black	One Parent	19	21	40
	Two Parent	10	13	23
White	One Parent	16	23	39
	Two Parent	54	69	123
	Total	99	126	225

---

[5] For more information about sampling procedures, the achieved sample, sample attrition, measures, and findings, see Cochran and Henderson (1986).

[6] Eighteen percent of the baseline sample was lost during the 3 years, 9 months between the start of Wave 1 data collection (October 1978 and the end of data collection at follow-up (July 1982). More than 70% of the 51 families lost from the study had left the Syracuse metropolitan area between baseline and follow-up. The remainder refused to participate in the second round of data collection or, more typically, failed to complete all three follow-up interviews.

They included change in number of primary ties between baseline and followup (both kin and nonkin), and number of kin and nonkin found in the primary network at followup who were nowhere present in the network at baseline (''new primary membership''). The *home–school contact* variables consisted of estimates by both parents and teachers for the numbers of conferences, notes, and telephone calls initiated from the home and from the school. Finally, the *school outcome* variables were drawn from a questionnaire completed by the children's first grade teachers, and included the following domains: personal adjustment, interpersonal relations, relationship to teacher, cognitive motivation, and report card score averaged across core subjects.

Summary of Statistical Methods

The core of our first stage statistical analyses involved single-equation models, using regression techniques (including analysis of variance and covariance). Here the interest was in how the program and control subgroups differed on the process and outcome variables, controlling for any differences in socioeconomic background factors.

Stage two analyses reflected a shift from initial interest in direct effects to concern with relations between ''intervening'' and outcome variables. Instead of concentrating on comparisons of means in analyses of covariance, we were concerned with the homogeneity, by program assignment, of the regressions of one ecological domain upon another. For instance, was the relationship between a change in networks over time and school performance different for families involved with the program than it was for those in the control group? The results generated for appropriate subsamples were control-program comparisons of regression coefficients representing relationships between pairs of ecological domains.

Summary of Findings

Composites created from the findings presented in detail elsewhere (Cochran & Henderson, 1985, 1986) are shown in Figures 2 and 3. The arrows in the figures represent *hypotheses regarding causality*; causality cannot be demonstrated with these data.

Program impacts *directly* related to each of the ecological fields of interest are shown as arrows connecting the program with each of those fields. The + and − signs on these arrows indicate that the program subgroup score was significantly higher or lower than the score for the control subgroup.

Of even greater interest is how involvement with the program might have affected *relations between* ecological fields—the link between social networks and school outcomes, for instance, or between social networks and perceptions of self as parent. A + sign on these arrows indicates a significant difference in regression coefficients between the program and control subgroups *in favor of the program families.* A − sign also represents a significant difference, but *in favor of the control subgroup.*

The pictures provided in Figure 2 for the single-parent subgroups suggest, as a hypothesis, that, for these families, the impacts of the empowerment program upon children's school performance are heavily mediated by changes occuring within and around their parents. In the case of the *Black one-parent family*, increases in the number of relatives included in the mother's primary network were associated with reports of more joint activity with the child. Joint activity involving household chores was linked in turn with higher performance in school. And expansion of nonkin membership in the primary networks of those mothers was also linked with their children's school outcomes, especially when those outcomes involved school readiness (personal adjustment, interpersonal relations,

Black, Single Mothers.

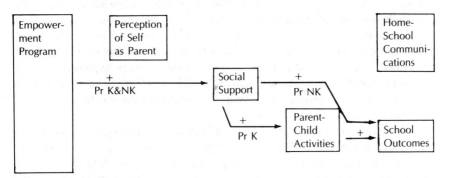

White, Single Mothers.

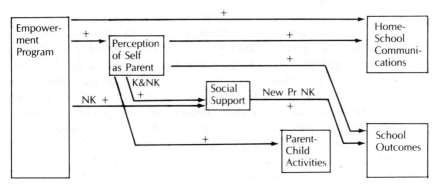

Key to abbreviations:
  Pr K - Primary network Kin
  Pr NK - Primary network Nonkin
  Pr K&NK - Primary network Kin and Nonkin

Figure 2.   Impacts of the Empowerment Program: One-Parent Families

relations with the teacher). *White single mothers'* perceptions of themselves as parents appeared to be a key determinant in whether positive performance was seen in the more distant reaches of their ecological fields. For these mothers, higher parental perceptions were associated with expansion of their primary networks, the activities they reported engaging in with the child, their level of communications with the child's teacher, and the teacher's report of the child's progress in first grade. There is evidence that the nonkin sector of the primary network played a positive role in its own right, with increase in nonkin linked to higher school outcomes, again primarily in the area of school readiness.

Figure 3 provides an overview of the findings related to two-parent families. These pictures are more ambiguous than were those for mothers and their children in one-parent families. Interestingly, a somewhat lower self-perception as parent by *Black married mothers* in the program was related to greater contact with the teacher. This was only true in those instances where the child was perceived as having difficulty in school. The self-perceptions of these women were the highest of any subgroup in the sample. As they dropped somewhat, perhaps becoming more realistic, involvement with the child's school increased. For these same mothers, increased involvement with kinfolk was related to greater amounts of mother–child activity. However, none of these hypothetical chains could be linked to better performance of the child in school. School performance was tied directly to program involvement, without any intermediate links to the ecological fields measured by us.

One set of possible mediating links did emerge for *White married mothers*, if those mothers had schooling beyond high school. The proposed sequence involved increased perception of self as parent, more mother–child activities, and better performance by the child in school. The reader can see from Figure 3 that there was also a direct link between program involvement and school performance for the children in this subgroup.

It is useful to elaborate somewhat upon what is shown in Figures 2 and 3 regarding the impact of participation in the empowerment program on performance of the children in first grade. A direct, positive impact was found for the children living with two parents whose educational backgrounds were relatively low—a high school education or less. There was also an impact for the children with only one parent living at home, but only when accompanied by other, empowerment-related changes. Thus the feature *common* to all of the sub-groups for which positive school effects were found was those families' *relatively less advantageous position in the social structure.* This makes sense—the more advantaged families were already empowered by the social system to assist their children in the academic arena, and so were effective regardless of their program or control group status.

Another interesting general pattern found in the data involved the slopes of the regressions of one ecological subsystem (mother's self regard, or change in her network) on another (contact with teacher or child's school performance). Re-

Black, Two-Parent Mothers

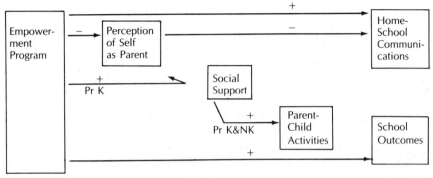

White, Two-Parent Mothers.

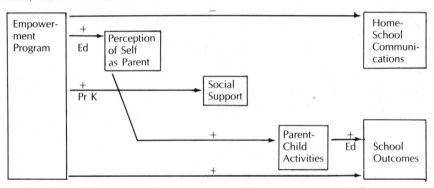

Key to abbreviations:
NK - Network Nonkin
K&NK - Kin and Nonkin
Pr K - Primary network Kin
New Pr NK - New Primary network Nonkin
Ed - Effect was observed only for mothers with education beyond high school.

Figure 3. Impacts of the Empowerment Program: Two-Parent Families

peatedly, when comparing the regression line for the program subgroup with that for the control group, we found a moderately positive slope for program families being contrasted with a rather more sharply negative slope for control families. Put in terms of program impact, these contrasts strongly suggest that this empowerment program has been *preventive* much more than it has been *enhancing*. We believe that this pattern has significance for how the impact of family support programs are understood and interpreted, and it is to that interpretation that I shall now turn.

Family Support as Relief from Stress

The traditional expectation associated with an intervention designed to affect outcomes in children has been that the children receiving the special treatment will then perform better than an equivalent control group. Historically, the assumption underlying such a model has been that the intervention was *compensating for* some *deficiency* in the child's life circumstances that would otherwise limit performance (Dokecki & Moroney, 1983). From our ecological orientation, we developed an alternative to this standard stance, based upon our assumption that *all* families have strengths and experience stress. This assumption has, in turn, led to an interpretation of our findings in which the intervention is thought of as *preventing the loss* of certain family or network functions, and therefore making possible the maintenance of child performance at an acceptable level. The assumption here is not that there is a deficiency that needs correction, but rather that *a system capable of functioning adequately deserves protecting*. The concept of supporting the family, or family supports, is based on this second model. From this perspective, the family is viewed as a system which, if given an opportunity to function in a relatively supportive environment, can fulfill the basic developmental needs of its members. Public policies designed to provide family support aim, through reduction of environmental stresses, to allow families to function effectively, rather than to "correct" their "deficits."

If the purpose of family support is to prevent loss of family functioning, then one would expect there to be instances in our data in which no change in the program group was accompanied by *decreases* for control families. The first example of this sort appeared in the relationship between family income and the child's performance in school.[7] In all control subgroups except the one containing married White families (the group with the highest income), lower incomes were associated with poorer school performance. This income-related decrement did not appear for the program families in these three subgroups, suggesting to us that participation in the program buffered those families against the effects of less income. This impression was reinforced by indications in the social network data that financial support from network members had eroded somewhat less for White, single mothers in the program than for those in the control group. It was underscored yet again in the relationship of the number of nonkin in the primary networks to school outcomes, parental perceptions, and home–school communications. The pattern for White, single mothers involved strong negative regressions for the control group balanced by flat or moderately positive ones for the program group, adjusting for mothers' educational level. This suggests, in the case of networks, that the program did more than simply increase the numbers of nonkin in the networks of these mothers. It also seemed to affect how those special nonkin were *brought to bear* on aspects of family life

---

[7] Detailed presentations of the findings reported here can be found in Cochran and Henderson (1985). The relationships reported were identified by examining the regressions of school performance scores on family income as reported at follow-up, within each of the four subgroups.

affecting the child either directly or indirectly (the financial situation, the mother's feelings about herself as a parent, daily routines conducive to school-related activities). The impression that accumulates from these data is that the strong positive *direct* associations between program involvement by White single mothers and both their perceptions of themselves as parents and the support they received from close friends served to buffer the child against problems in school. The details of this buffering process are only conjecture at this point, but a clue may be provided by the indication that, when their child showed signs of having difficulty in school, those same mothers were also found to be in much more frequent contact with the child's teacher than were their control group counterparts. The general point is that *interventions preventing a significant loss in the functioning of family members should be viewed with as much interest as those which produce gains in performance relative to controls.* In fact, one can argue that the preventive role is the more important one if it is accomplished by strengthening the family rather than usurping its role and functions.

The Utility of Process Variables

One contribution that an ecological orientation can make to research is to enrich our understanding of the processes through which a family support program achieves its effects upon child performance. At the same time, the inclusion of "process" variables in a conceptual model for evaluating the impact of an intervention complicates matters at virtually every stage in the life of the project. In the case of Family Matters, reams of additional data about self-perceptions, networks, and parent–child activities had to be collected both prior to and following implementation of the program. The costs of gathering, preparing, and analyzing these data were substantial. Did the results justify the investment?

One way to answer the usefulness question is to look at Figure 2. Imagine the diagrams as they would look if only containing the direct relationships between the program and school and home–school outcomes. The impression created would have been that one-parent families had not responded to our parental empowerment approach. Certain of the children in single-parent families showed improvements in school behavior that could only be linked to program involvement through their association with ecological variables associated, in turn, with program involvement. The removal of the "process" variables from the model virtually eliminates any opportunity to learn *what it was* about the program that seemed to make a difference to those involved with it. For instance, we invested a great deal of effort in discovering ways to give positive recognition to parents for the vitally important roles they were playing in the lives of their children. The supposition was that parents needed to feel confident about themselves as parents before they could be expected to become actively involved in the more "executive" aspects of the parenting role—those activities, like choosing among schools, or requesting a particular teacher for the child, that require assertiveness and confidence in one's analytic and decision-making skills. The summary of findings provided in Figure 2 certainly suggests that, for one of those two sub-groups, perception of self as parent played an active role in determining whether parents became involved with their child's teacher when there was indication that the child was having school difficulty. While the nature of our data permits only the generation of hypotheses, the findings are nevertheless intriguing. They are also not of the simple ''more is better'' variety, as indicated by the fact that, for married Afro-American mothers, more school involvement was accompanied by a *drop* in regard for self as parent.

Moreover, the findings about process can be translated into policy at the program level. If we are willing to assume what these data seem to imply—that White, single parents are much more likely to become actively involved with the teachers of their children if they feel reasonably good about themselves as parents—this suggests that programs should be designed to stimulate positive changes in such self-regard.[8] The same kind of argument can be made for social networks and school outcomes, again especially for mothers and children in single-parent families. If the development of important new relationships by the mother really does contribute to better performance by her child in school, then day care centers, schools, and other organizations heavily involved with young families could make a real contribution by designing into their programs ways to encourage the building of such relationships. The more general point is that such references to specific aspects of the content of the Family Matters program would not have been possible in the absence of data about process.

SHARPENING THE EMPOWERMENT APPROACH

The reader surely has seen from my description of the Syracuse Family Matters program that it evolved and changed over the 2½ years of existence, and that our understanding of the empowerment process was far more advanced at the end than at the beginning of the intervention. That is the purpose of research.

Eager to take advantage of what we had learned in a nonexperimental context, I applied for and received generous support from the W. K. Kellogg Foundation and Extension, USDA, to develop and pilot test training materials for the teaching of the empowerment approach and its applications. Thus the research in Syracuse became just the starting point for a program development, refinement, and utilization process that is still underway. The fruits of that process are described below.

Curriculum Development

We learned a great deal in Syracuse about how to articulate and apply empowerment principles and techniques in support of families with young chil-

---

[8] I am not arguing here that our data show causality, but only that they suggest a hypothesis with strong policy implications.

dren. The many improvements and refinements that resulted from that learning process now serve as the foundation of our continuing efforts, and have been encorporated in two major publications, one a workshop series for professionals and paraprofessionals, and the other a manual for group facilitators. The nine-session workshop series, called *Empowering Families: Home Visiting and Building Clusters* (Cochran, Dean, Dill, & Woolever, 1984) provides the preservice training that would have been made available to our workers in Syracuse if we had known better then what would have been most useful to them.[9] The series requires 25–30 hours of classroom activity, the first third of which focuses on the basic concepts of empowerment, positive recognition, balance of power, and differing value systems. The remainder of the time is equally divided between home-visiting and cluster-building skills, and includes exercises on active listening, information and referral, confidentiality, and avoiding dependency relationships, as well as on group cooperation, group facilitation, and group problem-solving.

The manual for trainers is called *Communications for Empowerment* (Vanderslice, 1984), and is designed both to introduce human service workers and teachers to the concept of empowerment and describe the myriad ways in which the concept can be applied. Examples of applications range from how a room is organized for a gathering of parents to a discussion of the power differences between the minilecture and brainstorming as ways of generating information in a neighborhood group.

Using these two sets of resources as a starting point, we have gone on to develop several workshop series that focus specifically upon the fit between families and particular social institutions. I mentioned earlier that, in our program work in Syracuse, we had been especially concerned about the transition from home to school, and more specifically relations between first grade teachers and parents. To capitalize on ideas developed in Syracuse we produced a set of companion curricula called *Cooperative Communication between Home and School* (Dean, 1983). This package of materials includes a six-session series for parents, a 2-day inservice training program for primary school teachers, and a monograph for school administrators. Skills developed with both parents and teachers include empathy building, creative problem solving, effective use of parent–teacher conferences and report cards, creative volunteering, conflict resolution, and cooperative communication.

The other set of materials is designed to help parents prepare for employment, and was developed for use in job-training programs, with displaced homemaker groups, and with teenaged and single parents. Entitled *The Employed Parent* (McDonough, Cherry, & Dean, 1984), this workshop series provides parents with skills in time management, asking for help and building helping networks, evaluating child care options, and organizing the work to be done inside the

---

[9] All of the empowerment materials described here are available through Cornell University (Cornell Distribution Center, 7 Research Park, Ithaca, N.Y. 14850), strictly on a nonprofit basis.

home. The ideas for these materials were heavily drawn from the responses of parents to the worklife section of a stress and support interview used as part of the Comparative Ecology of Human Development Study.[10]

Pilot testing

Once first drafts of the training materials had been developed, 18 months were invested in full-scale pilot testing efforts at 12 urban and rural sites in upstate New York. Participants in these workshops were human services professionals and paraprofessionals and parents ranging across the socioeconomic spectrum. Careful note was taken of what worked and wasn't successful, and why such successes and failures occurred. All of this feedback was received by the various authors, who used it in revising the materials. New drafts were then circulated for comment and revision before final copies were printed.

Utilization

This new, reworked version of our empowerment program has been available to the public for 2 years, and in that time demand for training in the use of it has far outstripped our capacity to respond. In New York alone, empowerment programs are under way in two-thirds of the State's 57 counties and in a number of agencies and organizations in New York City. The materials are currently in use in at least 20 other states, with especially heavy involvement in Minnesota, Wisconsin, Missouri, Iowa, Illinois, and Texas. Great interest in the empowerment concept and approach is being shown in Canada, including French-speaking Quebec, and in Great Britain, Norway, Sweden, and West Germany.

One theme strongly underscored by our research in Syracuse has been the interwoven nature of the stresses and supports experienced by American families. The interdependence of these forces is extremely difficult to communicate with the quantitative methods at our disposal, so I was resolved to make such a statement by more qualitative means—via case studies presented in semidocumentary format on film. Support provided in 1981 by the Office for Families, HEW, allowed the project to begin, and it was completed 3 years later with financing by Head Start (Region II), the Harris Foundation and the College of Human Ecology at Cornell. The film, called *Family Matters* (Cochran & Gluck, 1984), provides

---

[10] This stress and support interview was held separately with the mother and the father (when he was available and willing). It provided perceptions of many ecological domains external to the family (neighborhood, work-place, day care situation, social services), information about the distribution of housework, and data about perceptions of family members, including the "perception of self as parent" information reported as part of our program evaluation. In the case of the *Employed Parent* workshop series, those materials were especially influenced by our international perspective, which came in large measure from comparable data on family stresses and support collected by colleagues in Sweden, Israel, Wales, and West Germany.

audiences with a window into the evolving lives of two families struggling with the tasks of child-rearing in straitened economic circumstances. It is used in all of our workshop series as an opportunity for participants to practice identifying strengths in parents, and to develop a more systematic way of recognizing environmental stressors and mobilizing supports. The film is also being used heavily nation-wide as a freestanding educational resource, having won a ribbon at the 1985 American Film Festival, and been broadcast twice on national public television (PBS).

While we have not yet found the energy or money to do a extensive assessment of the effects on behavior of this multifaceted, refined version of the Family Matters program, reports by users emphasize especially increases in respect for self and others, stronger feelings of efficacy, closer relationships inside the family, and better understanding of both informal and formal supports. Professional human service workers in particular—public health nurses, Extension agents, day care workers, elementary school teachers—express relief at having found a positive, supportive approach to families which "feels right" and frees them from the punitive, "blame the victim" orientation that they have long felt was both inhumane and ineffective. Every major element in each of the components of what is now known nationally as Cornell Family Matters has roots that can be traced directly to findings, quantitative or qualitative, generated by our research in Syracuse.

ANOTHER PERSPECTIVE: FAMILY MATTERS AS BENEVOLENT INTENTION

It is always useful, and rarely possible, to see one's own work through someone else's eyes. Dr. Burton Mindick has written a book about implementation of the Family Matters program that provides us with that opportunity. Mindick describes his book, *Social Engineering in Family Matters*, as "both an extended case study, . . . and a comparative analysis of social programs, with Family Matters used as a detailed illustration of much of what is positive and negative in our attempts to better our society" (1986, p. 14). His basic thesis, detailed in Chapter 1 and restated at the end of the book, is that "attempts at social progress" show results not meeting expectations, "despite benevolent intention," because the problems they face are "large, complex and deeply rooted," and they "have inadequate resources to meet those problems" (p. 163). It is this thesis that he argues is demonstrated by the implementation of Family Matters, based on the data collected and analysed by his research team.

I include a presentation of Mindick's critique in this chapter, not because I agree with the overall thrust of his presentation. Rather, it seems to me that the points about which we disagree, as well as our areas of agreement, serve a useful purpose for the reader by underscoring and extending several of the themes introduced earlier. In an effort to do justice to Mindick's argument, I present below six points that appear central, beginning with the most general and then moving to the more specific. Presentation of each point is followed by my own perspective on that issue. Taken together, my responses to Mindick's conclusions can be expressed as follows:

1. Family Matters in Syracuse was a research project, not a social program. We were testing an approach to family support that was *very different* from those developed in the 1960s, because it was built on the premise of strengths rather than deficits. What has been written earlier in this chapter makes these differences clear to the reader. Dr. Mindick failed to recognize the paradigmatic shift this different approach represented, and so mistakenly uses the weaknesses in our project to explain the shortcomings of social programs developed in the 1960s.

2. The conceptual framework guiding our research—called the ecology of human development—led us to hypothesize that families living in different environmental circumstances, with access to different constellations of educational, economic, and social resources, would respond differently to an external stimulus—in this case, the Family Matters program. Mindick, in his eagerness to equate Family Matters with the social programs of the past, does not come to grips with the significance of this conceptual framework, and so is disappointed when the impacts of the program are not felt equally by all participating families.

3. Our program staff was not organized very efficiently, we responded too slowly and ineffectively to the needs of program workers for additional skills, and our monitoring of worker performance was insufficient. These problems in implementation are carefully documented in Mindick's book and deserve close attention from both the designers and those implementing social programs. They are not insurmountable; we have since found solutions to most of them. They should not be used to obscure the real accomplishments produced by our experiment.

Solving Intractable Social Problems

The first part of Mindick's 1986 thesis is stated succinctly on page 13:

> Social programs confront problems deeply rooted within interlocking human and physical environmental systems. The solutions to these problems are not at all obvious; and even where effective betterment strategies can be found, there is invariably a risk-benefit tradeoff that must be accepted.

In support of this point, he devotes an entire chapter of the book to analysis of the economic and social conditions prevailing in Syracuse at the time of our study. He concludes by asserting that "our detailed, ethnographic analysis of the urban environment, in addition to suggesting the difficulties experienced by Family Matters and likely to be the lot of other programs as well, also demonstrates very graphically the magnitude and interrelatedness of the problems Family Matters and other interventions seek to remedy'' (p. 565).

I strongly agree with the assertion that the problems of families in urban America are complex and deeply rooted. Mindick and his colleagues have done a fine job of demonstrating that families in Syracuse face many of the problems more commonly associated with much larger cities. The problem arises for me with his assertion that a primary—and perhaps *the* primary—purpose of the Family Matters program was to solve those problems. This was simply not the case. Our task was not to solve those problems, but to understand their impact on the attitudes and behaviors of parents, and the development of children. We took the problems of urban America very seriously, as witnessed by selection of an urban site for the research and inclusion of substantial numbers of those families most vulnerable to the stresses of urban living—families with minority status and those headed by a single parent. But Family Matters was not a social program; it was a program of research. This purpose was made explicit in our original proposal (Bronfenbrenner & Cochran, 1976), and it remained in force throughout the life of the intervention. Mindick himself acknowledges the scientific purpose of Family Matters (1986, p. 37). It presents a problem for him, however, because to give the research the prominence it in fact carried would be to seriously weaken the value of Family Matters as a case study example of a broader class of social programs.

The Dearth of Information Resources

Mindick includes as part of his basic thesis the fact that social programs don't have the basic information about powerful intervention needed to remedy the problems faced by families in urban environments. He concludes his chapter on information resources as follows:

> We have engaged in this lengthy exercise to demonstrate how brilliant men, leading experts in the area of human development and men who were aware of family and child interventions between the mid-1960s and the mid-1970s, simply did not yet have a solid informational foundation on which to build their intervention. (1986, p. 134)

Once more, I find myself agreeing with Mindick's general point; too little is known about either the workings of the great variety of American families or their reactions to different kinds of intervention to permit the a priori construction of a superpotent intervention. But, again, he has the cart before the horse in the particular case of Family Matters. As a research project, our purpose was to gather information precisely *because of its paucity*. We were not to be put off by lack of information, but to proceed in ways that would insure responsible information gathering and dissemination. This lack of information was one of the reasons we took an information-gathering rather than a "we are the experts" approach to participating families. The Family Matters research project was launched precisely because of the shortage of "information resources" that Mindick argues leads to disappointing results. We wish to be judged, not by what was known going in, but by what we have to share with others now that the research is complete.

The Program Changed over Time

In his overview of the chapter on information resources, Mindick criticizes what he calls "the conceptual uncertainty and the back and forth of Family Matters Program designers as they first pre-planned, then changed, and then changed again in major ways the blueprints for the program" (1986, pp. 133-134). In the chapter, he documents the debate between Bronfenbrenner and myself, prior to field testing of the program, that led to a shift in the home visitor's role from parent–child specialist to activities coordinator. He describes, as I did earlier in this chapter, the merging of the home-visiting and cluster-building approaches into a single program with a range of options. And he details shifts in the program workers' roles as they expressed discomfort with the passivity required by our initial attempt to empower parents, and we worked with them to better define their areas of responsibility and initiative.

What Mindick and his co-workers witnessed during 3 years of observation and interviewing was the evolution of a new approach to family support, an approach that Mindick himself calls "radical" (p. 15), which had a two-pronged research purpose. It was to "nudge" the social ecologies embracing participating families, and it was to experiment with delivery of support to families in a manner that built on their strengths rather than dwelling on their deficits. The model was a responsive one. We were to listen to the expressed needs of both families and workers as the intervention progressed, and make modifications to the program where such changes would further its goals as I earlier outlined them: to recognize parents as experts, to exchange information with them, to encourage parent–child activities, to stimulate social exchange beyond the family, and to facilitate concerted action on behalf of the child. Mindick does a first-rate job of documenting the changes in thinking and practice that occurred as we learned from our innovative new approach to family support. But the purpose of the undertaking was learning, and we learned a great deal. The real world is made up of difficult choices. We believed that we were plowing new ground in our attempt to develop a family support program based on the premise of strengths rather than deficits. In our effort to implement (and, so, to understand) that approach, we created changing expectations for our workers, and so made their work difficult. Certainly it is fair to criticize our mid-course corrections. They would not have been nearly necessary, had we started with a finished product.[11] But to

---

[11] It is important to emphasize that a certain amount of adjustment is always necessary, even when the program is established social policy, rather than research. In Sweden, heavy use is made of what they call "rolling reform," which simply means that, when those implementing policy see better ways to operate, they share those ideas, discuss them, test them on a small scale, and, if successful, implement them more broadly.

concentrate on our inadequacies without at the same time giving recognition to our accomplishments seems unreasonable. The glass partly filled with water is half full. Why judge its contents only by what is missing?

The Innovation Confused both Workers and Families

The most important point that Mindick makes about our efforts to develop the empowerment approach is that it confused both the program workers and some of the participating families. About the workers he says,

> the problem of workers who didn't know quite how to relate to their families or who didn't know when to initiate and when to wait for family initiative, were general problems that persisted for most of the program's history. (1986, p. 148)

In discussing those families who were what Powell (1983) calls "staff oriented," Mindick has this to say about the attempts of workers to learn from them about their needs and wishes:

> Yet workers said they were there to learn. This is probably what caused the greatest confusion in the minds of families who were staff oriented, and were waiting for the worker to tell them what to do. It also explains many of the difficulties we have described about the worker role. (p. 175)

The empowerment approach is different. It represents a very serious effort to shift the balance of power from primarily in the hands of the workers to substantially in the hands of the parent. This process was uncomfortable, both for workers used to displaying their expertise and those parents used to passive reception of those recommendations. The discomfort was especially strong in the early going, when we ourselves—as program designers—didn't understand the practical ramifications of our innovation. Mindick captures the dimensions of this problem well, and underscores its importance appropriately. He himself points out, however, that families also responded positively to our approach, quoting a participating father who said, "The good thing about your program—not like other programs—is that you're not always telling us what to do!" (p. 125). I remember well how identified with the empowerment approach our workers became in the last year of the program—so identified that they were sometimes too direct with visitors from other programs who dwelt at too much length upon the deficits of their "clients." So the initial confusions about the empowerment process were resolved in good measure by the end of the program. They have been further resolved through the curriculum development, testing, and utilization effort I described earlier in the chapter.

Staff Organization was Flawed, and Training Inadequate

Mindick refers to the work of Elmore (1978) in identifying a variety of organizational models implicitly adopted by social programs. He gives particular attention to two of those models: systems management and organizational development. Systems management is described as characterized by goal directed behavior, hierarchical organization, rational allocation of responsibilities, a defined set of objectives, the monitoring of performance, and the application of appropriate adjustments. Mindick sees the organizational approach as different from the other models in putting policy making in the hands of the implementors, rather than operating from the top down. He concludes that Family Matters was most aptly characterized by this organizational development approach, giving importance as it did to consensus building and accomodation between policy makers (the researchers) and implementors (the program workers). Speaking of this organizational approach, he says,

> It seems to be appropriate under conditions of "trust, truth, love and collaboration" (Bennis, 1969, p. 79). Furthermore, it is our observation that unless these ideal conditions prevail, the organizational development paradigm is a much less satisfactory model for organizations with short life cycles, low levels of information, and the need to learn rapidly, especially by comparison to the systems management model. (1986, p. 160)

Needless to say, such conditions prevailed only occasionally during the tenure of Family Matters, which was short in life span, was breaking new ground, and needed rapid learning.

Mindick's basic point here is sound; as designers, we knew too little about organizational theory and practice, and gave the subject much too little thought. In fact, he fails to discuss an aspect of our organization that contributed greatly to the general confusion: three principal investigators, administering jointly, each with a somewhat different interpretation of directives developed to guide staff. Communications improved considerably when one of us became sole Project Director, two-thirds of the way through the life of the program. At about that point, the organization did shift in the direction of systems management. It is important to emphasize, however, that the *research task required of us during the early stages of the program was better served by information flowing from below than by a rigid, top-down structure.* The workers, and through them the parents, were our eyes and ears, and they needed to feel free to express themselves.

Mindick also documents the marginal quality of the inservice training provided to program workers, citing as culprits unclarity of goals, uncertainty of the worker's role, lack of authoritative written materials, lack of highly specific skills-based techniques and time wasted on irrelevant organizational details. I agree with his analysis and conclusion. The kinds of training needed by our workers did become clear to us part way through the program, and we could have moved more quickly to implement them. Those training exercises make up the bulk of the *Empowering Families* training materials described in the previous section of this chapter.

The Effects of the Program were Neither Universal nor Large

Finally, we come to the effects of the program. Mindick repeatedly expresses two major complaints about the impacts of Family Matters. They are neatly capsuled in the following statement,

> "The outcomes may be of importance in future efforts to strengthen families, but they and other quantitatively measured outcomes obtained also represent what we have come to expect from early childhood intervention programs: small effects, neither general across participant sub-groups nor across outcome domains." (pp.107-108)

Let's begin with the "universality of effects" question. Mindick's expressions of dismay over the fact that all participating families did not respond to the program in the same way strongly suggest a lack of understanding of the ecology of human development. We initiated this research in the first place in good part because previous assessments of program impact had taken such a narrow, intrapersonal, cognitive focus. Our suspicion was that measures with such a narrow focus missed some, and maybe many, of the impacts of programs designed to affect families, neighborhoods and communities, as well as individuals. Our ecological orientation also led us to believe that families came into programs with differing needs, and so would be affected by different kinds of support. That is in fact what the data presented earlier in this chapter indicate was the case with Family Matters families. Children whose parents were less educated showed improvements in school performance. Those with more educated parents couldn't have been affected by the program; their performance was already being sustained by their parents. Program parents were in more contact with the teachers if their children were having difficulty in school; those whose children were doing fine didn't see the need. The primary networks increased for every sub-group of program parents; but single mothers responded to non-kin, while for mothers in two-parent families it was kinfolk who proved especially salient. Parental self-perceptions were affected by the program only when they were especially high or especially low. Parent–child activities were dependent upon self-perceptions or social supports. Increases in self-regard were associated with more parent–child activity for White mothers, while, for Black mothers, parent–child activity was contingent upon growth in the primary network. These patterns make sense in terms of the circumstances surrounding the different sub-groups of parents. The fact that the program did not have universal effects is ecologically sound, and can be used to advantage to design future programs. Such findings should not distress Dr. Mindick; they should please him, for they are the very "information resources" that have been absent in the past.

Regarding the magnitude of effects, what is most noteworthy is that they were at all discernable, given the ruckus caused by our scientific preoccupations. Mindick documents the discomfort with the evolving nature of the program, the organizational difficulties and the weaknesses in our inservice training program. I have written elsewhere (Cochran & Woolever, 1983) about other ways in which the research interfered with program activities. The accomplishments of program families and neighborhoods were kept out of the media for fear of "contaminating" control families exposed to those same media, thus severely limiting our capacity to provide program families with the "positive recognition" we hypothesized was necessary to motivate them. The home-visiting and cluster-building approaches were introduced separately rather than as a package initially, despite the strong conviction that the combination would prove more powerful, to permit scientific comparison of the two modalities. Program workers lost valuable programming time each week filling out documentation required by the research arms of the project.

What is a large effect? We think that the biggest effect of the Family Matters program was to prevent disruption and disorganization, rather than to promote great leaps in development. Does prevention count? Societies in Europe seem to think so; they devote most of their expenditures for social programs to prevention, and recent analyses indicate that their children are far less costly to society as teenagers and young adults than are ours.[12] The primary networks of the white, single mothers in the program increased by an average of about four network members. Is that a big increase? I don't know, but certainly it deserves our attention. Those mothers' new relationships with such close friends didn't turn their children into geniuses, but may well have made it possible for the mothers to invest more time and energy in childrearing.

My overall response to the critique offered by Burton Mindick in his book can be put briefly. I am in accord with the great bulk of his findings about how we implemented the Family Matters program. The data are sound, and the presentation of them is a valuable contribution. However, in my view the attempt to use Family Matters as a case study for understanding the social programs of the 1960s and 1970s is misguided. Mindick lost sight of the program as an instrument of research, and so generalized his findings inappropriately. This is surprising, given the constant tension created by our scientific orientation. Equally surprising is the apparent blindness to the purpose of the ecological orientation to research, as demonstrated by his repeated concern with the non-universality of program impacts. Most disappointing of all was Mindick's decision to dwell upon our inadequacies without acknowledging our achievements, thus dismissing Family Matters as just another in a series of overblown and underachieving social programs. This is the very deficit orientation we set out to counter in the first place.

---

[12] See, for example, the comparison of German and American youth behavior carried out by Hamilton (1987), which shows dramatically greater per capita amounts of school drop-out, teen-aged pregnancy, drug abuse, and suicide in the U.S. than in the German population. I have recently examined equivalent statistics for the Norwegian youth population, and found them much more similar to those of Germany than of the U.S.

Family Matters in Syracuse was a research program through which we studied the ecology of urban family life and experimented with an empowerment approach to supporting families with young children. That empowerment approach proved to have been more than simply benevolent; it produced positive results both in the systems surrounding families and in the performance of family members, despite scientific distractions and blemishes in implementation. One major strength in the empowerment approach is that it compensates for lack of knowledge about the needs of specific families by involving them in shaping the program, and in so doing takes advantage of the vast reservoir of general knowledge lodged in the culture as a whole. By taking a truly ecological approach to program delivery, the approach gives recognition to the real state of affairs with American families, which is the great variety both in their types and in the circumstances surrounding them. Another major strength in the approach is that it builds upon strengths rather than emphasizing deficits, thereby acknowledging what those studying psychology have known for a long time: that positive reinforcement is far more effective than punishment at producing sustained change in behavior. We are greatly heartened by our experiences with the empowerment approach to the support of families, parents, and children, and heartily recommend it to others. The glass really is at least half full!

REFERENCES

Bateson, G. (1972). *Steps to an ecology of mind: Collected essays in anthropology, psychiatry, evolution, and epistemology.* New York: Ballantine Books.

Berger, P., & Neuhaus, R. (1977). *To empower people: The role of mediating structures in public policy.* Washington, DC: The American Enterprises Institute for Public Policy Research.

BØ, I. (1979). *In support of families: The pilot testing of two experimental programs.* Paper prepared for the Carnegie Corporation of New York. Ithaca, NY: Cornell University.

Bronfenbrenner, U. (1974). A report on longitudinal evaluations of preschool programs. In *Is Early Education Effective?* (Vol. 2). Washington, DC: Department of Health, Education and Welfare.

Bronfenbrenner, U. (1979). *The ecology of human development: Experiments by nature and design.* Cambridge, MA: Harvard University Press.

Bronfenbrenner, U., & Cochran, M. (1976). *The ecology of human development. A research proposal to the National Institute of Education.* Ithaca, NY: Cornell University.

Bronfenbrenner, U., & Cochran, M. (1977). *A study of processes in the Family Matters Program.* Proposal to the Carnegie Corporation, Cornell University, Ithaca, NY.

Caplan, G. (1974). *Support systems and community mental health.* New York: Behavior Publications.

Cochran, M. (1985). The parental empowerment process: Building on family strengths. In J. Harris (Ed.), *Child psychology in action: Linking research and practice* (pp. 12-33). London: Croom Helm.

Cochran, M., & Brassard, J. (1979). Child development and personal social networks. *Child Development, 50,* 601-616.

Cochran, M., Dean, C., Dill, M., & Woolever, F. (1984) *Empowering families: Home visiting and building clusters.* Ithaca, NY: Cornell University Media Services.

Cochran, M. (producer), & Gluck, D. (director). (1984). *Family Matters* [Film]. Ithaca, NY: Photosynthesis Productions.

Cochran, M., & Henderson, C. (1985). *Family Matters: Evaluation of the Parental Empowerment Program*. Final report to the National Institute of Education. Ithaca, NY: Cornell University.

Cochran, M. & Henderson, C. (1986). *Family Matters: Evaluation of the Parental Empowerment Program*. Summary of a final report to the National Institute of Education. Ithaca, NY: Cornell University.

Cochran, M., & Woolever, F. (1983). Beyond the deficit model: The empowerment of parents with information and informal supports. In I. Sigel & L. Laosa (Eds.), *Changing families* (pp. 225-245). New York: Plenum Press.

Collins, A., & Pancoast, D. (1976). *National helping networks: A strategy for prevention*. New York: National Association of Social Workers.

Dean, C. (1983). *Cooperative communication between home and school*. Ithaca, NY: Cornell University Media Services.

Dokecki, P., & Moroney, R. (1983). To strengthen all families: A human development and community value framework. In R. Haskins & O. Adams (Eds.), *Parental education and public policy* (pp. 40-64). Norwood, NJ: Ablex Publishing Corp.

Ehrenreich, B., & English, D. (1979). *For her own good: 150 years of experts' advice to women*. New York: Anchor/Doubleday.

Elmore, E. F. (1978). Organizational models of social program implementation. *Public Policy, 26*, 185-228.

Florin, P., & Dokecki, P. (1983) Changing families through parent and family education: review and analysis. In I. Sigel & L. Laosa (Eds.), *Changing Families* (pp. 23-64). New York: Plenum Press.

Gourash, N. (1978). Help-seeking: A review of the literature. *American Journal of Community Psychology, 6*(5), 413-424.

Hamilton, S. (1987). Adolescent problem behavior in the United States and the Federal Republic of Germany: Implications for prevention. In K. Hurrelmann & F. Kaufman (Eds.), *The limits and potential of social intervention* (pp. 185-204). Berlin/New York: de Gruyter/Aldine.

Kamerman, S., & Kahn, A. (1981). *Child care, family benefits, and working parents*. New York: Columbia University Press.

Killilea, M. (1976). Mutual help organizations: Interpretations in the literature. In G. Caplan and M. Killilea (Eds.), *Support systems and mutual help*. New York: Grune & Stratton.

Kirschner Associates. (1970) *A national survey of the impacts of Head Start centers on community institutions*. Washington, DC: Office of Economic Opportunity (Eric Document Reproduction Service No. ED 045195).

McDonough, J., Cherry, F., & Dean, C. (1984). *The employed parent*. Ithaca, NY: Cornell University Media Services.

Mead, G. H. (1934). *Mind, self, and society*. Chicago, IL: University of Chicago Press.

Mindick, B. (1980). *Salt City and Family Matters: Supporting families in the urban environment*. Report to the Carnegie Corporation of New York. Ithaca, NY: Cornell University.

Mindick, B. (1986). *Social engineering in Family Matters*. New York: Praeger Publishers.

Mindick, B., & Boyd, E. (1982). A multi-level, bipolar view of the urban residential environment: Local community vs. mass societal forces. *Population and environment, 5*(4), 221-241.

Powell, D. (1983). Individual differences in participation in a parent-child support program. In I. Sigel & L. Laosa (Eds.), *Changing Families* (pp. 203-224). New York: Plenum Publishing.

Sarason, S., Carroll, C., Maton, K., Cohen, S., & Lorentz, E. (1977). *Human services and resource exchange networks*. San Francisco, CA: Jossey-Bass.

Stack, C. (1974). *All our kin: Strategies for survival in a black community*. New York: Harper and Row Publishers.

Tolsdorf, C. (1976). Social networks, support and coping. *Family Process, 15*, 407-418.

Vanderslice, V. (1984). *Communications for empowerment*. Ithaca, NY: Cornell University Media Services.

Chapter 3
Lessons Still to be Learned in Parent Empowerment Programs: A Response to Cochran*

Burton Mindick
Cornell University

Social Engineering in Family Matters was not an easy book to write. It wasn't that we did not have enough material or data. Now, nearly a decade after the research began, we have several file cabinets full of detailed, analyzed ethnographic observation reports, interviews, questionnaires, and archival material, enough to produce several more volumes of the same size. After painstakingly gathering and analyzing data for 5 years amidst judicious silence to all outside the Comparative Ecology of Human Development Project, I was quite anxious to make my findings known. In this I was encouraged by my own staff members and many of the staff members of the Family Matters program, as well as by some of the graduate students who worked with the larger Ecology of Human Development Project.

What was difficult about writing *Social Engineering in Family Matters* was the need to evaluate its program processes accurately—and that meant, unfortunately, having to include some negative comments along with the positive aspects of the handiwork of very talented, very high-minded colleagues whom I respected and liked, men to whom I also owed a debt of gratitude for giving me the opportunity, first, to direct a study of program processes, and then to become its principal investigator. When I raised this issue with my colleagues, they reminded me that my role as a process evaluator meant that I had to have the independence to assess their intervention in a way that might not always accord with their own views. Dr. Bronfenbrenner went even further. He reminded me that, as painful as it might be to criticize certain aspects of the implementation of the program, it was my "scientific responsibility" not to shrink from a fair assessment.

In writing *Social Engineering in Family Matters*, I therefore tried to fulfill that scientific responsibility by evaluating program processes as candidly as I could, consistent with a concern to avoid pettiness or excessive personalization of the research findings, and consistent with a desire that those findings be less a matter

* Grateful acknowledgement is hereby given to the Carnegie Corporation of New York for support of the research here described, with particular thanks to Project Officer Barbara Finberg. The views expressed here are those of the author and not necessarily those of the Carnegie Corporation.

of critiquing a single program and more a matter of identifying those generalities of wisdom and unwisdom of program implementation that might be helpful to those who might design and carry out comparable interventions in the future. It is therefore with considerable concern that I must comment on Dr. Cochran's chapter in this volume, where he not only disagrees in several major ways with my views of the Family Matters Program, but expresses disappointment in what he calls my "decision to dwell on our inadequacies without acknowledging our achievements, thus dismissing Family Matters as just another in a series of overblown and underachieving social programs" (p. 48).

Was Family Matters a Social Program, a Public Policy, or Neither?

The largest and most fundamental issue raised in Cochran's chapter is my supposedly "mistaken belief that Family Matters was a public policy, when in fact it was a research program" (p. 25), and his assertion that "Family Matters in Syracuse was a research project, not a social program." We can dispose of the question of Family Matters being "a public policy" fairly readily. Nowhere in *Social Engineering* does it state that Family Matters was a piece of public policy. Bronfenbrenner in his work as one of the originators of Head Start, was responsible for a "piece of public policy." It is very clear from the original proposal (Bronfenbrenner & Cochran, 1976), which begins and ends prominently with the relationship of the research project to public policy, and from Bronfenbrenner's (1979) book, which bears what is essentially the same title as the research project, that it was hoped that research would allow the investigators to *contribute to future public policy*. This emphasis is found in *Social Engineering in Family Matters*, on pages 34, 35, and 135. But there was never any statement that Family Matters was itself a "piece of public policy."

Allegations that I was unaware of Family Matters' status as a research project will astonish anyone who might read the *Social Engineering* volume in anything other than the most desultory manner. Pages 38–40 of the volume in question describe the "Research Design" of Family Matters. The section is headed by the words "Research Design," and the text begins, "Because of the interventive and experimental nature of Family Matters," and then proceeds to describe the pilot neighborhoods, the treatment neighborhoods, and the control neighborhoods. It would have been utter *nonsense* to describe in detail the research design of a program that I did not consider to be a research project. The status of Family Matters as a research project was never in question. The question is, what kind of research was it. On page 34, I quote Bronfenbrenner's (1980, p. 3) own description of the program as an "ecological intervention" and "an alteration of those aspects of the wider external environment that offered the greatest possibility of influencing the functional effectiveness of developmental settings such as the family, the day care center, and the classroom."

Thus, Family Matters was also an intervention. It was certainly not comparable to foreign components of the Ecology of Human Development Project where nature was simply allowed to take its course. Cochran uses the word *nudge* to describe what the Program was trying to do. He says that he and his collegues were just trying to nudge the family and the surrounding social settings, and see what happened. But "nudging" is very different from "*alterations that offer the greatest possibility of influencing developmental settings*" and from the "super-potent" intervention that Bronfenbrenner (1979, 1980) mentions in the same context and elsewhere.

Both research as well as potent intervention and amelioration were explicit aims of the program. Both kinds of language were used. As I have discussed in my book (Mindick, 1986, p. 37), sometimes the program was described as simply a "heuristic tool" or a "voyage of scientific discovery." But sometimes it was part of an attempt to influence families' lives profoundly. The original proposal (Bronfenbrenner & Cochran, 1976) not only dealt with the family in the home, but with the neighborhood and the wider community as well. Families were to be brought to schools. Employers of parents were to be brought into contact with their employees' children. Children were to visit the work place. Many of these ambitious plans were never realized in actual practice, partly because of theoretical retrenchment, partly because of resource scarcity, and partly because of implementation problems. But to label this kind of intervention into the home, the school, the neighborhood, the workplace, and the community broadly as just a "nudge" is the quintessence of understatement.

Because of its attempts to make some fundamental changes in the social structures of the families involved, I characterized the Family Matters as "radical." Its designers often used similar, if not stronger, terminology. My characterization, however, does not mean (as Dr. Cochran suggests in his chapter) that Family Matters was radically new. Unfortunately, as I have shown in *Social Engineering*, it was a great deal less novel than its designers liked to believe. I used the word *radical* in its simple denotative sense of dealing with root causes. Bronfenbrenner, Cochran, and Cross saw the problems of contemporary families, especially low-income families, as being very much tied to the social system.

The use of the word *empowerment* in the Family Matters pantheon of values was no accident. As noted in *Social Engineering*, empowerment "is a pivotal concept in the thinking of Paolo Freire (1971)," and throughout the world this term has very strong social-change and political connotations. Its resonances were to be heard in this country in the "power to the people" rhetoric during the sixties and seventies, and its quieter echoes reverberate in the empowerment theme Dr. Cochran sounds repeatedly today in his chapter and yesterday in the Family Matters Program. Like many other childhood interventions (cf. Mindick, 1986), Family Matters urged its participants to confront the political system (occasionally quite successfully), the social service system, neighborhood problems, and the educational system for their own benefit and for that of their children. Much of this I believe to have been good (though by no means all); but to call all this emphasis on social change "nudging" is quite anomalous.

Also, the attempt to make an impact by Family Matters was not trivial when judged by staff size. The approximately 15 persons who were employed (and the annual budget that implies) over the course of 3 to 4 years do not suggest a light-weight intervention. Indeed, as I have pointed out, because of the magnitude of the task the designers set themselves, the considerable resources the project received were insufficient, again not unusual for interventions of this kind.

As for the question of whether Family Matters was a social program, a great deal depends on one's definition of social program. If one means by "social program" an intervention that is distributed fairly broadly across a society, then clearly Family Matters did not qualify. It took place at only one site, Syracuse, New York, and cannot be considered to have been broadly distributed at that time. But if, by the phrase *social program*, one means an intervention which is targeted, not at separate persons, or even at individual families, but rather at the social structure broadly (and there is abundant evidence in Cochran's own words in this volume for this), then Family Matters would certainly be considered a social program. Furthermore, if one uses *social program* in the generic sense, to describe an intervention that has very much the same goals and implementation strategies as programs that are broadly based within a society, then Family Matters certainly qualified as a social program. Anyone knowing the early childhood intervention field who visited the program, if not informed of its specific name or affiliation, would have characterized it (based on goals and activities) as a Head-Start—or even more likely as a Home-Start-like—program having greater emphasis on home activities than Head Start, and having a little success in neighborhood organizing, but essentially very much like other early childhood intervention programs.

But rather than stating explicitly that Family Matters was a social program, *Social Engineering* refers to it as being in the context of "other family and childhood interventions" (p. 43). Rather than quibbling about its designation, I asked in the book's opening chapter what I believe what was an even more important question. Were the characteristics of Family Matters sufficiently representative of those of social programs to allow it to serve as a case study? I tried to answer that question as follows:

> It may of course be argued that the intervention was not necessarily totally representative of all social programs. In some respects, e.g., its knowledge base, the sincerity of its intentions, its leadership, the worthiness of its aims, and the genuine need for its offerings among a good number of its participants, it might have been expected to be superior to many other programs. In other respects, e.g., intervention knowhow and organizational management, it might have been expected to be less adequate. But in those respects that we see as being typically problematic in many contemporary and innovative social programs vis-a-vis the circumstances

they seek to alter, Family Matters serves as an example of considerable heuristic value. (1986, p. 14)

In other words, I stated that, while Family Matters might not represent all innovative social programs in some respects (mostly for the better, though sometimes for the worse), its implementation raised issues that are typical of many other programs of the sixties and seventies. And in this respect, at the very least, I hoped that readers would find value in the identification of problems common to many or most of these interventions and Family Matters' attempts to wrestle with these issues both successfully and unsuccessfully.

One of the most distracting aspects of Cochran's argument that Family Matters was not a social program but a piece of research is his rigid dichotomizing of programs as either research/experimental or social. Many social programs of the sixties and seventies were experimental and research-oriented. *Social Engineering* discusses many of them in Chapters 1 and 2, most prominently the income maintenance programs and Head Start and Head Start-like programs. Admittedly, the ratio of research energies and funding resources to intervention energies and resources was probably higher for Family Matters than for many others, but the hard and fast dichotomy between research and experiment as against social programs is certainly inappropriate.

Indeed, as a scientific program, Family Matters has produced a surprisingly small harvest to date. The findings Cochran presents in this volume are characterized strangely as "hypotheses." I do not know quite what is meant: Family Matters was a true experiment with both experimental and control groups. Yet we are told that the data do not allow us to infer causality. I do not know when Cochran will ever have a better opportunity to show program efficacy and causality for Family Matters or for his more recent efforts. More than 10 years after the original proposal, the scientific community still has from Family Matters only hypothesized relationships, some which seem to show improvement in the program group over the controls, and at least three relationships that suggest that it may have been better in that respect not to have participated in the program.

By its products, i.e., Extension publications and book chapters about intervention, I believe that it would be better to characterize the Family Matters component of the Comparative Ecology of Human Development Project as a demonstration and research program that achieved some modest success in its intervention and that produced some useful intervention expertise out of the good ideas and mistakes of its past. But based on its products, to proclaim its value as a piece of scientific research as opposed to being a "social program" is a bit much. What is most important, however, contrary to Cochran's assertions, *Social Engineering* never characterized Family Matters as a "piece of public policy," or explicitly called it a "social program." I have clearly stated that the program was *not* a prototypical social program, but in target, size (at the individual site level), philosophy, methods, and, most importantly, in terms of the strengths and weaknesses I was addressing in my book, Family Matters provided an important case study and afforded an excellent heuristic example.

Family Matters—A Paradigmatic Shift?

Cochran (this volume) states that, in addition to missing the scientific nature of Family Matters, I have also "failed to recognize the paradigmatic shift" that the empowerment approach represented historically. In responding to this criticism, I would here like to restate my purpose in writing this commentary. In addition to setting the record straight about *Social Engineering in Family Matters*, I would also like to contribute substantively to the purpose of this volume; and one of the most substantive contributions that I can make is to argue as forcefully as I can against the "empowerment approach," if by that it is meant that families participating in an intervention and staff members carrying it out are to be confused from beginning to end about who is to provide information to whom; or if empowerment means undertaking an intervention without careful assessment, planning, and use of available information before the intervention actually begins.

Empowerment *should* mean giving people a sense of their own worth, a sense of efficacy, in their lives. It is a concept that I have been studying in my research on fertility since 1973 (see Mindick & Oskamp, 1975). Nearly a decade ago, I proposed and found empirical support for a generalized model of adaptive behavior in which early relationships and socialization efforts lead to positive self-concept, cognitive coping style, and planfulness, which are shown to be pivotal correlates of adaptive behavior (Mindick, 1978). Distinguished researchers such as Rotter (1966) and Seligman (1975) have stressed the importance of personal efficacy (or the lack of it) for many years. Neighborhood groups and neighborhood mobilization in this country are at least several decades old (see Taylor, 1986).

As *Social Engineering* documents, other childhood intervention programs have stressed similar concepts in their objectives long before Family Matters, most notably Head Start in its third major goal of "community change." The Child and Family Resource Program (Abt, 1981) had, if anything, a greater emphasis on this kind of approach. The Family Development Research Program (which was a combination of research and social intervention much like Family Matters) preceded Family Matters by about half a decade in Syracuse, and had as one of its aims "to increase their [parents'] *potency* in fostering the development of their children" (Lally et al., 1982, cited in Mindick, 1986; emphasis added). Empowerment as an idea (though not necessarily the word) was hardly new with Family Matters on the childhood intervention scene. Several site teams reminded the program designers that empowerment, and the approaches used to bring it about, were far less novel than Bronfenbrenner, Cochran, and Cross liked to believe; and these same site visitors pointedly reminded those concerned that they ought to be benefitting from the previous research and intervention experience of others (cf. Mindick, 1986).

In an empowerment-oriented program, it has long been fairly clear from other interventions that participants should have a voice in the important decision making processes of the intervention. But this should not mean simply allowing workers to enter homes of families who expect information about worthwhile parent–child activities, which are supposed to promote development of cognitive sophistication, social skills, and the ability of a youngster to persevere in the pursuit of long term goals, and then simply to ask, "What kind of activities do you engage in?" without workers making significant substantive contributions of their own. Of course Bronfenbrenner, Cochran, and Cross were correct when they did not send their workers into homes with a patronizing, "we-know-best," Lady Bountiful attitude. But well-trained home visitors don't really have to choose between being overbearing and simply staring at families and waiting for them to say something (cf. Mindick, 1986, p. 147).

How might program designers have better empowered parents in the decision making associated with intervention? Kaplan (1976) offers some worthwhile suggestions in the context of social policy generally and housing specifically. Kaplan points out that attempts to construct housing or other kinds of programs for the elderly or for low-income families are often condemned to failure because no consultation takes place with such individuals in advance. He recommends, therefore, that advisory committees be formed *before* the design and the construction of such housing, so that decisions, planning, and information seeking take place in advance. He also urges that any participation in the decision-making process not be mere tokenism.

There was an advisory committee for the Family Matters program. It was made up of some community leaders and some program families. Unfortunately, the council was convoked almost as an afterthought, well after the pilot research had been undertaken and well after programs had begun. Furthermore, the kinds of issues that were raised for its consideration rarely gave it the opportunity to make decisions that could have markedly affected the outcome of the intervention. The result was that, with its relatively few meetings, its limited agenda, and the narrow interpretation of power given to it, the advisory committee rarely had little more than token power and merely ratified decisions already made elsewhere. This advisory committee could have served both to provide information and to make parents really feel empowered. Unfortunately, it did very little of either.

But probably the most unwise use of the "empowerment" theme is documented by Cochran himself in this volume. He states, "One major strength of the empowerment approach is that it compensates for a lack of knowledge about the needs of specific families by involving them in shaping the program." (p. 49). In light of Cochran's comment, one wonders just how little information one needs to plan a program in advance? And just how much can one depend on information gathering by program workers from families after a program has already begun? These are questions that we will address in the next section, which deals with the issue of whether or not Family Matters utilized the information at its disposal in an appropriate way, not just coming out of the project, but also "going in" and throughout its duration.

The Dearth of Information Resources

Cochran has faulted *Social Engineering* because of its comment about the dearth of information resources available to the Family Matters program designers and to other comparable interventions, including major social programs and policy interventions. He claims that he and his colleagues should not be faulted for the little that they apparently knew "going into" the project. Instead, they should be judged on the basis of information gain after the project was over. But we have seen that Cochran was willing to allow the "empowerment" approach to substitute for adequate information resources. This was a serious error. This was true, first, because Drs. Bronfenbrenner, Cochran, and Cross between them had a good deal of expertise in the area of child development, expertise displayed in their previous work and in the various research proposals that they submitted to funding sources and which indeed gained them the support to conduct the research and intervention programs that made up the Comparative Ecology of Human Development Project. Indeed, what I question in *Social Engineering in Family Matters* is the fact that the design elements put forward in these proposals were in large part abandoned before the pilot program even began, much less the mainstream intervention. In the correspondence documented in the book, the two earliest players, Bronfenbrenner and Cochran, decided that their thinking had been wrong and based on a priori assumptions, and simply discarded much of the information resource material that they already had, as well as much that previous studies had shown.

In addition, the original proposal had proposed several assessments of the needs and conditions of participant families, several of them to be carried out during the early stages of the project while program workers were being trained (Bronfenbrenner & Cochran, 1976). This was an attempt to make certain that the training of the workers would be well suited to execution of the interventions that were to be carried out. Furthermore, the original proposal also promised that data from the baseline assessment, the most important assessment of families in five major areas, would be used to help to guide the intervention. Workers were to be made aware of their families' needs at least as a group, and a "treatment profile inventory" was to be constructed for each family. In addition, there were to be "annual assessments" of participating families, once again with a view to fine-tuning the program so that the program goals would be reached.

Because of the dearth of financial resources that I discuss in *Social Engineering*, these annual assessments did not take place, and it would have been unrealistic to expect that this kind of measurement could take place in light of the financial situation. However, baseline assessment was made. Unfortunately, however, there was an undue delay in the analysis of those findings. Dr. Cochran's chapter shows that the final report on this baseline assessment was not completed and sent to one of its sponsoring agencies, The National Institute of Education, until 1982, a year after the program was completely over. Preliminary reports were made along the line, but there was considerable delay even in these tentative findings of the first wave of data collection, and it was not shared with workers. Treatment profile inventories were not instituted and updated *on a weekly basis* (as originally proposed) *describing in detail* the program resources that had been devoted to each family.

Several site teams visiting the project and several members of the project's senior staff commented that the program had failed to benefit from the literature describing the work of other investigators carrying out comparable early childhood interventions and similar research efforts (Mindick, 1986). Dr. Heather Weiss, then director of analysis for the project, was particularly concerned about this lack of cross-pollination. After repeated urgings by her, the program designers were at last persuaded to allow two or three other nationally reputed investigators to talk about their findings in relevant research or intervention areas. But it was the conclusion of the above site teams that the program designers had simply not used or shared their own information resources sufficiently, and that they had benefited insufficiently from the information resources that could have been provided by other experienced experts in the same area (Mindick, 1986).

Instead, Cochran states that workers were used to collect information about family needs. But this is a practice about which I would caution other program designers. Program workers have their own aims and interests at heart when they assess the "needs" of their clients. In *Social Engineering* (1986, p. 160), I point to the research literature that shows that, very often, organizations become self-sustaining in a way that makes them more concerned with perpetuating the organizational structure and fulfilling the needs of employees than meeting the needs of clients. This is a typical pattern found in many an organization, and we may not expect Family Matters employees or any organizational employees to be angelic. Also, program workers generally only reach people who choose to participate. There are certain demand characteristics implicit in the way they contact people and obtain information.

Thus, I believe it to have been a very serious error to depend on program workers to give feedback to the program designers when the families in the project had given at least four lengthy interviews lasting 2 to 3 hours each (and in some cases even longer), dealing with the very areas needed to make program policy decisions. A far better human resource was to be found in the research interviewers whose self-interests were not bound up with the kinds of program interventions that would be carried out. As *Social Engineering* mentions, some families spent more time with their research interviewer than with their program worker. In many cases, the relationship was even better with this kind of person than with the program worker.

Two additional sources of information that Family Matters could have had "going into" and during the duration of the program were both the Pilot Study and the Process Study. The Pilot Study was carried out in two neighborhoods in Syracuse very comparable to those that participated in the main study program. Supported by the Mott Foundation, the pilot program's dual rationale was: to pretest the research instruments before they were administered in program neighborhoods, and to perfect the intervention so that it would be more effective in those neighborhoods. Program materials and techniques were to be introduced into the pilot neighborhoods 9 months before their use in program main study neighborhoods (a highly appropriate gestational period) and these were to be used as a source of information.

Cochran (this volume) is curiously silent about this fairly large, long-lasting and relatively expensive pilot program, I suspect because it weakens his case somewhat about Family Matters being just an experimental research program. If one is just "nudging the environment" to see what happens, what is the point of the pilot program? The reality is that the pilot neighborhoods, in addition to helping in research instrument development, were used in order to establish a more potent treatment for the main study program; and some of the information from the pilot neighborhoods did in fact guide the main study intervention. Unfortunately, there was not sufficient flexibility early on in program history to benefit fully from what was learned in the pilot neighborhoods, i.e., that the very loose intervention that went by the name of "empowerment" was not terribly effective, and this information was not properly utilized "going in" to the main study programs.

Additional information that could have been utilized and was not used sufficiently was supplied by the Process Study itself. The Carnegie Corporation of New York had sponsored the process study to allow the program designers to better their understanding of the implementation of the program. This was to help assess the intervention en route and to aid in tracing the roots of its successes or failings at program's end.

We have discussed in *Social Engineering in Family Matters* the problems of organization that occurred in the Ecology of Human Development project, though not a great deal of prominence has been given the confusion and disagreement that sometimes prevailed at the senior staff levels, an understatement which apparently Dr. Cochran sees as a fault (p. 47). But there *was* considerable discord associated with the first two directors of the process study and, after the departure of both, the position of Process Study Director remained vacant for approximately a year. Unfortunately, this year coincided with the work being done in the pilot neighborhoods and with the first 7 months of program activity— months that were vital in terms of feedback to the program designers concerning the problems of the program. The year's time when the Process Study directorship was vacant, plus the startup time after that vacancy was filled, denied the program designers and implementors the kind of information resources that they might have used to improve the intervention. This meant that the Process Study was not able to provide information until the program was almost half over. Ingrid Bø and several students did assume some of the work of the Process Study temporarily, and indeed came to many of the same conclusions, both then, about 1979, and later, that I come to in my book *Social Engineering in Family Matters*, especially with regard to the excessive passivity of program workers (Bø, 1979). But their recommendations and mine were implemented only very slowly and rather tardily.

Thus, when Dr. Cochran argues that Family Matters should have been judged on what its designers knew coming out rather than what they knew "going in," my argument is that, although we do not have all the information we need to conduct successful interventions with human beings, especially in delicate areas like child development, one should still take maximum advantage of those resources that are available. We need to analyze and disseminate premeasurement data in timely fashion. We must fill staff positions promptly, especially when precious information resources are at issue. The relevant work of other investigators must be examined; and we cannot forswear our own expertise. We cannot place *excessive* reliance on program workers for information gathering, recognizing that they are not totally disinterested parties. We should use participant advisory committees which are convoked at a time and in a manner which will allow true decision making, true participation, and true "empowerment" to occur. Under these circumstances one may expect that interventions will be more potent and their effects more generalized.

The Generality of Effects of Family Matters

Cochran also takes issue with my concern that the effects of Family Matters were not more general than they were. According to his hypotheses, presented in his chapter is this volume, it is the less educated parents who benefited most from the Family Matters Program. He implies that we have no right to expect that the gains as a result of program implementation would have been more broadly felt. In *Social Engineering*, I cite the work of Schlossman (1976), which shows that, since the early seventies, there has been a trend in family and parent education programs toward democratization. This means that such interventions are no longer considered important only for low-income or racial-minority families. Family Matters did not point its intervention only at low-income or racial-minority families. *Social Engineering* discusses the two reasons for this; "the first was inherent in the study's interest in understanding the effects of *different* social structural characteristics on child rearing and family life" and second was "the belief of the principal investigators that many of the problems of child rearing in the contemporary urban environment are not confined to low income families'' (Mindick, 1986, p. 48). With two-earner families, the poor are *not* the ''only parents who don't or can't spend enough time in optimal forms of joint activity with their children'' (ibid.) or in networking with their neighbors.

As a matter of fact, it was middle class participants and well educated mothers who participated most actively in the program (Mindick, 1986). *Social Engineering in Family Matters* documents 17 quantitative indices of program participation that we in the Process Study constructed to assess levels of participation in the program. If Cochran is right that it was the less-educated mothers who benefited most, then we have another anomaly of the program, comparable to the anomaly previously mentioned: that, for black and for white mothers from two-parent families, participation in the program seemed to worsen some school relations and outcomes, as well as self-esteem for some of the subgroups of these mothers. The additional anomaly is that the mothers who participated the least benefited most. And while it is true that, as Cochran asserts, ''more is not necessarily better,'' and that it is possible that middle-class mothers had their own sources of support which were not markedly improved by participation in the program, it is a strange sort of intervention where those who participate the least benefit the most.

One may see the findings that Cochran reports as the result of the modest amount of empowerment given by the intervention to mothers of low education having its desired effect. Alternately, one may question whether or not the findings that he presents are in part attributable to: (a) incomplete control of several of the social and economic differences between the program and the control groups which differed significantly in several ways, both before the program began and after it was over; (b) regression artifact; (c) an interaction between the treatment and the pretest (cf. Campbell & Stanley, 1966) which worked for the program participants but not for the control group, who got no treatment; (d) measurement error; (e) genuine worthwhile effects; or (f) a combination of some or all of the above. Personally, I believe the last mentioned to be the most likely answer.

But the issue that must be raised and examined, rather than being dismissed out of hand, is the question of program effectiveness among families of low education, who apparently needed the treatment most, and seemingly benefited most, when these families participated least. Clearly it has not been the experience of other investigators, including Bronfenbrenner (1974), that families whose stresses are great and whose supports are not so great (or any kind of family, for that matter) benefit from a low-intensity parent–child intervention. The relevant research literature shows virtually no instances of interventions where low levels of participation in programs of modest intensity are especially beneficial, unless the intervention itself is counter-productive. There are, of course, ceiling effects that might have worked on the more highly educated mothers; but, given the modest intensity of the program generally (families received a mean of about 15 home visits and attended a mean of about 4 group or cluster meetings over the course of the entire program), and given the even lower levels of participation by less-educated mothers, further investigation of the phenomenon certainly seems indicated.

Summing up, I ask questions about the generality of the effects of the Family Matters program, given the fact that causality cannot be shown, given the fact that there has been a democratization of parent-education programs to which Family Matters subscribed, and given the fact that higher levels of participation did not produce in reasonably well-supported families many of the expected positive changes, but did produce some of those changes and apparently some negative ones among families with poor supports and low levels of participation.

Family Matters—A Process-Oriented Assessment

Cochran concludes his chapter by expressing his disappointment that the overall assessment of Family Matters in *Social Engineering* was not more favorable, because of a "decision to dwell upon our weaknesses without acknowledging our achievements, thus dismissing Family Matters as just another in a series of overblown and underachieving social programs" (this volume, p. 48). I find this to be a curious statement, for two reasons: first, because I made a very conscious attempt to present the affirmative side of the case, and, second, because the phrase "overblown and underachieving social program" was never applied to Family Matters in my book. As a matter of fact, this is not the only instance where Cochran puts pejorative, emotion-laden words into my mouth in alleged characterization of Family Matters. He states on p. 25 that I dismissed "Family Matters as another of those 'big ideas' that 'seem to have become caricatures of themselves the moment they ceased to be ideas and began to be translated into action (p. 186)' 4." Yet that statement, which was a citation of Elmore (1978), was not a characterization of Family Matters. It was a characterization of social programs of the fifties, sixties, and seventies by another scholar. Cochran not only confuses the issue by explicitly attributing it to me and applying it gratuitously to Family Matters, but he reinforces the perception of my being hard on Family Matters by not using the appropriate form of citation. The citation of "(p. 186)4" makes it sound like the words were mine and came directly from my book, but the appropriate citation should have been "(Elmore, 1978, p. 186, cited in Mindick, 1986, p. 7)." Only the conscientious reader who looks up endnote 4 knows that the quotation is Elmore's and that the statement applies to social programs prior to Family Matters; and only readers who read *Social Engineering* and look at page 7 know that I never applied Elmore's quote to Family Matters. In both of these cases, Cochran incautiously and inappropriately attributes highly charged statements of a negative nature to me about Family Matters. He then complains to the reader that I have been excessively unfavorable, "without acknowledging [Family Matters' designers'] strengths."

There are many positive elements of the program described in *Social Engi-*

neering, most notably "The Reaction of Families to Program I" (pp. 83–84) and "Taking Concerted Action" (pp. 99–101), as well as most of the description of both the home visit and neighborhood group program in Chapters 5 and 6. Indeed, Chapter 5 is entitled "Benevolent Intentions and Deeds," even though these two chapters are not *unfailingly* uncritical of Family Matters.

My task was not to present only the brighter side of program implementation. As a process analyst, my job was to look at *all* of this program's implementation, and Dr. Cochran says that he agrees with the "great bulk" of my analyses of those processes. I cited the project's own outcome analyses available to me in 1983 and 1984, when I was writing my book, to show the relationship between implementation and outcome. In preparation for writing this comment, I have had a brief opportunity to examine the recent final reports to NIE Cochran cites in his chapter. My conclusions remain basically unchanged. There were some excellent ideas inherent in the design of Family Matters program. Drs. Bronfenbrenner, Cochran, and Cross deserve credit both for those that were original and those they rightly derived from the experience of others. In some instances, these ideas, plus good implementation and the work of some of the devoted and idealistic workers, produced marked positive effects. Unfortunately, in some instances, much of the proposal design was abandoned prematurely, and some of this material was reinstituted belatedly. Some of what was planned was implemented poorly or not at all. This led to nonsignificant effects, noneffects, and perhaps even to some negative or reverse effects. The overall impact of the program cannot be said to be overly great, whether as positive change or as prevention. Indeed, in the two reports cited by Dr. Cochran, it appears that the .10 level of significance is adopted in much of the text and the .20 level of significance for most of the tables. Even though a sample of 225 is not inconsiderable in psychological research, these unconventional alpha levels are adopted precisely because effect size was not great.

The implication of blame because of the lack of large effects must be avoided. Expectations of very large or very general effects are not realistic (Mindick, 1986, pp. 178–179). My book presents the reasons why Family Matters and other social interventions cannot expect large and universal effects: shortage of information resources, inadequate organizational models, scarce financial resources, problems of living in the urban context, a short program life cycle, etc.

But I cannot overlook the problems of implementation in Family Matters as a source of small or noneffects. My job was to look at implementation. It would be no help to future program designers to avert my gaze from weaknesses and to describe only strengths. It is also no help to the research mission of the project and of the scientific community broadly to look at the kinds of effects produced by Family Matters as if the program had been implemented with great excellence, when there were serious implementation inadequacies.

If Dr. Cochran has now "sharpened empowerment," and his current programatic efforts are indeed potent and free of such inadequacies, then I rejoice! If important effects can be demonstrated scientifically and convincingly, then I will be among the first to wend my way to his door and wish blessings on his head, because his benevolent intentions and goals are extraordinarily worthwhile. But, based on the evidence available thus far, there are still many lessons that all of us may yet learn about the implementation of parent empowerment programs.

REFERENCES

Abt Associates, Inc. (1981, April). *Child and family resource program*. Paper presented at the biennial meeting of the Society for Research in Child Development, Boston, MA.

Bo, I. (1979) *In support of families: The pilot testing of two experimental programs*. Paper prepared for the Carnegie Corporation of New York. Cornell University, Ithaca, NY.

Bronfenbrenner, U. (1974) *Is early intervention effective? A report on longitudinal evaluations of preschool programs*. (Vol. 2.). Washington, DC: Department of Health, Education and Welfare.

Bronfenbrenner, U. (1979). *The ecology of human development*. Cambridge, MA: Harvard University Press.

Bronfenbrenner, U. (1980, February). Paper delivered to the Executive Staff of the National Institute of Education, Bethesda, MD.

Bronfenbrenner, U., & Cochran, M. (1976). *The comparative ecology of human development: A research proposal*. Ithaca, NY: Cornell University.

Campbell, D. T., & Stanley, J. C. (1966). *Experimental and quasi-experimental designs for research*. Chicago, IL: Rand McNally.

Elmore, E. F. (1978). Organizational models of social program implementation. *Public Policy, 26*, 185–228.

Freire, P. (1971). *Pedagogy of the oppressed*. New York: Herder & Herder.

Kaplan, S. (1976, September). On the fear of cognitive chaos. In D. Stokols (Chair), *Environmental design and policy implications of behavioral research and theory*. Symposium conducted at the annual meeting of American Psychological Association, Washington, DC.

Lally, J. R., Mindick, B., Darlington, R., Honig, A., Barnett, W. S., & Haiman, P. E. (1982) *The effects of the family development research program on families, children, and staff: A follow up study of low income/low education families whose children received continuous health, social, psychological and cognitive services from birth to five years of age*. San Francisco, CA: Far West Laboratory for Educational Research and Development.

Mindick, B. (1978). *Personality and social psychological correlates of success or failure in contraception: A longitudinal predictive study* Doctoral dissertation, Claremont Graduate School, Claremont, CA. *Dissertation Abstracts International, Volume 39* p#3051-B.

Mindick, B. (1986). *Social engineering in Family Matters*. New York: Praeger Publishers.

Mindick, B., & Oskamp, S. (1975). Population, planfulness, and the environment. *Man-Environment Systems, 5*, 311–312.

Rotter, J. B. (1966). Generalized expectancies for internal versus external control of reinforcement. *Psychological Monographs, 80*(1), Whole No. 609).

Schlossman, S. L. (1976). Before Home Start: Notes toward a history of parent education in America, 1897–1929. *Harvard Educational Review, 46*(3), 436–67.

Seligman, M. E. P. (1975). *Helplessness: On depression, development, and death*. San Francisco, CA: Freeman, 1975.

Taylor, R. B. (Ed.) (1986). *Urban neighborhoods: Research and policy*. New York: Praeger Publishers.

Chapter 4
Generic Issues in Parent Empowerment Programs: A Rejoinder to Mindick

Moncrieff Cochran
Cornell University

Dr. Mindick's response to my chapter is, to my mind, much like his book; it contains useful insights, but in the wrong cause. In the chapter I agreed with many of Dr. Mindick's criticisms of our program implementation process. But I argued that his comparison of our difficulties with the social programs of the 1960s was inappropriate, because ours was basic research rather than an effort to implement public policy. With regard to his response to my chapter, I again find myself agreeing with some of the points he makes, but convinced that they are presented for the wrong purpose. Dr. Mindick's overall concern is with what he calls his scientific responsibility, and he expresses that concern succinctly at the end of his response by saying,

> It would be no help to future program designers to avert my gaze from weaknesses and to describe only strengths. It is also no help to the research mission of the project and of the scientific community broadly to look at the kinds of effects produced by Family Matters as if the program had been implemented with great excellence, when there were serious implementation inadequacies. (p. 64)

This claim, that in the chapter I have proclaimed the strengths of the Family Matters project without acknowledging its weaknesses, is a red herring. If that had been my purpose, then I would never have brought in Dr. Mindick's book at all! What I *did* indicate was that interesting differences between program and control families were found *despite* inadequacies of program implementation, and that there is good reason to believe that the empowering processes involved in the program led to those changes.

Dr. Mindick could have used his response to my chapter as an opportunity to identify for the reader a series of challenges facing those interested in parent support and parent education. This rejoinder is organized in that way. Five generic issues are identified below. Each is articulated briefly, and then related to the Mindick response. Following these is a section for the record briefly summarizing other areas of disagreement.

Basic Research vs. Program Evaluation

This distinction is not a quibble. In basic research, the purpose is to identify predictive relationships between phenomena, and develop theories composed of laws derived from those relationships. With program evaluation, the goal is to understand what effects the intervention had upon program participants and how those effects were accomplished, usually in order to decide whether to continue the program or how best to modify it. Thus, with basic research the primary interest is in the social or physical environment intervened upon, while with program evaluation the intervention itself is the primary focus.

In the case of Family Matters, the primary emphasis of the project is stated on page 1 of the original proposal:

> This document presents a plan for a methodological, cross-cultural, and experimental research on the *ecology of human development.* Specifically, the aim of the investigation is the analysis of real-life settings, both immediate and remote, as they effect the activities of parents and other caretakers with the child, and thereby influence the development of the child's intellectual and social competence in the outside world." (Bronfenbrenner & Cochran, 1976)

On page 4 of that proposal, we describe the purpose of the "contrived experiment" as "to illuminate critical conditions affecting processes of socialization, education and development as they operate at the individual, family, school and neighborhood level." In later writings, Dr. Bronfenbrenner refers to the program as a way of "nudging" the ecological systems surrounding program families, in order to better understand those systems by observing their response. (How much intervention constitutes a "nudge," in scientific terms? Dr. Mindick argues at one point that ours was more than a nudge, and at another that we failed to intervene as comprehensively as promised. From his perspective, we were damned if we did, and damned if we didn't.)

As a research project, we made a major investment—3 full years—in developing new instruments for describing and evaluating the environments containing families with young children. This process was carried out jointly with research teams from three other countries. A year was spent pilot-testing these instruments in two Syracuse neighborhoods. The result was a set of complex, in-depth interviews, which had never been used before to assess program processes or impacts.

Our research experience contains several lessons for those who would evaluate parent support programs. First, gather some data at baseline that can be analysed quickly, if you wish to shape the program with baseline findings. As Dr. Mindick indicates, we had hoped to make such use of baseline data. Unfortunately, it took a full year after data collection to develop reliable coding schemes for use with the open-ended interview responses. This precluded the use of the data for program design. Thus, what hampered us was our emphasis on cross-national research, to the detriment of maximally effective program development. Second, include a pilot study if at all possible. In our case, 30 families in two neighborhoods participated both in a pilot version of the baseline interviews and in our initial attempts at home-visiting and building neighborhood clusters. Dr. Mindick claims that we did not "benefit fully" from the pilot study, and that information gathered from the experience was not "properly utilized." In fact, the pilot was invaluable for what it taught us about a wide range of key research tasks, like explaining the project to parents and community members, scheduling interviews, and shortening and tightening interview protocols. It also provided very useful information about the responses of families to initial program initiatives, and the roles of home visitor and neighborhood worker. As a direct result of the pilot study we made the following changes related to workers and staffing:

- shifted away from part-time jobs
- increased emphasis on regularly scheduled office time
- placed greater emphasis in training on staff relations
- created a written set of guidelines for workers and families
- hired a research and development person to support each program approach

The following aspects of the home-visiting approach used in the main study stemmed directly from the pilot experience:

- the activities notebook, containing suggestions from parents and others
- the newsletter for parents
- clarification of program boundaries

Cluster-building benefited from the pilot in the following ways:

- identified the need for initial home visits prior to group meetings
- emphasis on several smaller clusters, rather than one large group
- the shift to a more active worker role

In addition, the pilot study provided all of us with a practical understanding of the deficit perspective, and of ways to avoid it. Perhaps most importantly, the pilot provided us with the initial data regarding the need to fold the separate home-visiting and cluster-building approaches together into a single set of program options (see my chapter).

Dr. Mindick, with the benefit of hindsight, concludes that the intervention would have been more effective if we had made still more changes based on the pilot. I agree—with the benefit of hindsight.

I argued in my chapter that the emphasis given in the Family Matters Project to basic research hampered the program. The delays mentioned earlier, caused by development of new research techniques and tools, underscore that point. But the research orientation also has its benefits. One of those benefits is its emphasis on caution when interpreting findings. This caution is manifested partly in heavy emphasis on consideration of alternative hypotheses regarding cause and effect. In our case, we believe with a high degree of certainty that participation in the Family Matters program *caused* the differences between the program and comparison groups in perception of self as parent, network size and composition, parent–child activities, and school outcomes reported in my chapter. However, *one alternative hypothesis could not be ruled out.* We had no baseline measure of innate ability for the parents or the children in the two groups at baseline. Therefore, it is possible (although unlikely, given our sampling procedure) that some innate prior advantage on the part of program families caused the differences seen at follow-up. Because of this, and because several different "paths" can be argued for the sequencing of the process variables in Figures 2 and 3 of my chapter, I was careful to term the arrows in the figures "hypotheses." Dr. Mindick apparently would not have been so careful; he decries my use of the term.

The issue of care when interpreting findings also comes up when one wishes to apply the terms *positive* and *negative*, as there is always great pressure to do with regard to program impacts. The advantage of the more "detached" research perspective is that it reduces that pressure. For instance, the black, married mothers in our program showed a somewhat lower perception of themselves as parents at follow-up, when compared with their contrast counterparts. But the scores for these two subgroups were substantially higher than those for the other six subgroups, whether program or control. And, for that program subgroup, involvement with the child's school increased as the perception scores decreased. Was this program effect positive or negative? It can be argued either way. Another example of this dilemma involved the personal networks of white, married mothers. The networks of program mothers declined somewhat at the *overall* level in relation to the contrast group, but at the *primary* level the program mothers showed the greater increase, a difference that reached significance in relation to kinfolk. Thus, less growth in overall size was accompanied by more growth in the number of kinfolk viewed by the mother as "especially important." Is this finding positive or negative? I assume, because he is nonspecific, that these are the kinds of findings Dr. Mindick is referring to as negative in his response to my chapter. It is important to underscore that he is making a *personal judgement* about findings that could be interpreted in several different ways.

The Meaning and Importance of the Ecological Perspective

In my chapter, I emphasized that Family Matters research was built upon an ecological framework. In describing that perspective (p. 26) I stressed differentiation of the various environmental systems impinging on family life, and the importance of recognizing both environmental and intrapersonal systems as the *processes* through which a program achieves its impacts upon the attitudes, behavior, and development of individuals. Several key research strategies flow from this perspective. The first is that assessment of program impact must include a broad rather than a narrow range of "outcomes," and that some of those measures must be focused on the intrapersonal and environmental features viewed as processes rather than on change in the individuals viewed as the ultimate beneficiaries of the program. In our case, processes included parents' perceptions of themselves and their children, parents' personal network, and parent–child activities, while the child was the family member of ultimate interest. The second crucial strategy is to distinguish among families, in the analysis of the data, according to the combinations of ecological circumstance that social science suggests have significance for the ideologies, attitudes, and behaviors of their members. The reader of my chapter knows that we used race and family structure to distinguish four subgroups, and can see from the findings presented in Figures 2 and 3 how important those distinctions proved to be for understanding the patterns of process and outcome. In more qualitative analyses, not presented in the chapter, we have found real utility in still finer distinctions; for instance, between the single parents of one or the other race who receive public assistance and those who do not, and between those same parents who live without another adult in the home and those living with a partner or with their parents.

In my chapter I pointed out Dr. Mindick's concern with effects that were not "general across participant subgroups or across outcome domains." (Mindick, 1986, p. 108), and argued that this concern suggested a lack of understanding of our ecological orientation to human development. Several aspects of his response to the chapter reinforce that impression. First, when discussing the generality of effects issue, he bases his argument only upon the higher scores on school-related cognitive outcomes displayed by program children with less educated parents (p. 62). In so doing he is caught in the same fallacy that weakened the interventions of the 1960s and early 1970s, and that we consciously set out to avoid with the Family Matters research: the tendency to concentrate upon a narrow range of outcomes within a single segment of society. The Family Matters program was delivered to a broad cross-section of Syracuse families. Differences between program and comparison families were found *in all four subgroups.* Cognitive school outcome differences were greater for children with less educated parents, but changes in perceptions of self and in personal networks occurred in all four subgroups. These changes are summarized in more detail on pages 33 and 34 of my chapter. Of course, the overall pattern of changes was different in each subgroup (Figures 2 and 3), which again underscores the importance of distinguishing among meaningfully different ecological niches.

The other indication that Dr. Mindick hasn't grasped the significance of our ecological approach comes on page 64, where he claims that we adopted "unconventional alpha levels" in several reports "even though a sample of 225 is not inconsiderable in psychological research." In fact, as Dr. Mindick knew and as any reader can see in Table 1 of my chapter, the largest subgroup size in our analyses was 69, and one cell contained only 10 families. I can only conclude from such an obvious misreading of the research design that Dr. Mindick does not appreciate the importance of distinguishing among ecological niches in research of this kind. (My specific response to the "unconventional alpha levels" claim is found at the end of this rejoinder.)

What is Empowerment?

In his response to my chapter, Dr. Mindick presents his own version of the empowerment process, without any attempt to do justice to the process described in my chapter. Perhaps that is because nowhere in the chapter did I present a concise definition of the process as I have come to know it. This definition has emerged both from what we learned in Syracuse, and from 5 years of literature review and visits to support programs both in the United States and in other countries (Cochran, 1985, 1987).

> *Empowerment* - an interactive process involving mutual respect and critical reflection, through which both people and controlling institutions are changed in ways that provide those people with greater influence over individuals and institutions that are in some way influencing their efforts to achieve equal status in society.

In the two book chapters cited above, I evaluate our Family Matters program in terms of the seven empowerment criteria contained in this definition, and conclude that the Syracuse program was incomplete. While rather successful at interacting respectfully with families and at changing certain attitudes and behaviors, the program was only partially able to stimulate peer interaction and critical reflection, and failed to address the question of the balance of power between families and controlling institutions. I believe that, in our empowerment work since the Syracuse program was completed in 1981, we have continued to progress toward implementation of the process as embodied in the definition.

Several misconceptions about the empowerment process are generated by Dr. Mindick in his response to my chapter. The first is that the process had been understood, articulated and applied to programming in support of families well before 1977, when we began our work in Syracuse. The example he cites "most notably" is "Head Start in its third major goal of 'community change'." But Head Start programs did not operate with the explicit assumption, as we did, that *all* families have *some* strengths. Head Start was a program only eligible to families with incomes below a given cut-off point, which gave it a clear deficit orientation. And those operating Head Start programs did not assume, as we did and still do, that much of the most useful knowledge about the rearing of children is to be found among the people actually engaged in that undertaking. Yet I argue that it was these two assumptions that made it possible for our workers to develop the mutually respectful relationships with parents—not every parent in the program, but a large proportion of them—that set in motion the empowerment process.

What *are* the elements in the empowerment process? Dr. Mindick gives most weight to a sense of efficacy in parents. He also tells us that neighborhood groups and neighborhood mobilization are several decades old in this country, and he mentions a "generalized model of adaptive behavior" involving early socialization, positive self-concept, cognitive coping style and planfulness. But nowhere does he, *or does anyone else prior to 1983*, describe the process that we observed occurring with some parents in our Syracuse program, which we began to refer to as the "empowerment process" *only after those observations*. The first phase in the process involved a change in the parent's perception of herself as a parent, probably much akin to what Dr. Mindick and others refer to as a sense of worth.

This initial step, while important, is only the beginning. Next, we believe, came change in parents' relations with family members. In the case of Family Matters, emphasis was given by home visitors to the parent–child relationship. The third element involved informal relationships with relatives and friends outside the immediate family but in the parents' personal network. Family Matters' cluster group approach was an effort to facilitate this part of the process. The final stage in the process is, in our view, the most challenging; it involves interaction with formal institutions in an effort to obtain services needed by family members. In the case of Family Matters the focus was on home–school communications. We believe that successful accomplishment at this fourth stage is dependent upon a certain minimum level of accomplishment in each of the earlier phases. The most essential point is that the empowerment process involves *all four elements*, and is based on a specific set of assumptions about parents.

Contrary to what Dr. Mindick implies in both his book and his response to my chapter, the concept of an empowerment process that emerged from our Syracuse program is not the same as that used by Paolo Friere, although the two have some aspects in common. Our concept emphasizes a developmental sequence of steps focused both on the individual and the social surround. Friere (1973, 1978) emphasizes development of a group consciousness based on a process of critical reflection.

One major strength of the empowerment approach, I argue late in my chapter, is that it compensates for lack of knowledge about the needs of specific families by involving them in shaping the program, and in so doing takes advantage of the vast reservoir of general knowledge lodged in the culture as a whole. In his response, Dr. Mindick takes me to task for this statement, wondering "just how little information one needs to plan a program in advance?" (p. 57). The easy answer to that question is, "The more you can know in advance about the families you serve, without impinging on their rights to privacy and confidentiality, the better." But the real world is not that simple. Anyone who has worked with large numbers of families knows that they consist of an infinite combination of strengths and needs. No program can gather all of the information needed to gauge the resources and needs of the families to be served prior to service delivery. We also believe that families are in a better position than anyone else to judge their own needs. Therefore, we developed an approach to family support that involved parents as *partners* in needs assessment, and in the selection of a combination of program options specific to those particular needs. I am convinced that this partnership approach was an essential ingredient in the empowerment process and strongly recommend it to others interested in empowering parents.

Dr. Mindick faults us for being late in organizing an advisory committee and giving that committee relatively little say in the running of the program. It is accurate to say that we placed relatively little emphasis on the advisory committee as a part of the empowerment process. Our primary focus of empowerment was on individual families, and on cluster groups at the neighborhood level.

Dr. Mindick also states that the program design elements put forth in the original proposals "were in large part abandoned before the pilot program even began, much less the mainstream intervention." That is a statement of opinion rather than fact. Upon re-reading our original proposal, I come to a conclusion directly apposed to Dr. Mindick's. I am struck by how *closely* we adhered to the original plan, within the limits of available resources. The only dramatic shift was away from the "toy demonstrator" approach to home visiting developed by Levenstein (1972), because of a concern that the approach left too little room for validation of parental worth. In that regard, it was interesting to hear a paper presented at the 1987 SRCD meetings in Baltimore, Maryland, in which the authors were unable to find any positive effects for program children from a large-scale intervention in Bermuda using the strict Levenstein model (Scarr & McCartney, 1987).

The Value of Program Workers as Sources of Useful Information

We met with our program workers weekly, to discuss problems they were having in the field and to hear from them how families were responding to program initiatives. These meetings were very important for three reasons. First, they provided an opportunity to give support to the workers, who were performing a difficult set of tasks under difficult circumstances. The building of a support system for staff is especially important in interventions involving families, where demands are high and monetary rewards small. The second important function of the meetings was to provide a forum for discussing specific aspects of the workers' roles. We were asking workers to find a balance in their roles that gave parents a good deal of responsibility for program structure and content. As Dr. Mindick documents well in his book, this role was confusing to workers. The meetings were used to discuss what was unclear and efforts to provide more clarity. Finally, we used the meetings to listen to workers as they described how families were responding to their initiatives. This information was anecdotal. It did not take the place of either baseline or follow-up data collection. What it did do was to give us clues about *how* the program was having its effect. For instance, after about 6 months of pilot program activity, several different workers commented at different times upon the fact that the mothers in some of their families had begun to take better care of their physical appearance. After hearing this kind of observation three or four times, I began to wonder whether this was because these women's perceptions of themselves were becoming more positive. Later on, home visitors began to indicate that a number of their families were asking why they couldn't meet together in groups, rather than being visited separately by the home visitor. It occurred to me that these inquiries might have been stimulated in part by confidence stemming from more positive perception of self. They led to a proposal that those home-visited families who wished be encouraged to form cluster groups, and ultimately the folding together of the home visiting and cluster grouping approaches. Such observations were not made by workers in their own interest, as Dr. Mindick suggests on page 59. They resulted in considerable discomfort for the workers, who had to undergo training in home visitor or neighborhood worker roles for which they had not originally been hired. Dr. Mindick cautions program designers against engaging in the feedback process I have described. He and I differ in this regard. I believe that the practice was scientifically appropriate, and essential to our emergent understanding of the empowerment process.

Relationships between Program Outcomes and Participation Rates

Dr. Mindick raises the issue of differential participation rates by families in the program, in an effort to cast further doubt upon the veracity of our findings. He claims (page 62) that those families who benefited the most participated the least. What our analyses have in fact shown is different; we have found *no relationship between level of participation and program impact*. Dr. Mindick claims an inverse relationship, when the finding was of no relationship.

Should a finding of no relationship between participation rate and amount of change be of concern to those involved with parent support and education programs? Of course it should, because it is counter-intuitive. Our own surprise at the lack of relationship led to months of additional analysis, in an unsuccessful attempt to shed further light on the finding. But, along with further analysis came further thought, and greater appreciation for how our universalist and choice-directed approach to family support had complicated the otherwise simple assumption of linearity between participation level and amount of change. By offering the program to the "haves" as well as the "have nots," we had actually limited the extent to which the program could have impact, especially upon those who were likely to participate the most. Middle income families can buy the services they need to support the family. By so doing, they provide themselves with the time and energy to prepare their children for school, leaving little "room" for the program to have an effect not also achieved naturally by the equivalant contrast-group families. These parents also tend to be high participators. So, by providing universal entitlement, we had reduced the probability of a relationship between level of participation and amount of impact.

The other complicating factor was the range of program choices available to families. Parents could receive home visits, attend cluster gatherings, select a combination of the two approaches, or distance themselves from both. Whatever the choice, they could increase or reduce its intensity by selecting more or fewer home visits or attending more or fewer group gatherings. We still do not know how best to gauge the intensity of a program offering a wide range of options to families. We found ourselves in a situation where a complex array of data were being used to test a hypothesis of linear effects for a set of intervention circumstances that may have been related to impact in a nonlinear way. Viewed in this way, our finding of no relationship is not terribly surprising. Perhaps, as Dr. Mindick implies, our findings of program effects are suspect. We have considered this possibility with great care. It cannot be completely rejected with the data at hand. But we find it more probable that there is no linear relationship between level of participation and program impact, given present conceptions of participation level, *when an options-rich program is delivered to a broad range of family types living in a wide range of socioeconomic circumstances.* This is a hypothesis badly in need of testing by others, and we hope that it will be carefully examined by those evaluating the longitudinal effects of variable option family support programs.

It is clear from all that has been said here that Dr. Mindick and I disagree about many aspects of the Family Matters Project. One of the sources that he refers to several times in support of his arguments is the document prepared by Ms. Ingerid Bø for the Carnegie Corporation in 1979 as an interim report of the Process Study later directed by Dr. Mindick. He claims that, in this report, Ms. Bø came to "many of the same conclusions" that he does in his book. Upon re-reading Ms. Bø's report, I am struck by how *different* it is from the Mindick volume. Bø summarizes the strengths and weaknesses of the intervention after its first 6 months of operation with the kind of balanced perspective that I feel could appropriately have been applied to the program across its full duration. This perspective is evident in the first three summarizing paragraphs of her conclusion, with which I end the main body of my rejoinder,

> The most noteworthy and probably in the long run the most powerful quality of the intervention programs is their common emphasis on families' strengths and the commitment to finding ways of escaping the deficit model. The emphasis is noteworthy because it underscores a new approach in the field of family support programs and has powerful potential for building on perhaps one of the most powerful insights in human psychology: that we perform and grow best when we have a ba-

sic trust in our own ability and feel supported in what we do. Experiences from the first six months in the field should not reduce our belief in the value of this goal, but can teach us something about how to realize that end.

We have seen weak spots, some of which stem from a lack of balance between different forces and needs. For instance, the task of conveying the importance of our emphasis on what parents have, know, do, and want came across to the workers as very restricted. The workers were to ask and wait for input from parents, but had little opportunity for spontaneity, suggestions, or other active input. Workers thought that they should *receive* rather than give ideas.

Experience has pointed to a need for more balance between give and take—for the sake of having some variation and expectancy in the situation both for parent and worker. Workers as well as parents need to feel that they can contribute in a natural way; rapport between them, enjoyment, and the development of the work depend upon such an atmosphere. (Bø, 1979, pp. 77–78.)

Other Areas of Disagreement, Briefly Outlined

1. Dr. Mindick claims that Urie Bronfenbrenner and I wrote, in our original proposal, that "Families were to be brought to schools. Employers of parents were to be brought into contact with their employees' children. Children were to visit the work place" (p. 53). In fact, in the original proposal, descriptions of the activities included by Dr. Mindick were preceded by the phrase "Possible examples include the following:". Of the possibilities listed there, we chose to emphasize home–school communications. The Mindick claim is inaccurate.

2. Dr. Mindick presents no concrete evidence in support of items (a) through (d) on page 62, which are offered as alternative explanations for the findings we report. They are simply a textbook list of research issues always considered by the competent scientist. We considered all of them carefully, and came to the conclusions presented in this chapter and our other chapters and reports. Other scientists genuinely interested in the data can check our work, as the data sets are in the public domain, held in archive at the National Institute of Education in Washington, D.C.

3. Dr. Mindick claims on page 63 that I have inappropriately cited a quotation taken from his book, and that only the conscientious reader would read the endnote and see the correct citation. I assume that the reader is concientious, and stand by the citation and endnote.

4. On page 64, Dr. Mindick claims that in several reports we have adopted .20 in our tables "precisely because effect size was not great." In fact, we state clearly in both reports that only probabilities of .20 or better will be included in the tables, meaning that other relationships would be shown as nonsignificant. We could have simply included every probability, regardless of strength. Instead we adopted the convention used by many researchers, leaving blanks in the probability column where differences did not approach significance.

REFERENCES

Bø, I. (1979). *In support of families: The pilot testing of two experimental programs.* Report prepared for the Carnegie Corporation of New York. Ithaca, NY: Cornell University.

Bronfenbrenner, U., & Cochran, M. (1976). *The ecology of human development.* A research proposal to the National Institute of Education. Ithaca, NY: Cornell University.

Cochran, M. (1985). The parental empowerment process: Building upon family strengths. In J. Harris (Ed.), *Child psychology in action: Linking research and practice.* London: Croom Helm.

Cochran, M. (1987). Empowering families: An alternative to the deficit model. In K. Hurrelmann & F. Kaufmann (Eds.), *The limits and potential of social intervention* (pp. 105–120). Berlin/New York: de Gruyter/Aldine.

Freire, P. (1973). *Pedagogy of the oppressed.* New York: Seabury Press.

Freire, P. (1978). *Pedagogy in progress: Letters to Guinea-Bissau.* New York: Seabury Press.

Levenstein, P. (1972). *Verbal interaction project.* Mineola, NY: Family Service Association of Nassau County, Inc.

Mindick, B. (1986). *Social engineering in Family Matters.* New York: Praeger Publishers.

Scarr, S., & McCartney, K. (1987, April). Bermuda mother–child home program evaluation. In D. Phillips (chair), *Early intervention research: Myths, facts and new directions.* Symposium conducted at the Biennial meeting of the Society for Research in Child Development, Baltimore, MD.

Chapter 5
The Syracuse University Family Development Research Program: Long-Range Impact on an Early Intervention with Low-Income Children and Their Families*

J. Ronald Lally
Peter L. Mangione
*Far West Laboratory for Educational Research and
Development*
Alice S. Honig
Syracuse University

SECTION ONE
HISTORY OF THE PROJECT

Varieties of innovative intervention programs arose in the '60s and '70s. Their goal was to break the well-documented link between low-education, low-income households and children's later educational difficulties. Some programs focused on preschoolers, some on infants, and some on parents (Honig, 1979; Lazar & Darlington, 1982). The Family Development Research Program (FDRP) was distinctive in its *omnibus* conceptualization of program. A full complement of educational, nutrition, health and safety, and human service resources were provided to 108 families, beginning prenatally until children reached elementary school age (Honig, 1977; Honig & Lally, 1982; Lally & Honig, 1977a).

Very deprived families were recruited into the Family Development Research Program early in the last trimester of pregnancy. All the families had an income of less than $5,000 per year (in 1970 dollars). Mothers had less than a high school education, and no work or semiskilled work history. Their mean age was 18 years, and over 85% were single parent heads of households. Despite energetic attempts to maintain racial balance in the program, the majority of families served were black.

* The Family Development Research Program longitudinal follow-up study was made possible by grants from the W.T. Grant and Harris Foundations. The intervention program was supported by the Office of Child Development, Health, Education & Welfare, OCD-CB-100. The authors wish to thank Drs. Paul Casavant and William Collins of the Syracuse City School District for their invaluable assistance and supportive cooperation. We are most grateful to Dr. Donna Wittmer, who managed follow-up data collection on site in Syracuse.

The Family Development Research Program was an attempt to improve the ''well-being'' of these children born into environments sparse in the benefits that money, education, and job status can bring. It was hoped that, during these children's first 5 years of life a program of weekly attention to the issues and events in the family and community environment, coupled with supportive assistance in dealing with those issues, would serve to bolster family and child functioning. Additionally it was assumed that, if parents could be certain that their child would receive 5 continuous years of quality day care, this would greatly assist families meet the life challenges they faced and also positively influence the perceptions, emotions, and intellect of the children served.

The major thrust of the intervention was to influence and have impact on the more permanent environment of the child, the family, and the home, and to support parent strategies which enhance the development of the child long after intervention ceased. The pursuit of this goal led to an intervention strategy that viewed parent contact as the primary intervention, with child care as supplementary, rather than, as most child centered programs of the time were structured, enriched child care as the core of the program and parent contact as outreach. In actual operation, however, both components became crucially important and integrated aspects of the comprehensive and long term intervention.

Weekly contact with mothers and other family members in the home of each child was stressed as the key intervention component. Home visitors were employed to assist each family with issues of child-rearing, family relations, employment, and community functioning. The approach of this home-visit component was nonjudgemental family advocacy and oriented toward assisting families to become aware of, and operate in, the various systems in their environment. Staff were trained and instructed to act in support of, rather than as substitutes for, parents, to encourage the individual and cultural strengths of each family, and to treat parents as partners in providing children with rich environments.

The families were provided with child care for 50 weeks a year for the first 5 years of the program children's lives (one-half day care, 5 days a week, from 6 months to 15 months of age; and full day care, 5 days a week from 15 months of age to 60 months of age). Day care services, at Syracuse University Children's Center, were designed so that children could expect to be treated fairly and with loving kindness by adults and other children in a secure and consistent setting, that they would come to expect daily educational experiences, and that they would see the resources of their child care community as available for their use and to meet their needs. The staff functioned under the agreed-upon assumptions that these children were capable of: (a) learning something about anything in which they showed interest; (b) learning to understand that their actions and choices had an impact on others; (c) learning that cooperation and concern for the rights of others would ultimately allow them to express their own creativity, excitement, curiosity, and individuality more fully; (d) learning that wonder and exploration were encouraged by adults; and (e) imitating the actions of staff toward children and other adults. Additionally, these children were treated as special creations, each with particular skills and specialties that would be appreciated by, and useful to, the larger society, and that these special powers would be protected and allowed to rise to ascendance by the adults who spent the daytime hours with them. In summary, the context that was fostered set a daily tone of freedom of choice and awareness of responsibility, an expectation of success in each child, confidence in the fairness and consistency of the environment, an emphasis on creativity, excitement and exploration in learning, expectation of internal rather than external motivation, and a safe, cheerful place to spend each day.

Theoretical Foundations

Five theoretical rationales shaped the goals and objectives of the intervention program. Piagetian equilibration theory, which stresses judicious provision of toys, materials, and human interactions in sensitive relationship to the developing abilities and understandings of the child, helped to shape the infant curriculum both in the home and center. Piaget's attention to the crucial importance of *active* child participation in the construction of knowledge was also emphasized.

Language developmental theories suggested that adult modeling and expansion of child language, contingent responsiveness to early infant coos and babbles, interactive turn-taking talk, and frequent book reading would increase child language repertoire (Bernstein, 1964).

Erikson's theory of each child developmental stage as, optimally, the positive outcome of a series of nuclear conflicts or struggles between opposing emotional adjustments and attunements, focused program concern on the development of basic trust, sturdy autonomy, and learning initiatives in the children served (Erikson, 1950).

Saul Alinsky's (1971) theory of community organization shaped the way in which FDRP personnel perceived their role in the community served, and the tone with which parent contacts were maintained. Alinsky had theorized that "to give people help while denying them a significant part in the action contributes nothing to the development of the individual. In the deepest sense it is not giving but taking—taking their dignity" (p. 123).

From John Dewey and the British Infant School movement, the FDRP project drew the concepts of the importance of freedom of choice for children, encouragement of creativity, and design of an environment that supports exploration in a spatial rather than exclusively time-bounded organization of programmatic offerings.

The Parent Involvement Component

The major premise of the FDRP was that *parents are the primary teachers and sustaining caregiving persons in a young child's life.* Affective and interpersonal relations with the parent would have a profound impact on the learning motivation and competence of the developing infant. Thus, the major thrust of the intervention program was to maximize family functioning. Specifically, a cadre of paraprofessionals, called Child Development Trainers (CDTs), was recruited and trained intensively to work with families, particularly with young mothers of first- or second-born children beginning prior to birth of the baby.

The goals of the parent outreach component were to support a rich quality of family interactions and increase family cohesiveness. Home visitors encouraged an intense mother–child relationship that involved affectionate bodily loving contacts, yielding to children's needs for self-comforting activities, and responding positively to a young child's productions or efforts to learn. A learning game was taught to each parent during the weekly home visit.

The roles of the CDTs grew as the families grew. The major role played by the CDT was that of a knowledgeable friend. The CDT often acted as adviser and confidant on many family issues. When issues arose, the CDT was usually the first called. Often their advice was asked on personal relations, finances, career changes, and education. Many mothers looked forward to the weekly visit from the kind listener who had her and her child's well-being as her major priority. Specifically, during weekly home visits, CDTs:

1. Taught families *Piagetian sensorimotor games*, language interactions, and learning tasks appropriate to each child's developmental level. Particular emphasis was placed on helping parents carry out such learning games in the context of warm and loving interactions with children during daily routines and care situations.
2. Provided *nutrition* information, explanations, and demonstrations for families.
3. Modelled *processes of interaction* that facilitate involvement and enjoyment by children engaging in cognitive and language activities.
4. Offered positive support and encouragement to the mother as she herself carried out a given activity with her child. The mother, rather than the child, was the focus of the home visitor's attention and teaching.
5. Helped the mother to learn *ways to modify games* and activities so that the child was more apt to maintain interest in an activity and to learn. Meeting the "match" developmentally between parental learning goals for a child and the child's current developmental capability requires sensitive attention to the unique individual characteristics of a particular child.
6. Developed friendly working relations with personnel in service agencies and served as a liaison person between available community support services (such as pediatric clinics, food stamp programs, and legal counseling services) and the family. Community liaison function expanded and varied as the needs of the family were clarified or new needs arose.
7. Facilitated family members in taking an *active* role in their child's development. This involved helping families learn to *find and use neighbor-*

hood resources and learning environments, such as libraries, supermarkets, and parks.

8. Enhanced mothers' ability to *observe* their children's development and to *devise their own appropriate learning games* and activities as children continued to grow.

9. Responded positively and actively to the parent's need to fulfill her aspirations for herself. It was hypothesized that parental feelings of self-confidence and self-competence generated as the mother undertook a job or job training or further schooling would be reflected in more secure and positive relations between parents and child. Personal attention and friendship were offered to the mother by her home visitor. Different families need different personal support strategies.

10. Encourages the mother to take an active role in the child's classroom and school, when a child was ready to enter public school. Mothers were given specific practice in learning how to make and maintain contacts with school personnel (and how to access classroom interactions) so that the parents could continue to be positive educational agents and advocates for their children in the public school system (Honig, 1982a, pp. 51–52).

The home visitors did a good deal of liaison work with the Children's Center teachers. "They eased misunderstandings that could arise over messed rompers or lost mittens. CDTs alerted teachers to situations at home that could change a child's sociableness or responsiveness to adult expectations and to newly introduced learning situations" (Lally & Honig, 1977b, p. 29).

One baby did not dare to touch a doll to examine and label its features. His father punished him severely at home if he tried to play with a doll, since the father believed that doll play would cause homosexuality. Another child was causing major concern because of sexual acting out in the classroom. The CDTs explained what the parent had not to the teachers. The little girl had recently lost her beloved grandfather, her only male adult parenting figure, and was much disturbed by this loss. Thus, in myriad ways, the CDTs served families, not only directly, but indirectly.

The home visitors also created toy and book lending kits that parents could borrow freely. During the weekly home visits to families, each CDT also listened empathically to personal troubles. After each home visit, CDTs filled out a Weekly Home Visit report. Once a week, they escorted parents and any siblings to the Children's Center (the day-care component of the FDRP) for parent meetings, at which toy making, tye-dying, child-sized cardboard furniture making, or other constructive activities took place. During the once-a-month nightly parent meetings, CDTs also helped by providing transportation to parent meetings.

Weekly, all-day in-service training and review of formative evaluation information, with their own supervisor as well as with the Program Director and Project Director, furthered the home visitors' understanding of the aims, purposes, and methods of the Piagetian and other learning activities (Lally & Gordon, 1977) taught to parents each week.

These in-service sessions also provided opportunities for full discussion of difficult problems with case study analysis and group problem solving. Almost every week, a serious problem that faced one of the families was presented and strategies were drawn up with regard to the action the CDT or other project staff should take. Often, strategies were shared among CDTs with one who had already faced a problem, explaining possible approaches to a CDT with a similar problem. One CDT shared her frustration when, week after week, the home she visited was very chaotic. One day, on arriving with wet snowy boots, she asked the mother if she could please find some newspapers so those drippy boots would not mess up the mother's apartment during the home visit. "You know," she explained earnestly to the mother, "I sure would not want somebody messing up my apartment with snowy, muddy boots. I would really appreciate it if you could get some newspapers and I will leave my boots outside." The young mother agreeably found some newspapers. She also found ways during the next weeks somehow to straighten her own living place so that there was a clean place to sit down and more of a sense of order when the CDT came.

In-depth interviews with mothers, 3 years and 5 years after home visiting was initiated, generated overwhelmingly positive responses to the role and contributions of the home visitors. This positive response occurred even when mothers had missed many appointments.

Patience, courtesy, caring, and persistence were qualities the CDTs gave generously. As one mother remarked in response to the question "If your CDT has helped you, how has she been the greatest help?": "She's very understanding. She's gone through a lot with me. I don't answer the door or phone. It takes a person with a lot of nerve to try to see me. If she weren't so patient and understanding, my child wouldn't be in the Center. I don't think most people would put up with someone like me. I know I wouldn't!" (Honig, 1979, p. 53). Other comments about the CDT included: "She's always there to contact for every problem"; "She likes her job more than just for the money"; "She's not afraid to come into my house and eat my cooking"; and "She's one of the best friends I've got" (Honig, 1979, p. 54).

Choosing paraprofessionals as CDTs was an important project decision. The young mothers could identify with paraprofessionals who had come from a poverty background themselves and could serve as role models of competency. The CDTs were not only parent educators. They identified strongly with the needs of the families they served and felt themselves to be the most knowledgeable advocates and supports for parents in the project.

Staff–parent relationships.   Child Development Trainers were the critical link in parent–staff relationships. When parents were first becoming acquainted with staff and each other they often did so in the company of their CDT. Because children were bussed to the Children's Center, daily contact with teachers was rare. Therefore, staff created a welcoming atmosphere for parents, whenever the parents visited whether on a drop-in basis or for the occasional all-you-can-eat spaghetti, salad, and French bread suppers held at the Children's Center. During these suppers, slides were shown of the children in their activities. Teachers invited parents on a tour of the classroom areas, with the children proudly showing off "their" school. Polaroid pictures of the children were often given to parents who attended these events. Annually, an Open House was held. Parents baked cookies and helped prepare invitations. That they felt most welcome in the Children's Center seemed evident as they arrived with neighbors, friends, and relatives to attend the gala occasions of Open House.

Teachers further maintained positive relationships with parents by safety-pinning a "Memo to Mommy" note daily on each child's clothing. This note might contain a teacher appreciation of a toddler's fondness for another tot as a special friend, or a child's new skill in stacking six blocks, or venturing to try finger paint, or eating squash for the first time, or daring (finally) to pat the gerbil's fur as teacher carefully held the animal. Sometimes, a "Memo to Mommy" note brought a prompt telephone call of disbelief and relief, as when the note simply said "Jason did not bite anyone today."

The Parent Organization

As the project progressed, parents met and formed formal and informal associations. The formal parent organization met monthly, had elected officers, and functioned in similar ways to Head Start parent organizations. This group critiqued project plans, organized parent, child, and center events, and engaged in program advocacy. Another organization was called the Children's F.O.R.C.E., Families Organized for the Rights of Children in Education. This group of parents was specifically concerned about the continued education of their children after FDRP. They organized, asked for training in classroom observation and for information about parents' rights in relation to the schools. They set about observing in the Syracuse kindergarten and 1st grade classrooms and making their findings known to program parents so that they could make informed decisions about requests and demands for what they felt was proper placement for their children. A number of parents formed informal units for the purpose of purchasing food and supplies in bulk and at reduced prices. Two single-parent mothers who met in the program moved in together as a means to pool their resources and share evening child care responsibilities.

The Children's Center Component

The Children's Center, a pioneer child care and educational facility for infants, toddlers, and preschoolers, was founded in 1964 by Dr. Bettye Caldwell under a grant from the Office of Child Development. When FDRP began, the Children's

Center already had a well-trained staff and a strong reputation in the Syracuse community and nationally because of Dr. Caldwell's earlier work. This made recruitment and startup of FDRP a relatively easy process. In 1969, Dr. J. Ronald Lally became Project Director. He recruited a new population of families with infants, all from low income families, born in 1969, '70, or '71, and started the FDRP. He added the home visitation component and also implemented an open-education model in the Children's Center for the children from 18 to 60 months of age. Dr. Alice Honig remained Program Director and supervised staff training and assessments of the multiple components of the Family Development Research Program.

The Children's Center served children from all parts of the city. Children were picked up by bus driver and rider each morning and delivered home in the late afternoon. The manner of greeting and dropping off children was emphasized. The bus was equipped with special infant safety belts. Drivers and riders received in-service training so that the bus experience too could promote the social/cognitive/language goals of the program. Style and content of interaction were stressed. Each child was to be treated as a prince or princess. The bus driver even wrote a report on what Piagetian sensorimotor and preoperational learnings the children would experience on a bus trip to visit a park or the zoo or the airport!

Staff training.   All the caregivers and home visitors in FDRP participated, as did *all* staff, including the cook, secretarial staff, researchers, testers, and, as mentioned above, bus drivers and driver aides, in intensive annual 2-week training sessions each fall. Personal renewal and revival of motivation occurred as well as learning of increasingly subtle child observation skills and refresher understandings of Piaget, Erikson, etc.

During the year, staff held weekly case conferences, in which the progress, problems, and strengths of a particular youngster were discussed in depth. Every staff member who could contribute to a child's experiences at the Center was invited to participate in these case conferences. Plans were drawn up for possible ways to enhance the child's participation in program. For example, one preschooler who was beaten sometimes by his young mother's boyfriends seemed to have difficulty in concentrating on cognitive activities. He preferred running and found it hard to focus attention. Since he loved ball games, the teachers cut out paper footballs of varying sizes to interest him in size seriation. A small basketball hoop was erected on the outside play area to involve him in near and far shots. Several staff members participated in devising ways to help this particular child. Input from every staff member was valued when such a problem arose, and, over time, many became more skillful in helping individual children. The general philosophy was that the enhancement of staff skills was as integral a part of program as helping the children to flourish.

The Children's Center, lodged in a huge church basement, consisted of three main groupings designed to accommodate developmental stages of the children served.

Infant-Fold

Infants 6 months to 15 months were cared for in an "Infant-Fold." Each caregiver was assigned four infants. Caregivers worked in pairs with group size limited to eight infants. The caregiver assigned to an infant was expected to form the principal relationship with the child. The assignment was made clear to the parents and other caregivers. The team, however, worked quite closely, with one member often taking the one, two, or three infants from the group of eight for a special activity while the others cared for the rest of them. This team concept also was utilized to free caregivers for food preparation, room arrangement, and the like. During the half-day program, the infants received responsive loving attention, cognitive and social interactive games, Piagetian sensorimotor games, fine and gross motor activities, sensory stimulation and activities, and language and book experiences. The sensorimotor domains emphasized in games created by staff included object permanence, means–ends relationships, creation of new schemas, coordination of vision and prehension, causality learning, construction of spatial understandings, and imitation of gestures, sounds, and words. All games were carried out in a climate of respect for the personhood of babies and with the goal of building basic trust. Loving persistence paid off. Even babies who initially refused eye contact or were indifferent to interactive games eventually became animated, participatory, and happy in interactions with their living special persons—their caregivers.

Techniques that the caregivers used included praise and positive reinforcement for small tries, expressing pleasure at early perseverance at tasks, creating happy, nonfrustrating endings for learning activity times, and carrying out games with multiple curricular purposes. For example, singing and chanting "Up and down" while smiling and using baby's name enhanced language and social participation. Lifting a baby into the air so that she could venture to stretch to touch a paper mobile hanging by a string from the ceiling provided good experiences of body cuddling, building Eriksonian trust, while promoting coordination of prehension and vision, dexterity, and spatial understandings.

"Matchmaking" (Honig, 1983) was an important technique to enhance learning. Activities were tailored to the individual level of skill and capability of each child. Small steps, "dancing the developmental ladder" (Honig, 1982b), were created by modifying learning games to increase the child's chances of being able to solve a slightly new or novel task. All caregivers were encouraged to use creativity in findings ways to embed the curriculum in daily activities, in daily care routines, and in informal encounters, as well as in more formal learning experiences.

Transition Group

Babies from 15 to 18 months were in a special group with full-day care 5 days a week. They were offered a more varied program of sensorimotor activities. For example, they could make a zoom car go or work a jack-in-the-box. Self-feeding was encouraged, and larger spatial areas with sliding cabinets permitted more free choice of materials and encouraged early toddler autonomy. Yet body-loving, comforting, and emotional support remained freely available to the older babies. A handbook is available that describes in detail FDRP training procedures for preparing teachers to work with infants and toddlers (Honig & Lally, 1981).

Family Style Education (Multi-Age Differentiated Environment Groupings)

Children from 18 to 60 months were together daily in an environment designed by Lay (Lay & Dopyera, 1977) akin to the British Infant School in its philosophy and structure. The children had freedom of choice and access to four major environmental areas, replicated in two modules. Teachers were stationed in each area with some teachers "floating" to particularly popular areas. Within each module, the children could choose a:

1. Large-Muscle Area: Walkboards, large building blocks and cardboard boxes, slides, rocking boats, climbers, tumbling mats, and other such equipment encouraged the children to try activities involving large-muscle and kinesthetic development. A housekeeping corner and dress-up corner invited children to carry out dramatic play and bodily expression.

2. Small-Muscle Area: Fine motor coordination was encouraged by a plethora of materials (for example: pegboards, puzzles, and stringing beads) that invited practice of prehension skills. Many of these toys were made at the Children's Center. Often they consisted of items with which the toddler was already familiar at home, such as coffee cans that the child could fill with clothespins and bottle caps.

3. Sense-Perception Area: In this area materials and opportunities were provided for sensory experiences. Pasted in a cluster on a cardboard were bumpy kidney beans to touch. Stitched onto a burlap wall hanging was a puppy whose body was made of plush. Record players and rhythm and music instruments were available here. A reading corner had a comfortable couch and reachable shelves of attractive books. Taste sampling (for example, sweet honey, followed by sour lemon) and taste mixing (honey on lemon) were included in this area's ventures. Assorted gerbils, goldfish, and terraria were also available for sensory explorations—always, of course, with the teacher's gentle assistance.

4. Creative Expression and Snack Area: Furniture groupings permitted sev-

eral subdivisions of this major area, so that painting easels, a table for clay work or plastic arts, water-play tubs, sand or sawdust boxes, and a table set with mid-morning and mid-afternoon snacks were available choices for the children (Lally & Honig, 1977b, pp. 21–22).

Additionally, the children had a large variety of wheeled toys and equipment in the large gymnasium that was used in inclement weather, when the children could not go outdoors to their enclosed play area. Part of the gym served as a dormitory for the toddlers and preschoolers at nap time. In the large dining room, the Family Style children ate in groups with a teacher at each table. Parents were free to join the lunch and to visit whenever they chose.

The Family Style program was spatially structured rather than time oriented. Several rules pertained. No physical aggression was permitted. Materials had to stay in their appropriate areas, and materials had to be cared for and not destroyed. That is, books could not be torn and puzzle pieces could not be dunked in a water play tub, nor could dolls be banged with a hammer. Thirty-second time outs were used for flagrant transgressions.

Concept links were made from one area to another. For example, *fast* and *slow* could be acted out by running or walking or crawling in the large muscle room. Yet the concepts of fast and slow could also be taught in the sense experience area by singing or chanting faster or slower, and taught in the creative experience area by pouring sand fast from a cup into a pot or through a tiny hole in an orange juice can so that the sand poured slowly.

The opportunity to interact with children of different ages was used by the teachers to promote more prosocial behaviors and sensitive awareness of the differences between younger and older capabilities. One day in the lunch room, a 2-year-old spilt milk. The 4-year-old sitting at her table looked from the puddle on the ground to the toddler's face. Then he shook his head as if deciding that the younger child simply did not yet know the rules about cleaning up nor how to do so. He slipped off his chair, got some paper towels, and proceeded gravely to smear the milk puddle around in a helpful attempt to clean up the younger child's mess.

During the children's naptimes, the Family Style teachers often created learning activities for the children, such as a seriation game involving different size spoons in a shoe box. Or they cut up merchandise catalogues and prepared lotto games with household articles, clothing or recreational items of personal interest to young children, who could match one item with a similar one on a Center-made lotto card. Providing the caregivers encouragement and opportunities to be creative, develop, and work cooperatively was an essential part of the program.

Assessing the Family Development Research Program

The carefully spelled out goals of the FDRP program and the even more specifically defined roles and activities required of staff members made the tasks of assessment clear, if complex. A variety of psychometric tests and ecological observation measures in classrooms were administered to assess how the children were faring (see Lally & Honig, 1977a, b, for full details of all assessments). As noted earlier, parents were interviewed in depth after 3 and 5 years in the program to assess the effectiveness of the CDT's efforts. Weekly and Monthly Home Visit Reports permitted data gathering on the course of parental responsiveness to the CDT's work.

At 36 months of age, a longitudinal control group was established for the duration of the FDRP. The control children were carefully matched in pairs with Center children with respect to sex, ethnicity, birth ordinality, age, family income, family marital status, maternal age, and maternal education status (no high-school diploma) at time of infant's birth. Stanford-Binet IQ scores were compared at 36, 48, and 60 months between the Center children and their matched controls. Scores for the Center and controls were also collected at 72 months.

Short-term Impact on Child Functioning

The short-term effects of the Family Development Research Program have already been reported elsewhere (Honig, 1977; Honig, Lally, & Mathieson, 1982; Lally & Honig, 1977a). A synopsis of noteworthy program effects on child functioning during and at the close of the program follows.

Cognitive functioning. At 36 months of age program children scored significantly higher on the Binet test than their control counterparts (Lally & Honig, 1977b). However, as the children grew older, these differences disappeared. At the end of the program, when they were 60 months of age, the program and control children looked similar to each other across a variety of measures of cognitive development and intellectual abilities.

Social-Emotional Functioning. The Social-Emotional Observer Rating of Children (Emmerich, 1971) was used to observe study children in preschool, in kindergarten, and again in first grade. At 36 months of age, program children exhibited superior social-emotional functioning as compared to the control children. After leaving the program and starting kindergarten, program children continued to function better than control children in the domain of social-emotional functioning. During the time they were in first grade, program children continued to behave in positive ways toward other children but their behavior toward the teacher had changed. Program children displayed significantly more positive and negative behavior toward adults than control children did. Program children sought out teachers through many more negative bids than when in preschool or kindergarten and were observed to smile and laugh less frequently. In a complete report of this investigation, it was hypothesized by the researchers that the expectations of the children for personalized attention from the teacher were being violated, and their behavior changed accordingly (Honig et al., 1982). A number of parents reported that their children were frustrated with their school experiences, with one parent reporting that her child complained, "I'm not learning anything."

Whether it was the discrepancy between their expected interactions with teachers in preschool and first grade or some other factor that contributed to more negative behavior in program children, it is clear that the transition from the intervention to school went hand in hand with changes in social emotional behavior. This pattern corresponds to that found by Haskins (1985) in a study of an infant/preschool program which, though it emphasized cognitive goals rather than a balance between cognitive and social emotional goals, is in many respects comparable to the Syracuse intervention. Haskins reported that program children in his sample exhibited an increase in negative social emotional behavior once they entered the public school system.

SECTION TWO
LONGITUDINAL FOLLOW-UP STUDY: 10 YEARS LATER

The follow-up study was comprehensive in nature. We sought to gather information on the functioning of the study children in school, in their family, and in the community. We also wanted to investigate family functioning, both the family as a unit and how it relates to the community. Data were gathered from school records, court records, probation department records, and the like. In addition, teachers were asked to complete a questionnaire that involved rating the academic and social functioning of each study child in their class. The follow-up data collection also consisted of interviews with the study children and one of their parents or guardians. In almost all of the cases, the parent interview was conducted with the study child's mother. The interview session was multifaceted. Parents completed a demographic data form, filled out questionnaires, and responded to open-ended questions on their perceptions of their child's school and social functioning, the quality of their family life, their aspirations, and the like. The study children completed a questionnaire and responded to various interview questions about their functioning in school, their social attitudes and behavior, their family life, their aspirations and so forth. The entire interview session lasted 2 to 2 ½ hours. Parent and student interviews were conducted separately, usually in different parts of the home. The interviewers were advanced students in one of the helping profession fields. They were kept blind to family status in the study (program or control).

Research Sample

Of the 108 children who started the program, 82 completed the full 5-year intervention. Seventy-four of the matched controls remained in the sample through 60 months of age as well. Nine years later, when the longitudinal study commenced, we were able to obtain informed consent from 65 program families, which was 79% of the families who finished the program, and 54 control families, which was 73% of the control families who were still in the sample at 60 months of age. Two additional program and two additional control families were found, but these four families would not sign consent forms and were consequently dropped from the study.

We found the families for the follow-up study through various means. Publishing announcements that listed child and family names in local newspapers, and distributing information about the study in local schools, helped us make contact with a substantial number of families. Once families were aware that the study was taking place, many would contact the research team and arrange to participate. Occasionally, friends of a study family would either contact the research team or their friends, who would in turn contact the research team. Lists of other study families were shown to those already located; sometimes, study families could help us locate a few other families. These procedures helped us find about 80% of the families who consented to participate in the follow-up study. Finding the last 20% of the follow-up sample was much more difficult. We hired a recruiter who had vast experience doing community work in low-income neighborhoods. He located families through informal conversation on the street and, ultimately, through developing a network of contacts in the neighborhoods where the study families lived. It is noteworthy that this group of "hard-to-find" families who were eventually found and who consented to participate, about 20% of all families in the follow-up sample, consisted of by and large the least-organized and least-stable families in the entire sample.

Contact with the families was made by the research team first to obtain signed permission forms and then later to schedule and conduct parent and child interviews. Maintaining contact with the families turned out to be difficult in a substantial number of cases. A subgroup of families within the sample moved frequently, often without leaving a forwarding address. Some lost telephone service, some would fail to be home at an appointed time for an interview, or, in a few cases, because of severe problems in the family such as domestic violence, some avoided having continued contact with the research team. As it turned out, parent interviews were conducted with 51 of the 65 follow-up program families and 42 of the 54 follow-up control families. For the child interview, it was possible to perform 49 out of 65 possible program sample interviews and 39 out of 54 possible control sample interviews.

What the above data indicate is that it was impossible to maintain contact and conduct interviews with about 25% of both the follow-up program and control families from whom we were able to obtain parental consent. This is only part of the story, however. It was much easier to maintain contact with and perform interviews with 75% of the program families in the follow-up sample than with 75% of the control families. The last 10 interviews (about 25%) conducted with control families required an enormous amount of patience and persistence. Interviewers would arrive at a home at an appointed time only to find no one there. About half of these families had no telephone, so someone from the research team would have to stop by until the family was at home. Unlike the families with whom it was easy to maintain contact and conduct interviews, the "hard to study" families were very impoverished and disorganized. The larger proportion of the "hard to study" families in control follow-up sample, 25% of the control group interviewed versus 10% of the program group interviewed, was one indication that a substantial subgroup of families within the control group was functioning poorly.

Both the program and control follow-up samples did not differ from the make-up of the program and control samples at the close of the intervention. Attrition was studied by comparing the follow-up program sample with the original program sample, and the follow-up control sample with the original control sample on the following variables:

1. child's Stanford-Binet score at 48 months of age;
2. mother's years of education by the 60 month interview;
3. mother's age at the birth of the study child;
4. the presence or absence of a father figure in the house; and
5. family's annual income level when the study child was 60 months old.

The follow-up program sample was not significantly different from the original program sample, and the follow-up control sample was not significantly different from the original control sample on the five above variables.

Demographic Profile of Follow-up Sample

There was wide variation in the social and economic circumstances of both the program and control follow-up families. On one end of the continuum were two-parent families with both the mother and father earning average to better-than-average incomes. At the other end of the continuum were single-parent families that were completely dependent on public assistance. The majority of families in both the program and control follow-up samples, though not at the extreme, fell at the lower end of the continuum. As Table 1 shows, single-parent families with the mother working at a low wage made up a good part of both samples. This table also shows that the program follow-up sample consists of more single-parent households than the control follow-up samples, though this difference is not statistically significant.

School Functioning

School record data.   The Syracuse intervention had a positive impact on the school functioning of girls. This positive effect on the program girls started to appear during early adolescence. An analysis of grade report data, mostly for 7th

Table 1.   Median Family Income of Single-Parent
            and Two-Parent Households in Program
            and Control Follow-Up Samples

	Program n = 45	Control n = 39
Family Income		
Single-Parent Household	$10,000	$9.960
Two-Parent Household	$34,500	$25,500
Family Structure		
Single-Parent Households	78%	64%

or 8th grades, indicated that none of the program girls was failing school, while 16% of the control girls were found to have failing grade averages. Moreover, 76% of the program girls were performing at a C average or better, while only 47% of the control girls were performing at this level. This difference between program and control girls was statistically significant. When we analyzed recent grade report data for the boys no differences resulted between the program and control group.

School attendance data paralleled patterns found in the school grade report data. We were able to obtain school attendance data for 4 school years: 1981-82, 1982-83, 1983-84, and 1984-85. Poor school attendance was defined as having 20 or more absences from school, which was a criterion used in another intervention follow-up study (Seitz, Rosenbaum, & Apfel, 1985). The analysis of the first 2 years of attendance data resulted in no difference between the program and control group, for either girls or boys. In year 3, however, 14% of the program girls, as compared to 50% of the control girls, had more than 20 absences. And in year 4, none of the program girls had more than 20 absences. In contrast, a significant percentage (31%) of control girls had more than 20 absences. No such differences were found between program and control boys.

Unlike recent school data, information on the elementary school years indicated no differences between the program and control group. Grade retention in both the program and control group was similar to that in the entire Syracuse City School District. (As an aside, it is noteworthy that the Syracuse City School District, where all of the follow-up sample started school, and where over 85% of the study children are still enrolled, has had over the last decade a strong tendency to retain students. Using an age by grade data matrix provided by the Syracuse Schools, we estimated that about 60% of the students in the school district have been retained at least once by the time they reach 9th grades.) Finally, rate of placement in special education was similar for both the program and control groups for the school years 1980-81 through 1984-85.

Teacher ratings.   A questionnaire that consisted of 96 items was distributed to three current teachers of each of the study children (n = 119). Items on the questionnaire covered a variety of topics including the child's commitment to schooling, behavorial dispositions (e.g., animated and enthusiastic or depressed), confidence and social behavior (e.g., aggressive toward peers or friendly). Children were rated on each of the items according to a 6-point scale that ranged from "describes very well" to "does not describe well at all."

We were able to collect at least one completed questionnaire for 101 follow-up children. Since data from two or more teachers were available for only 46% of the 101 children for whom completed questionnaires were returned, we decided to use one questionnaire per child. For children for whom more than one questionnaire was available, one was randomly selected to be used in the analysis of teacher ratings.

Hans (1987) applied a facet theory analysis (as described by Guttman, 1980) to the questionnaire items. A set of facet categories was defined a priori according to a mapping sentence. This procedure resulted in 12 facet categories. These categories were in turn used to categorize the teacher questionnaire items; 43 items fit into the category structure across eight facet categories. (Chart 1 lists of these eight categories with examples.) Four categories failed to account for any items, and items failing to fit into the structure were not further analyzed. In order to study the hypothesis of a correspondence between the a priori category structure and the empirical organization of the 43 items, a smallest space analysis was applied to the data (Guttman, 1980). There was a high degree of correspondence between the facet categories defined a priori and the empirical organization of the 43 items resulting from the smallest space analysis. Although not necessarily part of a facet theory approach, sum scores for each of the categories were then computed, standardized, and used as a set of dependent variables in a multivariate analysis of variance with program and sex as independent factors in the analysis.

A multivariate analysis of teacher ratings resulted in a significant program group x sex interaction effect. To interpret this interaction effect, univariate analyses of variance were computed separately for the males and females; program group was the independent variable in this analysis. No significant group differences resulted for the males. However, program girls were rated as having more positive attitudes toward themselves and toward other people than control girls. Teachers also indicated that program girls had greater achievement in school and better control of their impulses with respect to other people. On the other four dependent variables, the mean scores for the program girls, though not significantly different, were always more positive than for the control girls. Figure 1 plots the mean scores for each sex and program group on each of the eight variables.

Thus, teacher ratings showed that program girls were functioning better than control girls in the areas of self-esteem, feelings toward others, control of aggression toward others, and achievement in school-related skills. The superior functioning of the program girls found in the teacher data corresponds to the findings from the analysis of school record data, which revealed that program girls were performing better in school and more regularly attending school than

Chart 1.   Eight Facet Categories Used to Categorize
43 Teacher Questionnaire Items

Direction of attitude toward self
      Examples: Seeks constant reassurance. (−)
                             Is animated and enthusiastic. (+)
Direction of attitude toward other people
      Examples: Is friendly. (+)
                             Gets pleasure from working closely with another student. (+)
Direction of attitude toward school
      Examples: Takes pleasure in a job well done. (+)
                             Values school and school activities. (+)
Involvement with school situation
      Examples: Is motivated to work and expends effort. (+)
                             Is alert and interested in school work. (+)
Achievement with regard to other people
      Examples: Is well received by other pupils. (+)
                             Has few or no friends. (−)
Achievement with regard to school
      Examples: Is good at school work. (+)
                             Reads poorly. (−)
Control of impulses with respect to other people
      Examples: "Loses head" easily. (−)
                             Would hurt someone just for the "heck of it." (−)
Control of impulses with respect to school situation
      Examples: Requires continuous supervision. (−)
                             Is easily led into trouble. (−)

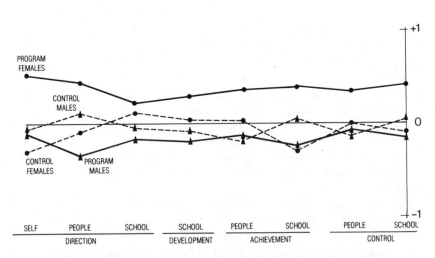

Figure 1.   Mean Scores for Eight Facet Categories of Intervention
and Control Males and Females.

control girls. Taken together, these data showed that the intervention clearly benefited the program girls in the domain of school functioning.

Family interviews

The parent and study child interviews consisted of open-ended questions on such topics as their use of leisure time, values, concerns, aspirations, accomplishments, and support systems. A content analysis was applied to the interview responses to identify categories for classifying them. Before categorizing interview responses, data coders segmented each response into thought units. A thought unit was defined as one piece of information in a response. For example, in response to the question in the parent interview on what advice she would give to a young parent on how to raise children in today's world, a mother said, "Listen to what they have to say," and "teach them about morals." In this response there are two thought units. The first was, "Listen to what they have to say," and the second, "teach them about morals." Once thought units were identified for a response to a particular question, each one was categorized into one of the categories defined for that question. Intercoder agreement ranged from 71% to 86% (median = 79%) across the coded responses for all questions. In the above example, the first thought unit was categorized as "Be Open or Responsive," and the second unit as "Teach Values."

Parent interview.   The most prominent findings in the comparison between the responses of program parents and those of control parents pertained to the parents' comments about what made them feel proud about parenting, and the kind of advice they would give to children growing up in today's world. In response to a question about what made them feel proud about raising their children, 28% of the program parents talked about their child having a prosocial orientation while only 10% of the control parents did so. An example of a thought unit that was coded as prosocial was, "He cares about other people." In addition, a significantly higher percentage of program parents (18% vs. 5% of control parents) mentioned that unity in their family made them feel proud of their parenting effort. Responses that were coded as indicative of family unity included, "We're all close with each other" and "We stick together."

When asked about what advice they would give young people today, 29% of the program parents said that they would advise young people to learn something about themselves and do everything they are capable of accomplishing. A significantly lower percentage of control parents (only 5%) expressed that they would give such advice. Thirty-three percent of the control parents, in contrast, responded cautiously, saying they would advise young people to avoid having too high of expectations and instead concentrate on getting by. Only 14% of the program parents said they would give such advice.

In sum, in comparison to control parents, program parents report feeling proud about the prosocial attitudes and behaviors of their children and the quality of family unity in their family. They also would more likely advise young people to seek to reach their full potential, while control parents would more likely counsel young people not to expect too much.

Child interview. In response to a question about what they liked about themselves, program children significantly more often expressed that they liked one or more of their physical attributes (e.g., their appearance or physique) than control students did. There was also a trend in which program children indicated liking one or more of their personal attributes (e.g., their personality or sense of humor) more frequently than control children. When asked what they disliked about themselves, program children tended to say "nothing" more often than their control counterparts. Taken together, these findings suggest that program children feel more positively about themselves than control students do. These results are shown in Table 2.

Other differences between program and control children in the analysis of interview data were in the area of school life and in the way they handle problems. In answer to a question about what they see themselves doing in 5 years, many more program children envisioned being in school, while control children tended to foresee having a job and being on their own. Another question about school asked the children to talk about the "worst things about school." Twice as many control students as program children responded to this question by saying "getting in trouble." In another domain, when asked about what they would do if faced with a serious problem, a significantly higher percentage of program children stated they would take an active approach to the problem. An example of an active response was when the children were asked what they would do if they were failing a class. Responses to this question that were coded as active included "going and talking to the teacher," "talking to my counselor," and "finding out if there was extra work I could do." If the children could not come up with a way of handling the problem or simply responded "nothing" in answer to the question, the response was coded as passive. These findings from the child interview are tabulated in Table 2.

In sum, the analysis of the child interviews indicated that, as compared to control children, program children feel more positively about themselves, envi-

Table 2.   Student Perceptions of Themselves and Their Schooling

	Percentage of Program Students	Percentage of Control Students	Chi Square
Like Physical Attributes	33	14	3.89*
Like Personal Attributes	31	14	3.18**
Dislike Nothing About Self	31	14	3.18**
In School 5 Years From Now	53	28	4.59*
Working 5 Years From Now	35	51	2.93**
Worst Things About School-Trouble	17	34	3.44**
Would Make Active Response to Problem	63	37	4.09*

*p < .05
**p < .10

sion education being a continued part of their life, and tend to report that they would handle problems more directly and actively. The more positive outlook reflected in the interview responses of both parents and students coincided with more positive functioning of program children in their community, as reported below.

Juvenile Delinquency in Program and Control Children

The strongest evidence of program and control children's functioning in the community came from involvement in the juvenile justice system. For this follow-up study effort, we sought to investigate the incidence, severity, and cost of juvenile delinquency in the program and control samples by collecting data from the Probation Department and court records. Data were available on 65 program children and 54 control children, ranging in age from 13 to 16 years old. The data on the incidence and severity of juvenile delinquency in the sample were collected from probation and court records by a specialist in social work.

Cost data were also collected in the study of juvenile delinquency. Fiscal officers from various agencies were interviewed to determine appropriate procedures for estimating the cost of each case identified in the longitudinal sample. Estimated costs included the cost of court processing, probation supervision, placement in foster care, nonsecure detention, and secure detention. The least severe cases, i.e., those in which the child was, on request by the parents, judged ungovernable or not under the control of the family, often required placement in foster care, which was the least expensive form of out-of-home care administered by the county probation department. The most expensive form of out-of-home residence was secure detention. Only the most severe cases in the research sample required secure detention. In general, those cases that involved delinquency often necessitated more extensive supervision by the probation department. The cost of supervising severe or chronic offenders was estimated from records that documented the amount of staff time devoted to each case.

Analysis of the data on juvenile delinquency revealed sharp differences between the functioning of program and control children. Only 6% of the program children in the follow-up sample, as compared to 22% of the control children, have been processed as probation cases by the County Probation Department. Moreover, the severity of the offenses, the degree of chronicity, and the cost of the cases were much higher in the control group. Table 3 shows that three of the four probation cases in the program group were ones in which the study child was found to be ungovernable or not under control of his parents at home. The other program case was a one-time juvenile delinquent. Table 3 shows a much different picture for the control group. Five of the 12 control cases involve chronic offenders. Control children have committed much more serious delinquent acts, including burglary, robbery, physical assault, and sexual assault. In addition, the cost to the court and the probation department for handling the cases was far greater for the control group.

Table 3. Summary of Probation Cases in the Syracuse Family
Development Research Program's Longitudinal Sample

Program Group (n = 65)			Control Group (n = 54)		
Sex of Subject	Case Type/Offense	Number of Times	Sex of Subject	Case Type/Offense	Number of Times
Female	Ungovernable	2	Female	Juvenile Delin.	1
				Petit Larceny	2
Female	Ungovernable	1	Female	Ungovernable	2
				Juvenile Delin.	1
Male	Ungovernable	1	Female	Ungovernable	1
Male	Juvenile Delin.	1	Male	Petit Larceny	1
Total = 4				Ungovernable	2
			Male	Ungovernable	1
			Male	Criminal Mischief	1
				Violation of Probation	1
Total Cost of Cases = $12,111			Male	Sexual Abuse	1
			Male	Ungovernable	2
				Attempted Assault (2nd)	1
			Male	Robbery	1
				Assault (2nd)	1
				Robbery (2nd)	1
			Male	Burglary	1
			Male	Juvenile Delin.	1
			Male	Ungovernable	1
			Total = 12		
			Total Cost of Cases = $107,192		

For the *program group*, the estimated cost per child (n = 65) was $186, and for the *control group*, the estimated cost per child (n = 54) was $1,985.

The findings in the area of juvenile delinquency correspond to those found in the longitudinal study of the Perry Preschool Project. (Berrueta-Clement, Schweinhart, Barnett, Epstein, & Weikart, 1984). Both studies suggest that the association of high-quality early education and family support with reduced delinquent behavior later on merits much more intensive investigation. We plan to continue to study the Syracuse sample to see if the differences between the program and control group in criminal activity extend into adulthood.

Discussion of Findings

The Syracuse Family Development Research Program clearly had a positive impact on the children and families who participated in the intervention. Thus far, the strongest program effects have been in the domain of social deviance and functioning in the community. The findings reported in this study correspond to other research that has shown high-quality early childhood programs prevent the incidence and severity of juvenile delinquency in children from low-income communities (Berrueta-Clement et al., 1984). The Syracuse children are still young. To the extent that early delinquent behavior predicts later criminality, we would expect the gap between the program and control group to increase. It is conceivable that the costs of criminal involvement in the control group, as compared to that in the program group, will continue to mount.

In addition to the findings on juvenile delinquency, family interview data indicated that program families tended to value prosocial attitudes and behavior, education, and family unity. Likewise, program children tended to express more positive feelings about themselves, take a more active approach to personal problems, and see schooling as a vital part of their life. Thus, the program appeared not only to prevent severely deviant behavior, but also to be associated with more positive attitudes and values in the children and parents. The message that came across in the interview from the program families was a proactive approach to life or a belief that one can act to better one's circumstances, that one can take steps to reach one's full potential. This stood in contrast to the control families, who tended to emphasize that one should seek to survive or get by.

In the domain of school functioning, the program girls benefited from the Syracuse intervention. Multiple sources of data support this conclusion including school grade average data, school attendance data, and teacher ratings. Though strong, these positive effects on school functioning did not start to appear until the program girls entered junior high school.

Another major early intervention study, the Early Training Project (Gray, 1983; Gray, Ramsey, & Klaus, 1982), indicated that an enduring effect of a high-quality preschool program (for 3- and 4-year-old children) was a more positive impact on the school performance of program female children than on male children. Gray (1983) offered several possible explanations for this sex difference in the program group. The two most plausible explanations, in her view, were either a sample fluke or that the transition to a public school environment was more difficult for the program boys than for the program girls. The Early Training Project gave the children a great deal of freedom. Gray speculated that boys in the preschool used the freedom more than the girls and that, once the children entered school, it was more difficult for the boys to adapt to a more restrictive environment.

The Syracuse Program differed from the Early Training Project in many ways, including the length of the intervention and specific research sample characteristics. Yet a similar sex difference in school functioning was found in both studies. This makes less plausible the explanation that a sample fluke can account for the superior functioning of both programs' girls in school.

In the Syracuse sample, the transition to elementary school was difficult for boys as well as for girls. No sex differences were found in the analysis of social emotional functioning of program children in first grade. In both program and control samples, girls were retained less often than boys during the elementary school years. However, only program girls showed improvements in school functioning as they entered junior high school. In effect, the Syracuse program strengthened the long-range school functioning of girls but not boys. It may be that, for a number of reasons, the school years are more difficult for the black male child (Stevens, 1982). Perhaps the impact of the intervention was not strong enough for the program boys to counteract an elementary school experience that routinely involved restrictions, conflict, and failure. This suggests that, to be optimally effective, intervention programs need to continue in some form throughout childhood, at the very least to support the positive effects of early intervention in a child's life.

One finding uncovered while doing this follow-up study must be addressed. We encountered what we believe to be a serious methodological issue in doing longitudinal research with low-income, "multi-risk" families. Both the "hard to find" and "hard to study" families were families whose long-range outcomes tended to be negative. This may have led to a positive bias in the follow-up data for both the Syracuse program and control follow-up samples, though this positive bias was much more pronounced in the control sample. As it was, in investigating the incidence and severity of juvenile delinquency, we found many more control children in serious trouble. Of the last 10 control families interviewed, each interview having required a tremendous effort to do, six had a study child involved in juvenile delinquency. Thus, in order to obtain results that are as accurate as possible, an investment must be made to find and study those families who are most difficult to find and study. Moreover, appropriate measures of difficulty in retrieving and investigating a follow-up sample need to be developed. With such measures, it will be possible to gauge more precisely the degree and type of attrition in longitudinal follow-up samples and how such attrition affects the interpretation of comparisons between program and control follow-up samples.

Finally, it is important to discuss, in general terms, just what worked, what did not and what we would recommend for future longitudinal interventions with similar populations. Although it is almost impossible to separate out the specific effects of parent participation from the child's participation in the Children's Center, it seems clear that our original notion to involve families intimately as intervention agents paid off. The advice that program parents gave their children about how to function in life, and the things program parents report they take pride in with regard to their parenting as compared with control parents, seem key to the prosocial, motivational, and educational differences reported in this chapter. One hypothesis that could be generated for the differences in the samples that appear at junior high school age is the continued input from parents after intervention ceased.

One discouraging finding was the relatively little impact the program had on family income and career advancement. It became painfully clear as follow-up data were being collected that many families, both program and control, still lived in poverty and in neighborhoods that they considered dangerous and harmful to the development of their children. A number of children interviewed discussed the discrepant goals of school and neighborhood, and the difficulty they had integrating the two. We had hypothesized at the start of the intervention that the permanent environment in which the child was raised would have a continuing effect on the child well after intervention ceased, and that is why parent participation was so strongly emphasized. What was not emphasized strongly enough was the power of the neighborhood and the need for special supports during the transition from program to school.

In many ways our program has been very successful, as our data suggest, with both the program boys and girls served. We feel that the findings would have been even more powerful if certain actions had been taken. In future programs of this type, we feel that it would be wise to design the program with three things in mind. One, that developmental transitions be carefully planned for, such as the transition from preschool to school, and that an inoculation approach (intervention ending abruptly) be avoided. Two, that the service institutions and agencies that are already a part of the existing community, including informal neighborhood organizations, be intimately involved in the creation and continuation of the intervention. Three, that programs be designed more dynamically and with opportunities to change and adapt services based on continued readings of the changing family needs.

REFERENCES

Alinsky, S. D. (1971). *Rules for radicals*. New York: Random House.

Bernstein, B. (1954). Social class, speech systems and psycho-therapy. In F. Riessman, J. Cohen, & A. Pearl (Eds.), *Mental health of the poor* (pp. 194-204). New York: Free Press of Glencoe.

Berrueta-Clement, J. R., Schweinhart, L. J., Barnett, W. S., Epstein, A. E. & Weikart, D. P. (1984). *Changed lives: The effects of the Perry Preschool Program on youths through age 19*. Ypsilanti, MI: High/Scope Press.

Emmerich, W. (1971). *Disadvantaged children and their first school experiences. Structure and development of personal-social behaviors in preschool settings*. (Report prepared for Project Head Start, Office of Child Development.) Princeton, NJ: Educational Testing Service.

Erikson, E. (1950). *Childhood and Society*. New York: W. W. Norton.

Gray, S. W. (1983). Enduring effects of early intervention: Perspectives and perplexities. *Peabody Journal of Education, 60* (3), 70-84.

Gray, S. W., Ramsey, B. K., & Klaus, R. A. (1982). *From 3 to 20: The Early Training Project*. Baltimore, MD: University Park Press.

Guttman, L. (1980). Recent structural laws of human behavior. *The Bulletin of the Institute of Communications Research* Keio University, *14*, 1-12.

Hans, S. (1987, April). *Syracuse University longitudinal follow-up study: Current teachers' ratings of subjects' behaviors, attitudes and achievement*. Paper presented at the Society for Research in Child Development's biennial meeting, Baltimore.

Haskins, R. (1985). Public school aggression among children with varying day-care experience. *Child Development, 56*, 689-703.

Honig, A. S. (1977). The Children's Center and the Family Development Research Program. In B. M. Caldwell & D. J. Stedman (Eds.), *Infant education: A guide for helping handicapped children in the first three years* (pp. 81-99). New York: Walker & Co.

Honig, A. S. (1979). *Parent involvement in early childhood education*. Washington, DC: National Association for the Education of Young Children.

104 LALLY, MANGIONE, AND HONIG

Honig, A. S. (1982a). Intervention strategies to optimize infant development. In E. Aronowitz (Ed.), *Prevention strategies for mental health* (pp. 25-56). New York: Neale Watson Academic Publications.

Honig, A. S. (1982b). *Playtime learning games for young children*. Syracuse, NY: Syracuse University Press.

Honig, A. S. (1983). Meeting the needs of infants. *Dimensions 11*(2), 4-7.

Honig, A. S. & Lally, J. R. (1981). *Infant caregiving: A design for training*. Syracuse, NY: Syracuse University Press.

Honig, A. S. & Lally, J. R. (1982). The Family Development Research Program: Retrospective review. *Early Child Development and Care, 10.*, 41-62.

Honig, A. S., Lally, J. R. & Mathieson, P. H. (1982). Personal and social adjustment of school children after five years in the Family Development Research Program. *Child Care Quarterly, 11*(2), 136-146.

Lally, J. R. & Gordon, I. S. (1977). *Learning games for infants and toddlers*. Syracuse, NY: New Readers Press.

Lally, J. R. & Honig, A. S. (1977a). The Family Development Research Program: A program for prenatal infant and early childhood enrichment. In M. C. Day & R. D. Parker (Eds.), *The preschool in action: Exploring early childhood programs* (pp. 147-94). Boston: Allyn & Bacon.

Lally, J. R. & Honig, A. S. (1977b). *The Family Development Research Program: A program for prenatal, infant & early childhood enrichment. Final Report*. Syracuse, NY: Syracuse University.

Lay, M. Z. & Dopyera, J. E. (1977). *Becoming a teacher of young children*. Lexington, MA: D. C. Heath and Company.

Lazar, I. & Darlington, R. (1982). Lasting effects of early education: A report from the Consortium for Longitudinal Studies. *Monographs of the Society for Research in Child Development, 45*, (203, Serial No. 195).

Seitz, V., Rosenbaum, L. K. & Apfel, N. H. (1985). Effects of family support intervention: A ten-year follow-up. *Child Development, 56*, 376-391.

Stevens, J. H. (1982). Research in review: From 3 to 20: The Early Training Project. *Young Children, 37* (6), 57-64.

Chapter 6
A Support Program for Adolescent Mothers: Predictors of Participation*

Donald G. Unger
University of Delaware

Lois Pall Wandersman
University of South Carolina

Teenage pregnancy continues to gain widespread national attention (Dash, 1986; Wallis, 1985; Stark, 1986). Over one million teenage American girls become pregnant each year. Nearly half of them carry to term, with approximately 90% of these teen mothers keeping their infants (Baldwin, 1983; Hayes, 1987; Zitner & Miller, 1980). Among developed countries, the United States has the highest rates of adolescent pregnancy and childbearing (Jones, Forrest, Goldman, Henshaw, Lincoln, Rosoff, Westoff, & Wulf, 1986).

The problems associated with children having children are numerous. Teenage mothers are more likely than older mothers to be at risk for perinatal complications and developmental problems (Sacker & Neuhoff, 1982). Early childbearing is associated with inadequacies in prenatal care, lower educational achievement and income, and a higher probability of marital instability and divorce compared to childbearing among women who become mothers at a later age (Field, 1981; Moore, Hofferth, Wertheimer, Waite, & Caldwell, 1981). Teen mothers tend to have inaccurate expectations of their infants and are less verbal than older mothers in their interactions with their babies (Field, Widmayer, Stringer, & Ignatoff, 1980). Teenage mothers are less likely to work and more likely to be on welfare (Group for the Advancement of Psychiatry, 1986). They also have a high incidence of repeat pregnancies (Furstenberg, 1976). Children of teenage mothers are likely to be low in birthweight and have lasting deficits in IQ and achievement (Broman, 1981; Monkus & Bancalari, 1981).

Programs for Pregnant and Parenting Teens

Several types of programs have developed in response to the problem of pregnant and parenting teens. These programs have been discussed elsewhere in detail and

*This research was supported in part by the NIMH Small Grants Program, the Robert Wood Johnson Foundation, the South Carolina Department of Health and Environmental Control, and the University of Delaware General Research Fund. We wish to thank Marion Hyson, Sharon Jacobs, Douglas Powell, and Karen Van Trieste for comments at varying stages of the manuscript.

will be summarized here (Anastasiow, 1984; Badger, 1981; Dryfoos, 1983; Field et al., 1980; Hayes, 1987; Jekel & Klerman, 1985; Nickel & Delaney, 1985; Pittman & Govan, 1986; Teenage Pregnancy, 1981).

Schools have begun to offer services to adolescent mothers, some having separate educational facilities for the pregnant or parenting teen. The school programs encourage completion of high school and usually include day care services. They typically offer a curriculum including parenting skills, child development, family life, health education, and family planning. They often provide counseling and referral to needed services.

Services for pregnant teens are offered through hospitals and health clinics, which are sometimes school based. These health clinics cater specifically to pregnant teens and can be sensitive to their needs and concerns. In addition to health education and prenatal care, health clinics get involved in the coordination of health services. Some clinics have incorporated peer counselors to provide counseling and outreach services. Specialized services include prenatal care, pediatric care, family planning, nutritional services, and health education.

Many community organizations such as the Ys and churches have programs for pregnant teenagers. They offer parenting seminars, discussion groups, counseling and referral, and recreation. Other community services provide help so that teens can complete their education by acquiring their GED, and provide them with job training and placement. Day care services have been offered by some agencies to increase the teen's opportunity for completing high school as well as obtaining employment.

There are many community services whose focus is on building and strengthening the teen's support system. Some programs will match volunteers with parenting teenagers. These volunteers are older women who often were teen mothers themselves. Mutual support groups are also held at such agencies which give the teen mothers an opportunity to share their experiences and concerns with each other.

Finally, there are programs which offer "comprehensive services." These programs try to provide all the needed resources under one roof or they rely on interagency coordination and collaboration to meet the needs of their clients. They attempt to provide a variety of health, educational, and social services.

We know very little about the overall effectiveness of these different services for pregnant and parenting teens (Harman & Brim, 1980; Hayes, 1987; Klerman, 1979; Shadish & Reis, 1984; Weatherly, Perlman, Levine, & Klerman, 1985). The lack of research makes it difficult to compare what types of programs are more effective than others. It is also unclear who in the programs are being helped and who the programs are not reaching. The high attrition rate common to programs working with this at-risk group of adolescents suggests there is a sizable number of teens not being served.

Most research on human service programs focuses attention on the outcome of the intervention and gives little consideration to the determinants of a client's decision to participate and their level of involvement in the program. Given the numerous problems, multiple needs, and complex lives of teenage mothers, it is unlikely that all teenage mothers will respond and be receptive to an intervention in similar ways. The high dropout rate for parenting programs, particularly for high risk samples, clearly suggests a need to examine more closely the relationship between the program, the clients, and the social context in which they interact (Johnson & Breckenridge, 1982; O'Connor, Vietze, Sherrod, Sandler, Gerrity, & Altemeier, 1982; Slaughter, 1983). Differing patterns of participation may be one clue in developing programs better matched with the needs and social environments of teen parents.

In this chapter we present an educational support intervention, the Resource Mother Program, which was developed for pregnant and parenting teens. Over the course of the program, some teen parents participated more than others. We suggest that prenatal differences of mothers in the program were related to differing levels of participation after their child was born. Implications of our exploratory findings for program development and future research are discussed.

THE RESOURCE MOTHER PROGRAM

The Resource Mother Program was a home-based educational support program for rural teenage mothers having their first child. The home visitors, or Resource Mothers, were experienced mothers and paraprofessionals who visited each teenager at home from early pregnancy through the baby's first birthday. The design of the Resource Mother Program was based upon a review of previous education and support programs developed for teenage and older mothers (Gray & Wandersman, 1980; Wandersman, 1981; Wandersman, 1987). The program attempted to build upon what we hypothesized were the successful components within the many different parenting intervention programs. These goals and approaches are discussed below. An evaluation of the program was conducted which was partly designed to provide information at the time of recruitment about characteristics of the teens and their families. These prenatal characteristics are later discussed in this chapter as they relate to differing levels of program participation among the mothers.

Goals of the Program

The overall goal of the Resource Mother program was to support the development of health and competence for rural teenage mothers and their babies. The emphasis was on enhancing the strengths of the mother and her social environment by identifying the positive motivations and skills of each mother and her family, reinforcing them, and using them as a foundation for growth and new choices for coping with problems. The specific aims included: (a) increasing appropriate use of medical and social services; (b) reducing perinatal complications; (c) improving maternal childrearing attitudes and parenting behaviors; (d) promoting maternal confidence, sense of control, and self-esteem; (e) promoting infant competence; and (f) reducing social isolation.

Approach of the Resource Mother Program

1. Home-based delivery of services.   There is ample literature which suggests that home-based interventions can be successful (Bronfenbrenner, 1974; Cappleman, Thompson, DeReimer-Sullivan, King, & Sturm, 1982; Cartoff, 1979; Gray & Ruttle, 1980; Gray & Wandersman, 1980; Larson, 1980; Olds, 1981). The Resource Mother Program was a home-based program designed to serve a rural population. We felt home visitation would be a useful way to reach teenage parents living far from many resources and usually having no transportation or even a telephone. A home-based approach also allowed the program staff to become familiar with the teen and her home environment and, therefore, to effectively respond to her individual concerns (Chamberlain, 1980).

2. Paraprofessionals as home visitors.   The home visitors or "Resource Mothers" were paraprofessionals. We believed the use of paraprofessionals would make the home visitors more acceptable and approachable to the teens than a professional. Growing up in the same community with similar values and problems, the teens could use the Resource Mother as a model of competence and feel less estrangement than they would with professionals. The Resource Mothers' familiarity with their rural community would also be helpful in developing sources for recruitment and referral.

3. Relationship between Resource Mother and teenager as critical element. Another major strategy of the intervention was to develop a supportive and encouraging relationship between the teen and Resource Mother. Research has demonstrated the important role social support plays in buffering the negative effects of stress and facilitating effective coping (Cohen & McKay, 1984; Crnic, Greenberg, & Robinson, 1984; Heller & Swindle, 1983; Unger & Powell, 1980). Previous evaluations of parenting programs suggest that the critical element in the success of parent education programs is that "the recipients come to believe that the service providers value them as people and consider their development and achievement as an important goal worth striving for" (Rescorla & Zigler, 1981, p. 12). A caring and supportive relationship between the Resource Mother and teenager was designed to help the teenager to feel valued as a person and to see her role as a parent as important to the development of her baby. The relationship was built by the Resource Mother in many ways—she began visiting early in pregnancy and empathizing with the mother's feelings, she expressed interest in the mother and her concerns, she reinforced the mother's strengths and efforts, she communicated acceptance of the mother, she was available when the teenager needed her, she provided tangible help when it was needed, and she was a real person who shared ideas and experiences.

4. Pragmatic and cost-effective.   The use of paraprofessionals in a home-based intervention was thought to be an economical way to provide services given the limited resources of this area (Chamberlain, 1980). The Resource Mother could be trained to provide multiple forms of support (e.g., informational/educational, emotional) and to refer the teen to other sources of support and assistance when appropriate. Many demonstration programs are too costly to be widely implemented. The program was designed to be cost effective and to build on available resources.

   5. Recognition of the strengths of the teenager.   Resource Mothers became adept at identifying and enhancing the teen's strengths. Helping the Resource Mothers develop skills to identify strengths was an important part of their training. When they initially viewed training videotapes, they could only describe what was "wrong" with the teen. Through training and working with the mothers, they began to describe the teen and her family in positive terms. They learned what was good about the family and how to build upon these strengths. It seemed as if they developed a whole new way of looking at people.

   6. Specific aims and a detailed curriculum.   The program offered focus, structure, and educational content to the supportive relationship between the teen and Resource Mother. Programs with more specific aims and structure appear to be more effective than less-structured programs (Gray & Wandersman, 1980). The program was designed to have specific aims and a detailed curriculum based on these aims. The regularity of needs, concerns, and interests which arise for parents during pregnancy and the postpartum period lent themselves to a curriculum useful with all teen mothers. The curriculum was aimed at communicating knowledge about health and development in ways that were easy to understand and involved the mother in developing realistic ways she could apply them to her own situation.

   7. Individualization of goals and approach.   Because teenagers vary in their needs, strengths, and resources, programs should be matched to the individual teenager. Resource Mothers developed individualized goals based on the needs, strengths and resources of each teenager. For example, a Resource Mother spent considerable time on helping a pregnant teen who had been kicked out of her home to find suitable housing. A frightened pregnant teen accompanied a Resource Mother on a visit to a mother with a newborn to find out more about what to expect when she has her child. Resource Mothers were present at labor and delivery for teenagers who did not have a support person from their network.

   8. Involvement of the social network.   Social support from a mother's family and friends has been found to be important in her adjustment to parenthood (Unger & Wandersman, 1985). The social network was involved in the Resource Mother Program in several ways. First, the teen's family and the baby's father were usually involved in the initial decision to participate in the program. Often, family members or the baby's father were part of home visits. Discussions of social relationships and effective ways to gain support from family and friends were an integral part of the curricula.

   9. Integration of the Program with the community.   Many excellent demonstration programs become extinct after the initial demonstration period. The

Resource Mother Program was designed to become a part of the community. The program was introduced into this rural community with town meetings in each community that were attended by local mayors, religious leaders, service agency representatives, and prominent citizens. Each community was involved in finding and funding a local base for the Resource Mother, one in a hospital day care center, one in a scout hut, and one in a hospital outreach center. A major component of the Resource Mother's role was maintaining cooperative relationships with schools, churches, and other services and facilitating the teenager's involvement with other parts of the community.

The Resource Mother Intervention

Resource Mothers located pregnant teenagers through referrals from the health department, prenatal clinics, private physicians, social service agencies, schools, and friends of teenage mothers. Mothers were recruited as early in pregnancy as possible. Each teenager was visited approximately once a month at home from early pregnancy through the baby's first birthday. The teen mothers were also given a phone number where they could reach the Resource Mother and were encouraged to call her with any questions or problems. The program served teen mothers in three rural counties in South Carolina. Program participation was voluntary and free.

The Resource Mothers. The Resource Mothers were selected from the community for their personal warmth, knowledge of the local community, parenting experience and attitude, interpersonal skills, responsibility, and leadership. They were recruited primarily through personal referrals and contacts at community meetings. Approximately one hundred people were interviewed before the six Resource Mothers were chosen.

All the Resource Mothers were parents. Several had been teenage and/or single mothers themselves. They were involved in community and church activities prior to being hired. For most of them, this was their first "real" job. The Resource Mothers had a strong sense of commitment and caring for their clients, or "their girls" and "their babies," as they would say. An example of the investment Resource Mothers showed in working with each particular family amidst the extreme challenges is seen in the report of one Resource Mother on a home visit in the baby's second week to a very poor, isolated home without running water. The report reads:

I praised her for getting a net to keep over her baby's face to keep the flies from playing on it. I checked the navel cord and found that she wasn't taking care of it like she should have. I went downtown and got her some alcohol and cotton balls to clean her baby's navel with. I also bought her baby a nipple. The one she had was stuffed with dirty cotton that came out of a mattress.

The Resource Mother had several different roles. She was a teacher who assessed the mother's needs and then provided the teen with appropriate information about pregnancy and prenatal care, childbirth, child development, parenting, and community resources. The Resource Mother modeled effective ways of interacting with adults and babies, and reinforced the mother's appropriate behaviors as well as her attempts at new behaviors. She was a source of emotional support, a person who listened to the teen mother in an accepting, caring manner and discussed the mother's concerns. In addition to providing support, the Resource Mother encouraged support from the mother's social network. Finally, the Resource Mother was a facilitator, making it easier for the mother to get the services and support she and her infant needed. She helped arrange transportation to well-baby clinics, referred the mother to community resources, and helped out with "red tape" involved in obtaining needed services.

The Resource Mother had a curriculum to guide her home visits. The struc-

Table 1. Outline of Resource Mother Home Visits

Visit	Focus of Visit
Prenatal:	
Recruitment	Explanation of project, consent to participate, prenatal interview
3rd month	Development of trusting relationship, assessment of strengths and needs, acceptance of fetus as real baby dependent on mother
4th month	Plan for adequate diet and limiting of adverse substances
5th month	Understanding of emotional, sexual, and psychological changes in mother and her relationships, explanation of conception and family planning
6th month	Understanding of stages of prenatal development, practice of good body mechanics and prenatal exercise
7th month	Recognition of signs and stages of labor, planning for labor and support person, practice slow breathing and relaxation
8th month	Preparation for hospital procedures and possible complications, practice rapid breathing and pushing, discussion of circumcision
9th month	Characteristics of newborns, feeding preparations, planning for baby care
Postpartum:	
1st week	Discussion of mother's feelings, individual needs of babies and ways to meet them, observing baby's responses and style
2nd week	Helping mother meet baby's needs for warmth, stimulation, safety in bathing, feeding, and changing; discussion of mother's feelings; teaching how to take temperatures
4th week	Discussion of how baby learns and issues concerning her adjustment to motherhood; learn to make a mobile
6th week	Making plans for family planning, immunizations, baby exercise; make a baby gym; facilitate attendance at well-baby clinic
3rd month	Caretaking of infant, importance of talking to baby, introducing solid foods, make rattle
4th month	Realistic expectations of infant, playing games with baby, mother's adjustment, make doll
6th month	Safe exploring, reinforcement, stimulation for baby, soft toy
8th month	Encouraging baby sounds and mother's labeling, mother's adjustment, realistic expectations of infant, make stacking cans
10th month	Increase positive reinforcement and effective discipline, make shape can
12th month	Review of progress, resources for future needs, expectations about toddlers, make string toy, receive diploma

tured curriculum for each home visit was geared to the young mother's changing interests and needs. The curriculum was based on a concrete, goal-centered approach which the Resource Mothers individualized for each mother. The curriculum dealt with such topics as (a) prenatal development, (b) conception and family planning, (c) preparation for labor and delivery, (d) nutrition, (e) baby's care, (f) infant development, and (g) stimulation for her baby. All visits emphasized the importance of the young mother in influencing the development of her baby. An outline of the focus of the Resource Mother home visits is presented in Table 1.

While the Resource Mother was to cover educational topics during her home visit, she had great flexibility and varied the particular visit depending upon the problems the teen was experiencing. For example, a teen's personal difficulty might receive special attention and the educational component would be covered in less detail. The Resource Mothers viewed the curriculum as important and usually found a way to cover the essential information on each visit. Table 2 gives an example of the stages of a typical home visit.

Training for the Resource Mothers was provided by an initial, intensive, 3-week-long workshop, followed by continual inservice training and supervision. Training focused on home visiting skills and perinatal well-being. Topics included: physical changes in the perinatal period, perinatal nutrition, preparation for labor, delivery, and the new baby, normal infant development and signs of problems, the role of family, friends, and community in promoting well-being, developing the Resource Mother's communication skills, assessment of

Table 2. A Resource Mother Home Visit

1. *Discussion of how teen is coping with problems and concerns:*
   "How have you been doing since I saw you last?" the Resource Mother asks. "Okay," the teen answers. The Resource Mother pauses when she notices a concerned look on her client's face. After a brief silence, the teen starts to mention concerns about her changing body and problems with her family's response to her boyfriend. The Resource Mother responds supportively, "I used to feel that way, too."

2. *Educational focus specific to the period of development:*
   "Do you know how big your baby is now and what it looks like?" The Resource Mother asks. "I guess it's about all developed by now." The Resource Mother opens a book to show her color pictures of different stages of development of the fetus . . . "I don't like milk. I go for a week without it. Does that matter?" the teen asks. "Yes, your body needs milk. Try making some rules for yourself. Like, 'I'll drink a half glass of milk each morning' . . . Why don't you try this? It might help you have less pain in your back . . ."

3. *Check on services: Knowledge of availability and use of services:*
   "Last time we talked about you getting on WIC. How did that go? . . . When is your next doctor's appointment? If you can't find anybody to take you, let me know."

4. *Developmental expectations and planning for next visit:*
   "When the baby is born, do you think he'll be able to see you? What do you think he'll be able to eat . . . Next time we meet we'll talk about what it's gonna be like when your baby gets home from the hospital . . ."

adolescent psychosocial and major health problems, and identifying appropriate referral sources. Supervision was provided by either a pediatric nurse practitioner or social worker, and by a developmental psychologist who served as the Program Coordinator.

PREDICTORS OF PARTICIPATION

Little is known about how interventions are affected by participant characteristics or about how the social context in which interventions occur influences the utilization of these services (Gray & Wandersman, 1980; McKinlay, 1972). Our research addresses how prenatal differences of mothers were related to differing levels of postpartum program participation. Four categories of predictors were chosen to explore what factors affected participation in the Resource Mother Program. These categories were based upon the available literature and our experience through pilot work with families in the program. First, it was hypothesized that certain "enabling" factors must be present in order for the teen to utilize the program's services (cf. Andersen & Newman, 1973). For example, social networks play an important role in a client's decision to use services by acting as an informal information and referral system (Freidson, 1960; Powell & Eisenstadt, 1982; Unger & Wandersman, 1983; Warren, 1981). Social networks may also influence a client's participation in parenting programs and services for parents and their children (e.g., Birkel & Reppucci, 1983; Gabel, Graybill, DeMott, Wood, & Johnston, 1977; Kammeyer & Bolton, 1968; McKinlay, 1973). For example, Kessen and Fein (1975) and Badger (1981) found that parents were more responsive to home-based parent education programs when the parents had more extensive family ties and support. Powell (1984) also found that mothers were more likely to remain involved in a neighborhood-based educational/support program when their parents, prior to program entry, were a greater source of instrumental help compared to parents of mothers who were later inactive participants.

Families may need to provide a sufficient level of emotional and instrumental support resources to the teen so that she has the means and encouragement to participate in the program. For instance, if the teen and/or her family are struggling and overwhelmed with the stresses of meeting daily needs, active program involvement where the focus is on parenting may be unlikely. Some research suggests that pregnancy for teens causes an interruption of their normal adolescent development, resulting in a loss of coping ability, abrupt changes in relationships, and increased distress (Cartoff, 1978; Group for Advancement of Psychiatry, 1986). Supportive family resources may be necessary to mobilize the teen to become involved in a pregnancy and parenting program.

In our research we assessed the mother's perceptions of social support from her family and the baby's father. We define social support specifically in terms of perceived social support or the extent to which individuals feel their needs for support are satisfied (cf. Procidano & Heller, 1983; Shumaker & Brownell, 1984). We also assessed the structure and functioning of the teenager's social interactions (Gottleib & Hall, 1980). For instance, we were interested in the frequency of contact she had with different network members, as well as the instrumental help she received or expected to receive from her network members, such as financial support, housing arrangements, and child care.

Second, the severity of problems experienced as a result of the pregnancy may increase the mother's perception of need for services (Bice & White, 1969). Most teens do not seek out services such as prenatal care as a result of the pregnancy (Bierman & Streett, 1982). It was expected, however, that, with more health-related problems, there would be a heightened sense of need and greater likelihood of participation in the program.

We also thought the teen's interest and investment in raising her child would predict more active involvement in the program. This included general preparations for the child's birth, involvement with professional agencies designed to provide services for prenatal care and parenting, and knowledge of pregnancy and infant development (Lochman & Brown, 1980; Wandersman, 1983).

Finally, the timing of the teen's contact with the program would likely influence whether she would remain involved with the program once the child was born. We thought having the time and opportunity to develop a relationship between the teen and the Resource Mother prior to delivery would help their relationship continue after the child's birth. For example, Larson (1980) found that having prenatal and hospital contact facilitated the development of a relationship between the home visitors and older mothers, with the mothers turning to the home visitors for advice and encouragement. If initial contact occurred several weeks after delivery, the mothers seemed less receptive to the intervention, having independently developed a style of coping and seeing little need for the home visitor.

THE STUDY

Participants

The participants in this research were 88 adolescent mothers of low socioeconomic status who were interviewed prenatally. These teens participated in the program between 1981 and 1983 and are a subsample of all mothers who were recruited over the course of the program. The subsample was chosen because detailed records of contact between the Resource Mothers and the teens were kept only during this time period. Ages of the mothers ranged from 13 to 18 years, with an average age of 16; 84.2 percent were black and 15.8 percent were white. Most of the teens (86.5%) were in school and 98 percent were unemployed. The majority (77.4%) lived with their parents, although some resided with nonparental relatives (16.7%) or the baby's father (6%). Ninety-two percent were single during their pregnancy.

We defined *active* program participation as having seven or more home visits after the baby was born. This criterion was selected since seven was approximately the average number of postnatal home visits for all teens in the program ($\overline{X}$ = 7.5; median = 6.2). The number of prenatal visits was not included in determining the participation level of the mothers, because their initial involvement in the prenatal program varied according to several external factors, e.g., time of referral to program and recruitment, and the teen's acknowledgement of the pregnancy to herself and others (cf. Bierman & Streett, 1982). Of the 88 adolescent females, 52 actively participated in the program. These "active" teens had an average of 9.1 postnatal home visits (range 7–17).

There were 36 mothers who received six or fewer postnatal home visits. Of these 36 mothers, we looked at two subgroups. The *inactive* subgroup included those mothers who remained living in the area throughout the baby's first year of life. Those in the second subgroup are called *movers*. These were mothers who moved and were not actively involved in the program after their baby's birth. We did not include movers in the inactive subgroup, so as to not confuse mobility with early program termination. The inactive subgroup (N = 22) had an average of four postnatal home visits (range 0–6) and the mover subgroup (N = 14) had 3.6 postnatal home visits (range 0–6). All movers and inactives had had prenatal home visits.

All teens initially had equivalent access to the Resource Mothers. The Resource Mothers were very ingenious in trying to complete their visits. They would wait at the teen's house for the bus to drop them off, wait for them at school, or look for them in K-Mart or even in the local bars. Especially throughout the prenatal period, the Resource Mothers were very aggressive in contacting the teens. Once into the postnatal period, they began to lessen their pursuit if they felt the teen still did not want to be involved.

Procedure

Teenagers were recruited as early in pregnancy as possible, most by their second trimester. At the time of recruitment, all teenagers who agreed to participate in our program were interviewed by a Resource Mother. A major function of the interview was to provide information about the client which we could use at the conclusion of the program to better understand the factors which were predictive of participation. The interview was also used by Resource Mothers to assess a teen's strengths and problems and to individualize their approach with the teen.

The interview was structured with closed-ended questions which assessed: (a) the teen's feelings about having a baby; (b) her preparedness for parenthood and her plans for child care; (c) a checklist of pregnancy related health problems; (d) her knowledge about pregnancy, labor, and delivery; (e) her knowledge about babies and their development; (f) her perception of social support from family and the baby's father; (g) dimensions of her social network including the provision of instrumental support resources, frequency of contact with network members, and characteristics of the baby's father; and (h) her participation in health and social service programs.

Throughout the course of the intervention, the Resource Mothers kept records of their home visits with their clients. When the mother's child was 1 year old, the client "graduated," and the file was completed. For mothers who terminated our program early, the file was, of course, completed earlier. We went through approximately a year's worth of completed files and recorded the number of home visits conducted after the child's birth. We also tried to determine whether early program termination was the result of a move that prohibited the mother from participating or that kept the Resource Mother from finding her, or because she was no longer interested.

RESULTS

The results are discussed in terms of differing patterns in the data between groups.

Actives

The active participants of the program were single (96%) and lived with one or both of their parents. When interviewed at the start of the Program, the majority felt they would have help with child care and would be sharing the responsibilities of the baby's care with others, as is shown in Table 3. They were getting prepared for the baby's arrival, for example, by receiving things for the baby or reading about what to expect. They also were participating in programs that would help their pregnancy and baby (e.g., WIC, prenatal care). Throughout their pregnancy, they were involved in the prenatal home visits of the Resource Mother Program, having an average of 4.5 visits.

About half of the active participants had only occasional or rare contact with the baby's father. Few were counting on the baby's father to be their sole source of financial support, and instead were planning to rely on some combination of assistance from their family, relatives, or the baby's father.

So far in their pregnancy, they had begun to experience a few health problems.

Inactives

Compared to the actives, more of the inactives lived with nonparental relatives and the baby's father rather than with their parents. The inactives also had much more contact with the baby's father, with 76% seeing the father daily (19% of the inactive mothers lived with the father). They expected to have contact with the fathers after the baby's birth and were depending on the father for future financial

Table 3.   Differences Between Active and Inactive Teen Mothers

Who are you currently living with? ($\chi^2(2) = 10.41$, p < .005)

	Inactive (%)	Active (%)
One or both parents	66.7	88
Family other than parents	14.3	12
Baby's father	19.0	0

How often do you see or talk to the baby's father now? ($\chi^2(2) = 6.46$, p < .05)

	Inactive (%)	Active (%)
Rarely or never	19.0	37.0
More than once a month	4.8	19.6
Nearly every day	76.2	43.4

Who will take care of the baby? ($\chi^2(2) = 5.48$, p < .07)

	Inactive (%)	Active (%)
Others all or most of the time	14.3	2.2
Share with others	57.1	80.4
Self most of the time	28.6	17.4

How will you support yourself? Money from . . . ($\chi^2(4) = 10.15$, p <.05)

	Inactive (%)	Active (%)
Government programs only	25.0	6.7
Both family and baby's father	10.0	31.1
Family, but not father	25.0	31.1
Baby's father, but not family	35.0	15.6
Don't know	5.0	15.5

What have you done to prepare for this baby? ($\chi^2(2) = 6.99$, p < .05)

	Inactive (%)	Active (%)
Nothing	45	14.9
Read things, received things	45	70.2
Made toys, furniture and/or bought things	10	14.9

assistance. One-third were expecting to support themselves from the father's income rather than from any help from their families.

As a group, there was more diversity about who they expected to care for their future child. Half of them expected to share child care responsibilities, but others felt they would have to assume full responsibility or would have to put the child in someone else's care.

The inactives were not making as many plans for their child. Only about half of the girls had started to get things ready for their baby and to learn about infant care. They also were not participating in many child related programs (e.g.,

Table 4.   Additional Differences Between Actives and Inactives

	Active ($\overline{X}$)	Inactive ($\overline{X}$)	df	t	p
Social service and prenatal care programs	2.3	1.6	72	−2.54	.02
Health problems	3.7	2.5	66	−1.94	.06
Prenatal home visits	4.5	3.5	72	−1.77	.08
Knowledge of prenatal care and infant development	11.3	11.1	66	−.28	>.10
Baby's father social support	8.4	9.6	70	1.5	>.10
Family social support	15.0	15.6	72	1.4	>.10

WIC) in preparation for the baby. Similarly, they had fewer prenatal home visits than the actives.

The Movers

Compared to the actives, more of the movers were living outside of their family's home (see Table 5). They were much less likely to anticipate receiving financial support from their families and instead were expecting to rely more heavily on government programs. More of the movers did not anticipate working in 5 years from the interview, and they were more likely to have dropped out of school. Throughout pregnancy they had approximately the same number of home visits with the Resource Mothers as the actives ($\overline{X}$ = 4.5).

When asked if they could go back and change things like magic, significantly more of the movers as compared to actives or inactives (36% movers: 8.5% inactive: 9.5% active) said they would choose to be pregnant. Many of these characteristics seem similar to Badger's (1981) description of the teen mother who has few hopes for personal achievement, resigns herself to being on welfare, begins to feel powerless, and often has a second unplanned pregnancy.

Table 5.   Differences Between Actives and Movers

Who are you currently living with? ($\chi^2(1)$ = 7.9, p < .05)

	Movers	Actives
One or both parents	58.3	88
Family other than parents	33.3	12
Baby's father	8.4	0

How will you support yourself? Money from . . . ($\chi^2(4)$ = 9.8, p < .05)

	Movers	Actives
Government only	30.8	6.7
Both family and baby's father	23.1	31.1
Family, but not father	0.0	31.1
Father, but not family	23.1	15.6
Don't know	23.1	15.5

Are you in school now? ($\chi^2(1)$ = 4.5, p < .05)

	Movers	Actives
No	28.6%	7.7%
Yes	71.4%	92.3%

Do you think you'll be working in five or so years from now?
($\chi^2(2)$ = 8.2, p < .05)

	Movers	Actives
No	35.7	8.5
Yes	64.3	72.3
Don't know	0.0	19.2

If you could go back and change things, like magic, would you be pregnant?
($\chi^2(2)$ = 8.2, p < .05)

	Movers	Actives
No	64.3	72.3
Not sure	0	19.1
Yes	35.7	8.5

Similarities Among Actives, Inactives, and Movers

The three groups did not differ in the teen's age, knowledge about pregnancy or infants, or their perceptions of support from their families. There was a trend for inactives to report more support from the babies' fathers than the actives did. However, this difference was not statistically significant. Most of the teens (84%) said they had never intended to get pregnant when they had. The majority (79%) felt they knew how to be a good mother, although half indicated some concerns about caring for their child.

DISCUSSION

The results suggest that there may have been a better "fit" between the Resource Mother Program and certain teen mothers than others. The teen mothers who actively participated were living with their families, felt they could rely on their families for financial assistance and instrumental support, and were not very involved with the baby's father.

As expected, the actives differed from the inactives by being more involved in preparations for their child. Living with their families, the actives probably had more access to information and resources as well as "prodding" from their parents to help them get ready for the baby. A certain level of interest and resources seem a necessary condition to support participation.

Most of the inactives had much more involvement with the baby's father. They had more contact with him and had expectations of his future help with child care and financial support. Their family's support seemed less certain and not their primary source of support. These different patterns of reliance on providers of support between the actives and inactives are consistent with Furstenberg's (1980) observation that support from the mother's family and the baby's father often do not function as complementary sources of support.

The prenatal involvement of the baby's father with mothers in the inactive group raises some interesting possibilities about the father's influence on participation. The inactive mothers may have expected the father to be supportive, but, after the pregnancy, this was not realized. With the lack of support, her life became more unstable and stressful, making consistent and regular participation difficult. Unger and Wandersman's (1985) finding that many of the teen mothers in this sample by 8 months postpartum were no longer involved with the baby's father lends some support to this idea. Without some kind of stability or support, whether from the family or baby's father, continued participation in a home visitation program is unlikely. Another explanation is that the fathers might not have "approved" of their girlfriend's involvement in the program, resulting in the mothers leaving the program. Badger (1981) also notes this phenomenon in her teenage sample. The teenage father often feels left out of the whole pregnancy and birth experience, and the maternal focus of the Resource Mother Program may have been perceived by him as one more isolating experience.

The narrative comments made by Resource Mothers in their case records about the inactive mothers suggest there is more than one type of inactive mother. Some inactive mothers, as discussed, were involved with the baby's father and planned to care for their infant either by themselves or with help from relatives. However, there also appears to be a group of inactive mothers who gave up responsibility for their baby to relatives. These inactives usually lived at home and seemed to return to their life as an adolescent but not as a parent. For example, the Resource Mothers wrote of these teens: "The baby was always left to someone else's care," "The baby was never with her but with her aunt," "The client started working, and she could never find time for our visits." Further research is needed to more clearly distinguish between these different groups of inactive participants.

The movers seemed less connected with potential informal resources than active participants. Their living arrangements were less stable and they weren't counting on their families for instrumental assistance. The sample size for this group is small, but case records by the Resource Mothers suggest these "movers" were a diverse group. Some of the mothers made several moves during the postpartum period to and from relatives and friends. Other movers got married, not necessarily to the baby's father, and moved out of the county. Finally, there was one older mother who came home to have her child and then returned to college in another state. Clearly, there was not a good "fit" between these mothers and a home-based program. The Resource Mothers found it very difficult to keep track of these mothers once their child was born.

The teen's lack of knowledge about infants and parenting was not a predictor of program participation. Since the Resource Mother Program was designed to meet a number of the teenager's needs, the educational component probably appealed to some of the active teens but not to others. For example, our data suggest some teens may have been motivated by concerns about their health. Within the same program, different teens may be using certain services more than others (e.g., Powell, 1983). Future research of multifocused support programs needs to look beyond the actives to identify subgroups of active participants and their differing needs and characteristics.

The earlier that teens were recruited in pregnancy, the more likely they would continue their participation once their child was born, given that they continued to live in the area. In fact, across all groups in the study, the number of prenatal visits was significantly positively related to the number of postnatal home visits ($r = .44$, $p < .001$). The movers had the same amount of prenatal contact with the Resource Mothers as the actives did. The results suggest that the movers had the opportunity to develop a relationship with the Resource Mother, but that the instability and stressors of their lives could not support their continued involvement in the program.

The data did not show significant differences in perceived social support from the families across the groups. This may have been due to the measure's lack of sensitivity to such differences. It also may have been due to the fact that provision of instrumental types of support such as financial aid and help with child care (which did vary across the groups) are not the same as the mother's perception of her family's "emotional support" (Cutrona, 1986). For example, even though the parents of the actives provided more help, all teens may have had difficulty in their relationships with their parents. For example, a Resource Mother noted in the record of an active mother: "Valerie would have done more with her baby, but her mother would tell her she did not know how to take care of a baby."

IMPLICATIONS FOR PROGRAM DEVELOPMENT

Families and Support Programs for Teen Parents

Teen pregnancy is a family problem, affecting all members of the teen's family. To understand teen parents and to develop effective intervention programs, it is necessary to focus, not solely on the teen, but rather on the teen within the context of her family (Authier & Authier, 1982; Furstenberg & Crawford, 1978; Ooms, 1984, Zitner & Miller, 1980). Prenatal predictors of later adjustment emphasize the importance of family support in effecting parenting competence (Furstenberg & Crawford, 1978; Unger & Wandersman, 1985). Support from their families, particularly instrumental types of support such as child care and financial assistance, are predictive of whether teens will actively participate in intervention programs for parenting teens. Families have a primary influence in enabling the teen's use of a program. How families influence the teen's use of services is not clear. It is likely that, when families provide sufficient support, the teen has enough resources to make use of a support program rather than having to attend constantly to daily stressors.

Teens who are estranged from their families, moving away from home, and relying on their own resources or resources of the baby's father fare much worse than those who remain living with their families (Barth, Schinke, & Maxwell, 1983; Furstenberg, 1980). These mothers are likely to be faced with more stressors and to be more economically strained. For example, relying on the baby's father for support in our sample was not typically a reliable source, given the high rate of unemployment among black male teens (Height, 1986). Engaging these mothers may need a different approach than when working with mothers having family resources. Mothers not receiving help from their families are in need of programs that can provide support resources to enable them to cope with parenting and adolescent developmental tasks. For instance, they need day care services so they can complete high school, obtain job skill training, and/or maintain part-time employment. In the rural counties of our program, these services were not available to refer the teen to.

Ideally, if a program could deal with the immediate environmental stressors first, mothers might later be able to make use of the educational and emotional support component of a program. Eisenstadt and Powell (1987), for instance, found that stress limited a parent's ability to initially use the peer-group component of a program but resulted in heavy reliance on the program staff services. Only later were the parents able to make use of the group's support.

The families of the teen are also in need of support. Strategies designed to help the grandparents, uncles, and aunts may further strengthen their ability to support the parenting teen. Some programs have tried to incorporate families in the services to the teen parent as the Resource Mother often did. Other programs have developed support groups and activities specifically for the grandparents (Nickel & Delany, 1985). There is a great need for developing interventions which can successfully address the concerns of families of parenting teens.

Involvement of the Baby's Father

The role of the baby's father needs to be further explored and taken into account when planning an intervention for some teen mothers. Possibly, if the teen fathers had been more involved in the services of the program, the retention rate would have been higher for our group of inactive teens. While many human service providers argue they do not have the funds to offer services to teen fathers, it may be more cost effective when working with some mothers to include the fathers so as not to lose the mothers. Research on programs for teen fathers is encouraging in that many teen fathers are willing to participate (Klinman, Sander, Rosen, & Longo, 1986) although their recruitment is typically very challenging. The benefits to the father, and his child, are likely to be numerous as a result of his participation.

The father's involvement is a very complicated issue for teen parenting intervention programs. For the actives, advocating father involvement may alienate the mother's family. It also may be counter to what the teen mother wants, particularly if she has started to be involved in a relationship with another man. There were a number of fathers who wanted to participate in raising their child, but many of the mothers active in the program did not want them involved. For the inactive group, however, father involvement may be one way of encouraging the mother's participation and helping the couple clarify their expectations of each other and their responsibilities to their child. Assessing the teen's relationship to her family and the baby's father seems critical in developing an appropriate intervention for the teen mother.

When planning programs which include fathers, differing concerns and characteristics of the fathers will need to be addressed and studied. For example, not all of the fathers of the babies in our program were teen fathers. Approximately 14% were 21 years of age or older. These men will have different emotional, legal, and economic concerns than the 14-year-old teen father.

Subgroups of Teens

In addition to differing patterns of support from their families and the baby's father, teen parents vary in other important characteristics, making them a very heterogeneous group (Quay, 1981; Hamburg, 1986). More research is needed to identify profiles of various subgroups of the teens to develop programs according to their needs. The concerns of older teens (aged 18–19) may be more oriented around employment and job skills, while younger teens (aged 11–15) may be more in need of personal, emotional support, in light of their developmental immaturity. Teens having planned versus unintended pregnancies may have different concerns and respond to interventions differently. For example, within certain subcultures, having a child as an older teenager may be an adaptive and responsible behavior (Hamburg, 1986; Stack, 1974). Our findings also suggest the need for future research to study subgroups within the active and inactive groups of participants.

Timing of the Support Program

The timing of the intervention seems critical to establishing participation. In our study, if the Resource Mothers had little contact prior to delivery, they had a great deal of trouble establishing a relationship and maintaining contact postnatally. Changes in the teen's level of distress over time may contribute to the difficulty Resource Mothers reported when trying to develop relationships with some clients. While much research details the continued stressful and disruptive influences of pregnancy and parenting for the adolescent (Group for Advancement of Psychiatry, 1986; Klerman, 1986), there may be periods which are less stressful than others (Furstenberg, 1980; Panzarine, 1986).

The disclosure of the pregnancy and the family's response, relationship difficulties with the baby's father and the mother's family, concerns about the mother's health, and preparations for the baby may initially be met with much apprehension and turmoil. Once the baby is born, the stress subsides for many mothers, particularly those with family support. Similarly, the need for supportive services may decline.

> In one conversation with an administrator from a large urban agency, a theory about services was presented that bears credibility, in as much as it was mentioned or alluded to by others also. The administrator stated that from a teenager's perspective, a pregnancy is a very short-term crisis, the greatest hurdle being the family's reaction. Once the family is informed and accepts her condition—with or without the agency's help—the crisis is over. (Forbush, 1981, p. 270)

The teen's distress, however, probably resumes later in postpartum, as it does for older mothers (Belsky, Lang, & Rovine, 1985; Miller & Sollie, 1980).

While the timing of the intervention affected the teen's interest in participating in the program, it also may have influenced how the Resource Mother responded to the teens. Earlier contact with the teen mothers was more reinforcing for the Resource Mother. If the teens and Resource Mother had more shared experiences, they were more likely to establish relationships which would carry over postnatally (cf. Larson, 1980).

Differences in how the teens responded to their pregnancies may affect when they join the program and their level of participation. Our study did not systematically assess these differences. However, our impressions are that the actives were more motivated to plan for their babies and consequently were responsive to a parent support program. During their pregnancy, the inactives were more ambivalent about becoming parents and probably were more likely to deny that they were pregnant (cf. Joyce, Diffenbacher, Greeve, & Sorokin, 1983). The inactives were, therefore, more difficult to identify and contact. Research is needed to address how teens' different reactions to their pregnancies affect the use of prenatal and postpartum services.

Community Support

Another factor which influenced participation was a community value structure which was supportive of the program and encouraged participation of the teens. While we cannot determine how this affected teens differently in terms of their level of participation, it is clear to us that the community's support for the program is important in achieving substantial service utilization. From the inception of the program, the local community was an important structural component. The administration of the program involved three institutions: a local hospital, the state health department, and two medical schools. The community had enough influence to feel ownership, yet the program had enough credibility from the professional community to encourage referrals. The Resource Mothers also actively cultivated contacts within the school systems and local agencies. The community acceptance and ownership of the program seemed to be a vital part of gaining access to the teens. In fact, these factors contributed to the program being currently implemented state-wide in South Carolina.

The Matching Process

The development and evaluation of support programs needs to focus on identifying what program characteristics work best for different teenage parents, taking into account the teenagers' families and social environments. Rather than trying to fit all clients and their social context to one program, it would be useful if we could better understand what types of clients and their social contexts are more likely to succeed in what different kinds of programs. Politser and Pattison (1980) illustrate how this process of matching clients and programs might work. They identified several types of community programs which had different structural characteristics and group functions. Some programs, for instance, solely provided recreation while others focused more on education. Programs were also structured differently, some requiring regular attendance and others having a drop-in policy. Effective matching between the client and programs could be done by using these identified differences in the community programs along with an individual assessment of the goals and needs of the client.

In regard to parenting support programs, a group program which emphasizes emotionally supportive contacts may be most appropriate for parents who are relatively skilled in their parenting and have adequate economic and personal resources to interact with the group. A program which focuses on specific parenting skills and multiple forms of support may be more useful for parents with less adequate parenting skills and with multiple problems. This matching process would have to be an ongoing endeavor. Education and support needs can change even during the span of participation in a program (Eisenstadt & Powell, 1987). For example, Haffey and Levant (1984) suggest that low-income parents may be more responsive initially to parent education that focuses on their interest in learning skills to increase their children's obedience. Once this concern is met, they may become more interested in learning ways to improve communication.

Support Programs are not Enough

Our previous research has shown that the Resource Mother Program can have many positive effects for some teens. As part of the evaluation of the program, teens were assigned to participate in the program or to be monitored only (comparison group) (Unger & Wandersman, 1985). Visited mothers demonstrated more knowledge about babies, more responsive behavior toward their infants, and greater satisfaction with mothering. They were more likely to seek medical care for illness and to return to school. The percentage of low birthweight babies for mothers visited by the Resource Mothers was significantly lower than for mothers in the comparison group.

The Resource Mother Program was not able to reach those high risk teens having few resources and unstable lives. Our program or any support program working with teen parents cannot overcome the massive problems of poverty (Gray & Ruttle, 1980). However, it is the low socioeconomic status and the associated inadequacies in prenatal care that primarily places teenage mothers at risk for perinatal complications and developmental problems (Baldwin & Cain, 1980; Field, 1981). Weatherly (1987) suggests that the politicalization of teen pregnancy has shifted the focus away from the critical social welfare issues associated with teenage pregnancy to the "inadequacies" of the teenagers and programs to correct individual deficits. Concerted efforts need to be made towards addressing the broader social issues placing these teens at risk along with the improvement of services to teen parents. To improve our ability to develop programs for pregnant and parenting teens, we will need to work towards effecting changes in social policy so that our policies more accurately address the social problem.

Summary

Developing programs for pregnant and parenting teens will continue to require the study of the differential effects of various interventions. To identify the impact of these programs, we will need a careful selection of the types of outcomes we can realistically expect to influence (Wandersman, 1987). However, evaluation research of support programs needs to look beyond "treatment versus control/comparison groups" to understand the process of the intervention (Belsky, 1986; Gray & Wandersman, 1980). Our understanding of the types of programs which are most useful for the varying needs and concerns of teens will only come about once we move beyond an outcome research approach. The challenge awaits us to build upon the many creative programs which have been developed for teen parents and to learn how to match these needed services with the patterns of strengths, needs, stresses, resources, and attitudes of teen parents and their families.

REFERENCES

Anastasiow, N. (1984). Preparing adolescents in childbearing: Before and after pregnancy. In M. Sugar (Ed.), *Adolescent parenthood* (pp. 141-158). New York: Spectrum Publications.

Andersen, R., & Newman, J. F. (1973). Societal and individual determinants of medical care utilization in the United States. *Milbank Memorial Fund Quarterly, 51*, 95-124.

Authier, K., & Authier, J. (1982). Intervention with families of pregnant adolescents. In I. R. Stuart & C. F. Wells (Eds.), *Pregnancy in adolescence* (pp. 290-313). New York: Van Nostrand Reinhold.

Badger, E. (1981). Effects of parent education program on teenage mothers and their offspring. In K. G. Scott, T. Field, & E. G. Robertson, (Eds.), *Teenage parents and their offspring* (pp. 283-310). New York: Grune & Stratton.

Baldwin, W. (1983). Trends in adolescent contraception, pregnancy, and childbearing. In E. R. McAnarney (Ed.), *Premature adolescent pregnancy and parenthood* (pp. 3-19). New York: Grune & Stratton.

Baldwin, W., & Cain, V. S. (1980). The children of teenage parents. *Family Planning Perspectives, 12*, 34-43.

Barth, R. P., Schinke, S. P., & Maxwell, J. S. (1983). Psychological correlates of teenage motherhood. *Journal of Youth and Adolescence, 12*, 471-487.

Belsky, J. (1986). A tale of two variances: Between and within. *Child Development, 57*, 1301-1305.

Belsky, J., Lang, M. E., & Rovine, M. (1985). Stability and change in marriage across the transition to parenthood: A second study. *Journal of Marriage and the Family, 47*, 885-865.

Bice, T. W., & White, K. L. (1969). Factors related to the use of health services: An international comparative study. *Medical Care, 7*, 124-133.

Bierman, B. R., & Streett, R. (1982). Adolescent girls as mothers: Problems in parenting. In I. R. Stuart & C. F. Wells (Eds.), *Pregnancy in adolescence* (pp. 407-426). New York: Van Nostrand.

Birkel, R. C., & Reppucci, N. D. (1983). Social networks, information-seeking, and the utilization of services. *American Journal of Community Psychology, 11*, 185-205.

Broman, S. H. (1981). Long-term development of children born to teenagers. In K. G. Scott, T. Field, & E. G. Robertson (Eds.), *Teenage parents and their offspring* (pp. 195-224). New York: Grune & Stratton.

Bronfenbrenner, U. (1974). *A report on longitudinal evaluations of preschool programs, Vol. 2. Is early intervention effective?* Washington, DC: Department of Health, Education, and Welfare.

Cappleman, M. W., Thompson, R. J., DeRemer-Sullivan, P. A., King, A. A., & Sturm, J. M. (1982). Effectiveness of a home-based early intervention program with infants of adolescent mothers. *Child Psychiatry and Human Development, 13*, 55-65.

Cartoff, V. G. (1978). Postpartum services for adolescent mothers. *Child Welfare, 57*, 660-666.

Cartoff, V. G. (1979). Postpartum services for adolescent mothers: Part 2. *Child Welfare, 58*, 673-680.

Chamberlain, R. W. (1980). Rationale for developing home visitor programs. In R. W. Chamberlain (Ed.), *Conference exploring the use of home visitors to improve the delivery of preventive services to mothers with young children* (pp. 2-8). Washington, DC: American Academy of Pediatrics.

Cohen, S., & McKay, G. (1984). Social support, stress, and the buffering hypothesis: A theoretical analysis. In A. Baum, J. E. Singer, and S. E. Taylor (Eds.), *Handbook of psychology and health* (Vol. 4 pp. 253-268). Hillsdale, NJ: Erlbaum.

Crnic, K. A., Greenberg, M. T., & Robinson, N. M. (1984). Maternal stress and social support: Effects on the mother-infant relationship from birth to eighteen months. *American Journal of Orthopsychiratry, 54*, 224-235.

Cutrona, C. E. (1986). Objective determinants of perceived support. *Journal of Personality and Social Psychology, 50*, 349-355.

Dash, L. (1986, January 26-31). At risk: Chronicles of teenage pregnancy (Special series). *The Washington Post.*

Dryfoos, J. G. (1983). *Review of interventions in the field of prevention of adolescent pregnancy: Preliminary report.* New York: The Rockefeller Foundation.

Eisenstadt, J. W., & Powell, D. R. (1987). Processes of participation in a mother-infant program as modified by stress and impulse control. *Journal of Applied Developmental Psychology, 8*, 17-37.

Field, T. (1981). Early development of the preterm offspring of teenage mothers. In K. G. Scott, T. Field, & E. G. Robertson (Eds.), *Teenage parents and their offspring* (pp. 145-175). New York: Grune & Stratton.

Field, T. M., Widmayer, S. M., Stringer, S., & Ignatoff, E. (1980). Teenage, lower-class black mothers and their preterm infants: An intervention and developmental follow-up. *Child Development, 51*, 426-436.

Forbush, J. B. (1981). Adolescent parent programs and family involvement. In T. Ooms (Ed.), *Teenage pregnancy in a family context* (pp. 254-276). Philadelphia: Temple University Press.

Freidson, E. (1960). Client control and medical practice. *American Journal of Sociology, 56*, 374-382.

Furstenberg, F. F., Jr. (1976). *Unplanned parenthood: The social consequence of teenage childbearing.* New York: The Free Press.

Furstenberg, F. F., Jr. (1980). Burdens and benefits: The impact of early childbearing on the family. *Journal of Social Issues, 36*, 64-87.

Furstenberg, F. F., Jr. & Crawford, A. G. (1978). Family support: Helping teenage mothers to cope. *Family Planning Perspectives, 10*, 322-333.

Gabel, H., Graybill, D., DeMott, S., Wood, L., & Johnston, L. E. (1977). Correlates of participation in parent group discussion among parents of learning disabled children. *Journal of Community Psychology, 5*, 275-277.

Gottlieb, B. H., & Hall, A. (1980). Social networks and the utilization of preventive mental health services. In R. H. Price & P. E. Polister (Eds.), *Prevention in mental health* (pp. 167-194). Beverly Hills, CA: Sage.

Gray, S. W., & Ruttle, K. (1980). The family-oriented home visiting program: A longitudinal study. *Genetic Psychology Monographs, 102*, 299-316.

Gray, S. W., & Wandersman, L. P. (1980). The methodology of home-based intervention studies: Problems and promising strategies. *Child Development, 51*, 993-1009.

Group for the Advancement of Psychiatry (1986). *Teenage pregnancy: Impact on adolescent development.* New York: Brunner/Mozel.

Haffey, N. A., & Levant, R. F. (1984). The differential effectiveness of two models of skills training for working class parents. *Family Relations, 33*(2), 209-216.

Hamburg, B. A. (1986). Subsets of adolescent mothers: Developmental, biomedical, and psychosocial issues. In J. B. Lancaster & B. A. Hamburg (Eds.), *School-age pregnancy and parenthood* (pp. 115-145). New York: Aldine De Gruyter.

Harman, D., & Brim, O. G., Jr. (1980). *Learning to be parents: Principles, programs and methods.* Beverly Hills, CA: Sage.

Hayes, C. D. (Ed.) (1987). *Risking the future: Adolescent sexuality, pregnancy, and childbearing.* Washington DC: National Academy Press.

Height, D. I. (1986). Changing the pattern of children having children. *Journal of Community Health, 11*, 41-44.

Heller, K., & Swindle, R. W. (1983). Social networks, perceived social support, and coping with stress. In R. D. Felner, L. A. Jason, J. Moritsugu, & S. S. Farber (Eds.), *Preventive psychology* (pp. 87-103). New York: Pergamon.

Jekel, J. F., & Klerman, L. V. (1985). Comprehensive service programs for pregnant and parenting adolescents. In E. R. McAnarney (Ed.), *Premature adolescent pregnancy and parenthood* (pp. 295-310). New York: Grune & Stratton.

Johnson, D. L., & Brekenridge, J. H. (1982). The Houston Parent-Child Development Center and the primary prevention of behavior problems in young children. *American Journal of Community Psychology, 10*, 305-316.

Jones, E. F., Forrest, J. D., Goldman, N., Henshaw, S., Lincoln, R., Rosoff, J. I., Westoff, C. F., & Wulf, D. (1986). *Teenage pregnancy in industrialized countries.* New Haven: Yale University Press.

Joyce, K., Diffenbacher, G., Greene, J., & Sorokin, Y. (1983). Internal and external barriers to obtaining prenatal care. *Social Work in Health Care, 9*, 89-96.

Kammeyer, K. C. W., & Bolton, C. D. (1968). Community and family factors related to the use of a family service agency. *Journal of Marriage and the Family, 30*, 488-498.

Kessen, W., & Fein, G. (1975). *Variations in home-based infant education: Language, play, and social development.* New Haven, CT: Yale University (ERIC Document Reproduction Service No. ED 118233).

Klerman, L. V. (1979). Evaluating service programs for school-age parents. *Evaluation and the Health Professions, 1*, 55-70.

Klerman, L. V. (1986). Teenage pregnancy. In M. W. Yogman & T. B. Brazelton (Eds.), *In support of families* (pp. 211-223). Cambridge, MA: Harvard University Press.

Klinman, D. G., Sander, J. H., Rosen, J. L., & Longo, K. R. (1986). The teen father collaboration: A demonstration and research model. In A. B. Elster & M. E. Lamb (Eds.), *Adolescent fatherhood* (pp. 155-170). Hillsdale, NJ: Erlbaum.

Larson, C. P. (1980). Efficacy of prenatal and postpartum home visits on child health and development. *Pediatrics, 66*, 191-197.

Lochman, J. E., & Brown, M. V. (1980). Evaluation of dropout clients and of perceived usefulness of a parent education program. *Journal of Community Psychology, 8*, 132-139.

McKinlay, J. B. (1972). Some approaches and problems in the study of the use of services—an overview. *Journal of Health and Social Behavior, 13*, 115-152.

McKinlay, J. B. (1973). Social networks, lay consultation and help-seeking behavior. *Social Forces, 51*, 275-292.

Miller, B. C., & Sollie, D. C. (1980). Normal stresses during the transition to parenthood. *Family Relations, 29*, 29-35.

Monkus, E., & Bancalari, E. (1981). Neonatal outcome. In K. G. Scott, T. Field, & E. G. Robertson (Eds.), *Teenage parents and their offspring* (pp. 131-144). New York: Grune & Stratton.

Moore, K. A., Hofferth, S. C., Wertheimer, R. G., Waite, L. J., & Caldwell, S. B. (1981). Teenage childbearing: Consequences for women, families, and government expenditures. In K. G. Scott, T. Field, & E. G. Robertson (Eds.), *Teenage parents and their offspring* (pp. 35-54). New York: Grune & Stratton.

Nickel, P. S., & Delany, H. (1985). *Working with teen parents.* Chicago, IL: Family Resource Coalition.

O'Connor, S., Vietze, P., Sherrod, K., Sandler, H. M., Gerrity, S., & Altemeier, W. A. (1982). Mother-infant interaction and child development after rooming-in: Comparison of high-risk and low-risk mothers. *Prevention in Human Services, 1,* 25-43.

Olds, D. (1981, April). *An ecological perspective on providing support to parents of infants: Problems and prospects.* Paper presented at the biennial meeting of the Society for Research in Child Development, Boston, MA.

Ooms, T. (1984). The family context of adolescent parenting. In M. Sugar (Ed.), *Adolescent parenthood* (pp. 217-227). New York: Spectrum Publications.

Panzarine, S. (1986). Stressors, coping, and social supports of adolescent mothers. *Journal of Adolescent Health Care, 7,* 153-161.

Pittman, K., & Govan, C. (1986). *Model programs: Preventing adolescent pregnancy and building youth self-sufficienty.* Washington DC: Children's Defense Fund.

Politser, P. E., & Pattison, E. M. (1980). Community groups: An empirical taxonomy for evaluation and intervention. In R. H. Price & P. E. Politser (Eds.), *Evaluation and action in the social environment* (pp. 51-68). New York: Academic Press.

Powell, D. R. (1983). Individual differences in participation in a parent-child support program. In I. Siegel, & L. Laosa (Eds.), *Changing Families* (pp. 203-224) New York: Plenum.

Powell, D. R. (1984). Social network and demographic predictors of length of participation in a parent education program. *Journal of Community Psychology, 12,* 13-20.

Powell, D. R., & Eisenstadt, J. W. (1982). Parents' searches for child care and the design of information services. *Children and Youth Services Review, 4,* 239-253.

Procidano, M. E., & Heller, K. (1983). Measures of perceived social support from friends and family: Three validation studies. *American Journal of Community Psychology, 11,* 1-24.

Quay, H. C. (1981). Psychological factors in teenage pregnancy. In K. G. Scott, T. Field, & E. G. Robertson (Eds.), *Teenage parents and their offspring* (pp. 73-90). New York: Grune & Stratton.

Rescorla, L. A., & Zigler, E. (1981). The Yale Child Welfare Research Program: Implications for social policy. *Educational Evaluation and Policy Analysis, 3,* 5-14.

Sacker, I. M., & Neuhoff, S. D. (1982). Medical and psychosocial risk factors in the pregnant adolescent. In I. R. Stuart and C. F. Wells (Eds.), *Pregnancy in adolescence* (pp. 107-139). New York: Van Nostrand Reinhold.

Shadish, W. R., & Reis, J. (1984). A review of studies of the effectiveness of programs to improve pregnancy outcome. *Evaluation Review, 8,* 747-776.

Shumaker, S. A., & Brownell, A. (1984). Toward a theory of social support: Closing conceptual gaps. *Journal of Social Issues, 40,* 11-36.

Slaughter, D. T. (1983). Early intervention and its effects on maternal and child development. *Monographs of the Society for Research in Child Development, 48* (4, Serial No. 202).

Stack, C. (1974). *All our kin.* New York: Harper & Row.

Stark, E. (1986, October). Young, innocent and pregnant. *Psychology Today,* pp. 28-35.

Teenage Pregnancy: A critical family issue. (1981). Flint, MI: Charles Stewart Mott Foundation.

Unger, D. G., & Powell, D. R. (1980). Supporting families under stress: The role of social networks. *Family Relations, 29,* 566-574.

Unger, D. G., & Wandersman, A. (1983). Neighboring and its role in block organizations: An exploratory report. *American Journal of Community Psychology, 11,* 291-300.

Unger, D. G., & Wandersman, L. P. (1985). Social support and adolescent mothers: Action research contributions to theory and applications. *Journal of Social Issues, 41,* 29-46.

Wallis, C. (1985, December 9). Children having children. *Time,* pp. 78-90.

Wandersman, L. P. (1987). New directions for parent education. In S. L. Kagen, D. R. Powell, B. Weissbourd, & E. F. Zigler (Eds.), *America's family support programs: Perspectives and prospects* (pp. 182-227). New Haven, CT: Yale University Press.

Wandersman, L. P. (1981, April). *Supportive parent education programs: What we are learning.* Paper presented at the Biennial meeting of the Society for Research in Child Development, Boston, MA.

Wandersman, L. P. (1983, April). *A support program for adolescent mothers: Who participates and effects.* Paper presented at the Biennial meeting of the Society for Research and Child Development, Detroit, MI.

Warren, D. I. (1981). *Helping networks.* Notre Dame, IN: University of Notre Dame Press.

Weatherly, R. A. (1987). Teenage pregnancy, professional agendas, and problem definitions. *Journal of Sociology and Social Welfare, 14,* 5-36.

Weatherly, R. A., Perlman, S. B., Levine, M., & Klerman, L. V. (1985). *Patchwork programs: Comprehensive services for pregnant and parenting adolescents.* Seattle, WA: Center for Social Welfare Research.

Zitner, R., & Miller, S. (1980). *Our youngest parents.* New York: Child Welfare League of America.

Chapter 7
A Family Systems Model of Early Intervention With Handicapped and Developmentally At-Risk Children*

Carl J. Dunst
Carol M. Trivette
Western Carolina Center

Early intervention practices for both handicapped and nonhandicapped preschoolers have traditionally been child-focused, deficit-oriented, atheoretical, paternalistic, and usurping in their methods and approaches. Many of the assumptions implicit in the more traditional ways of conducting intervention trials have increasingly been challenged and come under attack (e.g., Dunst, 1985, 1986a; Foster, Berger, & McLean, 1981; Hobbs et al., 1984; Stoneman, 1985; Reese & Overton, 1980; Zigler & Berman, 1983). This has occurred, in part, as a result of major advances in the behavioral and social sciences which now provide the types of broader-based social systems frameworks for understanding child, parent, and family functioning, and how interventions and the manner in which they are implemented can have either positive or negative consequences (Dunst, 1986b; Dunst & Trivette, in press a).

In this chapter we describe how the Family, Infant and Preschool Program (FIPP) uses social and family systems concepts for conceptualizing early intervention practices, conducting intervention trials, and assessing the manner in which different types of family systems interventions affect child, parent, and family functioning. FIPP is an outreach unit of Western Carolina Center, a regional facility providing services to handicapped persons and their families. The program is located in Morganton, North Carolina, in the foothills of the Blue Ridge mountains. FIPP provides home-, center-, and community-based services to families of both handicapped and nonhandicapped children birth to 6 years of age. Nearly 1400 children and families have been served since the program began in 1972. FIPP has evolved from a traditional child-focused early intervention program to a family-systems oriented program as a result of theoretical, clinical,

* Preparation of this chapter and support for the research described herein was made possible by a grant from the National Institute of Mental Health, Center for Prevention Research (MH38862). Appreciation is extended to Pat Condrey, Pam Lowman, Sharon Huffman, Norma Hunter, Judy Anderson, and Clara Hunt for assistance in preparation of the manuscript, and to Wayne DeLoriea, Sharon Propst, Peggy Mankinen, Mae Shell, and Debbie Smith for data compilation and analysis.

and research evidence suggesting the most efficacious strategies for strengthening family functioning and promoting growth and development in all family members.

The chapter is divided into three sections. In the first section we describe a social systems framework that has guided both our research and programmatic efforts. As part of the description of this model, we summarize and synthesize research data from a series of studies that provide a basis for disentangling the complex relationships among intrafamily factors and external influences that affect child, parent, and family functioning. In the second section we describe key aspects of our family systems early intervention model, and illustrate how we bridge theory, research, and practice. We also present the results from several additional studies that sought to test certain assumptions regarding the manner in which interventions were conceptualized and implemented. In the final section we briefly reflect upon what we have learned as a result of our research and programmatic efforts, and discuss what we believe to be both unanswered questions and unresolved issues, and thus future directions for research and practice.

TOWARD A SOCIAL SYSTEMS MODEL OF FAMILY FUNCTIONING

The conceptual and methodological approach we have taken in developing a social systems model of family functioning is best characterized as intervention research (Brandtstadter, 1980; Reese & Overton, 1980). We are specifically interested in the development of a family systems model of functioning that has both explanatory and heuristic value. First, we would like to have a conceptual model of development that permits greater understanding of family functioning, and thus can be used as a framework for generating and testing hypotheses about factors that are likely to influence behavior and development. Second, we would like to have a model that generates specific information and guidelines about the types of interventions that can be used to promote behavior and development.

The paradigm that is generally followed when one argues that intervention ought to be based on sound empirical evidence is:

$$(T + R) \rightarrow P,$$

where T = Theory, R = Research Evidence, and P = Intervention Practices. However, as we learn more and more about the complexities of family functioning, the shortcomings and limitations of this paradigm become increasingly obvious. The above paradigm implies that theory and research should govern or even dictate intervention practices, whereas we believe it should suggest and guide practice. Based on the theorizing of Brandtstadter (1980), Bunge (1967), and Reese and Overton (1980), we believe there has been a missing link between theory and research and its implications for practice. We propose a more useful paradigm that is stated as follows:

$$(T + R) \rightarrow SO \rightarrow P,$$

where T, R, and P are defined as above, and SO = substantive and operative rules and aids for promoting desired effects. "Whereas substantive technologies yield general rules for producing some desired effect, operative technologies supply decision aids for the effective implementation of substantive-technological rules in the concrete action context" (Brandtstadter, 1980, p. 15). Substantive principles are the rules derived from theory and research, whereas intervention operatives are the necessary actions that are taken in order to put the principles into practice. More specifically, substantive rules and intervention operatives constitute the smallest number of principles and practices that will produce a desired effect while at the same time reflecting what is known from theory and research.

In many respects, our research and programmatic efforts may be characterized as "model building" in both design and outcome. The focus of our research efforts has been the study of variables that can be operationalized as intervention techniques and strategies. Our research sharply diverges from common practice. Most family research has been comparative in nature. For example, one typically finds comparisons involving mothers vs. fathers, parents of retarded vs. nonretarded children, low vs. middle SES background families, retarded vs. physically impaired children, etc. that focus on establishing the fact that one can discern differences between groups on one or more dependent measures (e.g., stress). While such studies yield interesting information, we are of the opinion that comparative studies that use sex, diagnosis, and other stable, relatively unchanging variables as the principal or only independent variable produce essentially useless information from an intervention standpoint. This is the case because these types of variables *cannot* be manipulated in a clinical treatment sense, and thus cannot be considered interventions. In contrast, we emphasize the study of variables that are manipulatable and consequently constitute potential intervention variables.

Our model-building research has been carried out in two distinct phases. The first has involved a series of cross-sectional studies that have attempted to isolate the effects of different forms of social support on parent, family, and child functioning. This line of research has resulted in identification of the types of supportive experiences that are most likely to have the greatest impact on child, parent, and family functioning. A considerable amount of this work is summarized in this chapter. The second has involved a series of longitudinal intervention trials in which the provision and mediation of support is assessed with respect to predictions generated from our social systems model. This is work in progress, and reports of the results from these investigations are pending completion of the trials.

The evolution of the model described next can be traced through a number of papers and reports, including Dunst (1982, 1983, 1985, 1986a, 1986b); Dunst, Cooper, & Bolick (1987); Dunst and Leet (1987); Dunst and Trivette (1984,

1986a, 1987, in press a, b, c, d); Dunst, Trivette, and Cross (1986a, 1986b, in press a); Dunst, Trivette, and Deal (in press b); Trivette, Deal, and Dunst (in press); and Trivette and Dunst (in press a, b).

A SOCIAL SYSTEMS FRAMEWORK OF BEHAVIOR AND DEVELOPMENT

Our research has resulted in the development of a social systems model (Dunst, 1985, 1986b; Dunst & Trivette, in press a, c) that draws heavily from several conceptual frameworks, including human ecology (Bronfenbrenner, 1979, 1986; Cochran & Brassard, 1979), social support theory (Cohen & Syme, 1985), help-seeking theory (DePaulo, Nadler, & Fisher, 1983), and adaptational theory (Crnic, Friedrich, & Greenberg, 1983a). These four separate but complementary theoretical orientations indicate that ecological settings and social units, and persons and events within them, do not operate in isolation but influence each other both directly and indirectly, so that changes in one unit or subunit reverberate and impact upon members of other units.

Social support theory attempts to describe the properties of social units, the linkages among units, and how provision of support by network members promotes individual, family, and community well-being (Cohen & Syme, 1985). Social support refers to a "number of different aspects of social relationships" that has increasingly been found to have positive effects on various health outcomes (House & Kahn, 1985, p. 84). Human ecology emphasizes the interactions and accommodations between a developing child and his or her animate and inanimate environment, and how events in different ecological settings directly and indirectly affect the behavior of the person (Bronfenbrenner, 1979; Cochran & Brassard, 1979). For example, Bronfenbrenner (1979) argues "whether parents can perform effectively in their child-rearing roles within the family depends upon role demands, stresses, and *supports* emanating from other settings" (p. 7). Help-seeking theory examines the conditions which affect a decision to seek help, from whom help is sought, and the nature of help-seeking and help-giving exchanges (Dunst & Trivette, in press a). Research on the relationship between help-seeking, help-giving, and social support has increasingly shown the importance of informal social networks as sources of help and assistance in response to both normative and nonnormative life events (see Wilcox & Birkel, 1983). Adaptational theory attempts to explain how ecological influences affect reactions to the birth and rearing of an atypically developing child, and how different ecological forces, including social support, either positively or negatively influence a family's ability to cope and adapt to the birth and rearing of a handicapped child (Crnic et al., 1983a).

Collectively, the above four theoretical orientations provide a framework for understanding how resources and support either directly or indirectly affect family functioning. Our own research as well as that of others provides considerable support for the contention that adjustment to the rearing of a child with a poor developmental outcome is influenced by various forms of aid, help, assistance, and resources provided by others.

Social Support Construct

A major emphasis of our research has been the study of the role social support plays in influencing parent, family, and child functioning because *the social support construct holds promise for being a major form of intervention.* "Social support is defined as the resources provided by other persons" (Cohen & Syme, 1985, p. 4). More specifically, social support includes the emotional, psychological, physical, informational, instrumental, and material aid provided by others that influences the behavior of the recipient of the help and assistance.

Figure 1 shows graphically a simplified version of how we believe social support affects parent, family, and child functioning. According to this model, social support influences parent well-being and health; support and well-being influence family functioning; support, well-being, and family functioning influence styles of parent–child interactions; and support, well-being, family functioning, and interactive styles influence child behavior and development. Within this framework of direct and indirect relationships, well-being, family functioning, and interactive styles function as both independent and dependent variables depending upon the juncture at which one is assessing the influences of social support.

The social support construct includes at least five components (Dunst & Trivette, in press c; Hall & Wellman, 1985; House & Kahn, 1985). These are relational, structural, functional, and constitutional support, and support satisfaction. *Relational support* refers to the existence and quantity of social relationships, including such things as marital and work status, number of persons in one's social network, and membership in social organizations such as the church. *Structural support* refers to the characteristics of social networks, including network density, stability and durability of relationships, intensity of feelings toward network members, and reciprocity of relationships. *Functional support* refers to the source, type, and quantity and quality of help and assistance. *Constitutional support* refers to the perceived need for help, the availability of specific types of support that are needed, and the congruence (match) between needed support and the type of support offered.[1] *Support satisfaction* refers to the extent to which assistance and aid is viewed as helpful and useful.

Figure 2 shows the potential connections among the different components of

---

[1] The term *constitutional support*, as used here, refers to something that is basic and essential for individual and family health and well-being. Although the notion of constitutional support may conceptually be subsumed under the other support categories, factor analysis of our support data shows perceived need for support to be a clearly distinct category.

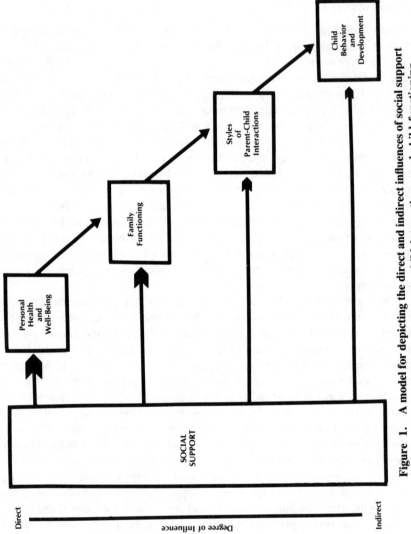

Figure 1. A model for depicting the direct and indirect influences of social support on parent, family, parent–child interactions, and child functioning.

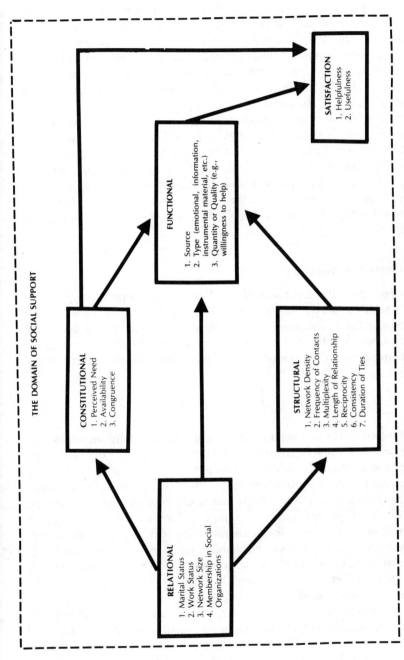

Figure 2. Conceptual framework for assessing the components of social support and the potential relationships among the five support components.

137

the social support domain. This conceptualization is derived, in part, from the work of Hall and Wellman (1985) and House and Kahn (1985), and has evolved from our own work on explicating the components of the social support construct (Dunst & Trivette, in press c). The existence or quantity of relational support is viewed as a necessary condition for and hence a partial determinant of (a) defining needs, (b) the structural characteristics of one's social network, and (c) the types of help and assistance available from network members. Similarly, both constitutional needs and network structure may partially determine the particular types of support that are sought and offered. Finally, the types of support provided, especially the relationship between constitutional and functional support, will in part determine the degree to which one finds the aid and assistance helpful, and thus the extent to which one is satisfied with the support. Taken together, these five components and the potential connections among them provide a basis for understanding the temporal and mediational relationships that set the occasion for "supportive" exchanges.

A Paradigmatic Framework

While we recognize the importance of social support as a factor affecting parent, family, and child functioning, we also fully recognize the influence of other intra- and extrafamily characteristics as explanatory, mediating, and moderating variables. Consequently, these factors are also examined as part of our research. This multiple determinant approach may be stated in the following paradigmatic framework:

$$B = f(S, P, F, C, E)$$

where B is an outcome or criterion measure (e.g., parent, family, and child functioning), and the relationship between B and the variables on the right side of the equation is in the form: B varies as a function of S (social support), P (parent characteristics), F (family characteristics), C (child characteristics), and E (environmental characteristics). Accordingly, one would expect to find *social support* (relational, structural, functional, etc.), *parent characteristics* (age, education level, locus of control, etc.), *family characteristics* (SES, income, etc.), *child characteristics* (age, sex, level of functioning, etc.), and *environmental factors* (living arrangements, neighborhood characteristics, etc.) having both cumulative and interactive effects on behavior and development.

Figure 3 depicts the model we are currently using to assess the effects of several major categories of variables on parent, family, and child functioning. The social support domain and relationships among the five components of support are as described above (see Figure 1). Both parent and family characteristics are considered partial determinants of support (Gore, 1985; Gottlieb, 1981; Heller, Amaral, & Procidano, 1978; Holahan & Wilcox, 1978; Mitchell & Trickett,

1980). Parent and family characteristics are seen as mutually dependent, although parent characteristics are seen as exerting a greater influence on family characteristics rather than vice versa (Duncan, Featherman, & Duncan, 1972; Sewell & Hauser, 1975). All three sets of variables (parent, family, and social support) are viewed as partial determinants of adaptation and coping mechanisms (Richman & Flaherty, 1985; Roskin, 1982; Shapiro, 1983; Tolsdorf, 1976) used in response to both normative (e.g., marriage) and nonnormative (e.g., birth of a handicapped child) life events (McCubbin, Cauble, & Patterson, 1982; McGuire & Gottlieb, 1979). The combination of all five sets of variables directly and indirectly influence parent and family health and well-being (Cohen & Syme, 1985). These six sets of variables are seen as directly and indirectly affecting interactional behaviors (Crnic, Greenberg, Robinson, & Ragozin, 1984; Crnic, Greenberg, & Slough, 1986; Dunst & Trivette, 1986a; Philliber & Graham, 1981), and all seven sets of variables may have direct and indirect influences on child behavior and development.

There is a growing body of evidence that social support directly and indirectly influences parent, family, and child behavior, including *personal health and well-being* (Cohen & Syme, 1985), *familial well-being* (Patterson & McCubbin, 1983), *adaptations to life crises* (Moos, 1986), *satisfaction with parenting* (Crnic, Greenberg, Ragozin, Robinson, & Basham, 1983b), *attitudes toward one's child* (Colletta, 1981), *parental styles of interaction* (Trivette & Dunst, 1987), *aspirations for self and child* (Lazar & Darlington, 1982), *child temperament* (Affleck, Tennen, Allen, & Gersham, 1986), and *child behavior and development* (Crnic et al., 1986). We now turn to a description of our own research findings to illustrate the manner in which different forms of support are related to parent, family, and child functioning.

EMPIRICAL EVIDENCE SUPPORTING OUR SOCIAL SYSTEMS MODEL

A series of eight cross-sectional studies have been conducted over the past 6 years designed to systematically assess the relationships between social support and child, parent, and family functioning. We briefly describe the methodology and procedures employed in each of the studies, and then present the findings from the studies organized according to parent, family, parent–child, and child outcomes.

Method

Subjects.   The participants in the studies were the families enrolled in FIPP, and included parents of mentally retarded, physically impaired, and developmentally at-risk preschoolers. (The number of subjects included in each investigation is shown in Tables 1 to 4 below.) The mothers and fathers were, on the

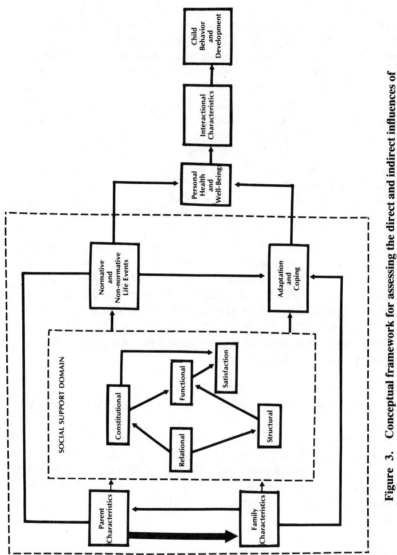

Figure 3.   Conceptual framework for assessing the direct and indirect influences of parent and family characteristics, social support, and life events on personal and familial health, interactional behavior, and child behavior and development.

average, 29 and 31 years of age, respectively. The average number of years of school completed was between 11 and 12 for both mothers and fathers. Their socio-economic status scores (Hollingshead, 1975) were between 27 and 30, indicating that the majority of the families were predominantly from lower to middle SES backgrounds. The families average gross monthly income was about $1200. Eighty percent of the subjects were married, while the remaining 20% were single, separated, divorced, or widowed. Approximately 55% of the mothers worked outside the home either full or part time.

The average chronological and mental ages of the children were 36 and 20 months, respectively. The children's average Developmental (DQ) and Social (SQ) Quotients scores were, respectively, 65 and 70. Approximately 55% of the children were male.

Procedure.   Data were gathered from a combination of self-report measures, in-home interviews, and observational ratings of parent-child and child behavior. Indices of social support were obtained from both self-report rating scales and extensive interviews with the subjects. Parental and familial well-being (emotional and physical health, time demands, and family functioning) were measured using self-report rating scales. Parent–child interactional behavior was assessed using both a self-report measure and behavior ratings of caregiver interactional styles displayed during parent–child play episodes. Child behavior characteristics were assessed using both a self-report rating scale and independent ratings of child behavior. Demographic information about the families and diagnostic and developmental information about the children was also obtained.

The measures of parent and family characteristics included father's and/or mother's ages (in years), gross monthly income, and socio-economic status scores based on mother's and/or father's education level and occupation (Hollingshead, 1975). The measures of child characteristics included age, developmental quotient (DQ) scores, and diagnostic group (mentally retarded, physically impaired, or developmentally at-risk). Contrasts coding (Cohen & Cohen, 1983) was used to render diagnostic group information into two orthogonal comparisons: mentally retarded and physically impaired vs. developmentally at-risk, and mentally retarded vs. physically impaired.

The social support measures employed in the various studies included the Family Support Scale (FSS; Dunst, Jenkins, & Trivette, 1984), Maternal Social Support Index (MSI; Pascoe, Loda, Jeffries, & Earp, 1981), Parent Role Scale (PRS; Gallagher, Cross, & Scharfman, 1981), Psychosocial Kinship Network Inventory (PKI; Pattison, DeFrancisco, Wood, Frazier, & Crowder, 1975), and Support Function Scale (SFS; Dunst & Trivette, 1985a). Each of these scales measures one or more components of support shown in Figure 2, and indices derived from each assessed a number of aspects of support received from informal social network members, including spouse/mate, blood and marriage relatives, friends, church members, etc. The various indices used as measures of social support included the number of persons in the respondent's social network, the total number of persons who provided different types of support, ratings of willingness of network members to provide support, intrafamily support (role sharing), and ratings of the degree to which support was helpful and useful. Additionally, the independent contributions of maternal work status (working vs. not working outside the home) and/or marital status (married vs. not married) were also assessed in the majority of studies as indices of relational support.

The well-being measures included the Questionnaire on Resources and Stress Emotional and Physical Health subscale (QRS; Holroyd, 1974, 1985), the Psychological Well-Being Index (PWI; Bradburn & Caplovitz, 1965), and the Personal Well-Being Index (WBI; Trivette & Dunst, 1985). Global indices of well-being or specific components of well-being (child-related, general life) were used as measures of physical and emotional health. Each scale includes items that tapped the respondent assessment of strains, feelings of depression, a sense of euphoria, physical energy level, etc. that, taken together, form a basis for an overall measure of well-being.

The time demand measures included the QRS Time Demands subscale, the Survey for Parents of Children with Handicapping Conditions Time Demands subscale (SPC; Moore, Hamerlynck, Barsh, Spieker, & Jones, 1982) and the Personal Time Commitment Scale (PTC; Dunst & Trivette, 1985b). The QRS and SPC scales yield a global index of time demands, whereas the PTC yields subscale scores for time demands related to childcare and general life events respectively. Each time demand scale assesses the degree to which the respondent had adequate time for the care of a child (e.g., I'm the only person who cares for my child) or performance of adult activities (e.g., I have sufficient time to enjoy hobbies).

The family functioning scales included the QRS Family Integration and Family Opportunities subscales, the SPC Family Impact subscale, the Family Functioning Environment Scale (FES; Moos, 1974), and the Family Inventory of Resources and Management (FRM; McCubbin, Comeau, & Harkins, 1981). The QRS, SPC, and FRM scales assess the degree to which different family members function in a cooperative, integrated manner (e.g., share household chores), and the QRS scales assess the influence of a handicapped or retarded child on family integration and family opportunities. The FES yields separate measures of family functioning in three areas: family relationships (cohesion, conflict, etc.), personal development (independence, achievement, etc.), and systems management (family organization and control styles).

The parent–child interaction scales included the Parent-Child Play Scale (PCP; Dunst, 1986c), the Parent–Child Interaction Scale (PCI; Farran, Kasari, & Jay, 1983), and the Caregiver Styles of Interaction Scale (CSI; Dunst, 1986d). The PCP assesses the degree to which caregivers play six different categories of "games" with their children. The PCI measures the amount, quality, and appropriateness of caregiver interactions displayed during parent–child play episodes. The CSI measures both the frequency and duration of six mutually exclusive styles of interaction that vary on a continuum from caregiver passivity to joint action between the interactive partners to caregiver control and coercion. The PCP is a self-report measure, whereas the PCI and PSI are scored by independent raters based either in vivo or video taped observations of parent–child play episodes.

The child functioning measures included the QRS Behavior Problems and Social Acceptance subscales and the Carolina Record of Individual Behavior (CRB; Simeonsson, 1979). The QRS subscales measure the respondent's self-ratings of perceptions of child functioning. The CRB assesses a number of behavior characteristics of young children, including social and communication development, child temperament, goal directedness, attention span, and positive and negative affective behavior (e.g., smiling and crying). The CRB was completed by a person highly familiar with the child, and was scored from observations made of the child in his or her home.

Methods of Analysis

The data in the studies were analyzed either by hierarchical regression analysis (Cohen & Cohen, 1983) or canonical correlation analysis (Levine, 1977; Thompson, 1984). Each of these procedures yields information about the unique, nonshared variance accounted for in the dependent measure(s) by the individual independent variables, and thus aids in the substantive interpretation of the effects of these variables. The order of entry of the variables in the hierarchical regression analyses was as shown in Figure 3 above, whereas the contributions of the independent variables in the canonical correlation analyses were done simultaneously.

Results and Discussion

The results from the studies are organized in terms of five major categories of outcomes: personal well-being (physical and emotional health), time demands placed upon a parent by his or her disabled or at-risk child, family functioning (familial well-being), parent–child interactions, and child functioning (both parent perceptions and ratings of the behavior characteristics of the children).

Well-being.   The role that social support played in affecting the emotional and physical well-being of parents of disabled and at-risk children was assessed in the eight studies using a variety of social support and well-being measures (see Dunst & Trivette, in press c, for a detailed presentation of the results). The independent variables were parent and family characteristics (mother's and father's ages and education levels, family SES and income), informal support (two or more types of support shown in Figure 2 above), and child age, DQ, and diagnostic group. The dependent variables included the various well-being measures described above (Bradburn & Caplovitz, 1965; Holroyd, 1974, 1985; Trivette &

Dunst, 1985). The data were analyzed by hierarchical multiple regression analyses with the order of entry as described above for the different sets of independent variables.

The 12 sets of analyses produced results that were both clear cut and convincing. In only 2 of the 12 analyses did any of the parent characteristics, and in only one of the analyses did family characteristics account for a significant amount of variance. In only one analysis did child age account for a significant amount of variance, and in none of the analyses did child DQ or diagnosis account for a significant amount of variance. *In every study and every analysis, social support accounted for a significant amount of variance in the dependent measures.* The average amount of variance accounted for was 26% (SD = 13, Range = 10 to 60). In general, the largest percentages of variance were accounted for in those studies which employed measures that assessed at least three or more components of the support domain (see Figure 2 above). Examination of the zero-order correlations between the various indices of support and the well-being measures showed that adequacy of resources and the perceived need for help (constitutional support) generally accounted for the largest percentage of variance, followed by satisfaction with support, functional support, structural support, and finally relational support.

On the one hand, the findings demonstrate the importance of social support as a moderator of health and well-being, and are consistent with both predictions from our social systems model and other research examining the influence of social support on health consequences (Cohen & Syme, 1985). On the other hand, the results show that support can promote adaptations to the rearing of a handicapped child, and question the commonly held belief that the more handicapped a child, the more stress the child will place on his or her parents. This contention is simply not supported by our data, and the fact that we have replicated the finding across eight studies, using different measures of support and different measures of well-being, makes our findings particularly robust. Collectively, the findings from the analyses of the well-being data provide substantive evidence for the contention that the stresses and strains associated with the rearing of a disabled or at-risk child are lessened by support available to individual family members, particularly support that matches family identified needs.

Time demands.   The extent to which social support lessened the time demands placed upon parents of disabled and at-risk preschoolers was assessed in three studies. The independent variables included parent and family characteristics (father's and/or mother's age, family SES and income, marital status, and maternal work status), social support, and child age, DQ, and diagnostic group. The dependent measures were the time demands scales described above (Dunst & Trivette, 1985b; Holroyd, 1974, 1985; Moore et al., 1982). The data were analyzed by hierarchical multiple regression analyses with the order of entry described above for the different sets of independent variables.

The results are presented in Table 1 and show that, in four out of five of the analyses, both support and child DQ accounted for significant amounts of variance in the dependent measures. In none of the studies were parental age or family SES related to the outcomes, and in two studies family income was related to time demands. Marital status and maternal work status were generally unrelated to the dependent measures.

The pattern of findings for the social support measures showed that availability and adequacy of support as well as satisfaction with support moderated time demands placed upon the respondents by both their children and other life events. Examination of the zero-order correlations between the different indices of social support and time demands showed that the latter was lessened in situations where network members (relational support) provided instrumental assistance (functional support) for both child care and other day-to-day tasks, particularly aid that matched perceived needs (constitutional support). It is noteworthy to observe, for example, that the correlations between time demands and support were the highest in instances where there was a match between an indicated need for child care assistance and provision of child care aid by network members.

In contrast to the positive influences of social support on lessening time demands, the more retarded the respondents' children the greater were the time demands placed upon the parents. Thus, whereas the well-being analyses showed DQ unrelated to health consequences, degree of retardation seemed to affect both child care and other life event demands. However, the fact that support moderated and lessened the time demands placed upon the parents by their children, albeit to a small degree, suggest that provision of support by social network members can have positive effects on the parents. Our findings are generally consistent with the theorizing of others regarding the importance of instrumental support for families of disabled children (see especially Salisbury & Intagliata, 1986) and are consistent with predictions based on our social system model.

Family functioning. The role that social support, well-being, and time demands played in affecting family functioning was assessed in five studies. The independent variables included parent and family characteristics (mother's and father's age, family SES and income, marital status, and maternal work status), social support, well-being, time demands, and child age, DQ, and diagnosis. The dependent variables included the various family functioning measures described above (Holroyd, 1974, 1985; McCubbin et al., 1981; Moos, 1974). Because there were two or more dependent measures in each study, canonical correlation analysis was used to assess the relationships between the various sets of variables.

Table 2 displays the findings from the five sets of analyses, each of which produced a significant multiple R. Family income and SES were the only parent and family characteristic variables consistently related to family functioning. Respondents from higher income and higher SES families reported better family functioning. Child diagnosis but neither child age nor DQ was related to family

Table 1. Multiple Regression Coefficients and Increments (I) in R^2 for the Analysis of the Time Demands Data

Independent Variables	Study 1 (N = 129) QRS Time Demands R^2	I	Study 3 (N = 63) QRS Time Demands R^2	I	SPC Time Demands R^2	I	Study 5 (N = 117) PTC Parent-Level Commitment R^2	I	PTC Child-Level Commitment R^2	I
Parent/Family Characteristics:										
Mother Age	013	013	015	015	000	000	001	001	022	022
Father Age	014	001	015	000	032	032	022	021	034	012
Family SES	018	004	024	009	062	029	024	002	034	000
Family Income	072	054**	026	002	062	000	057	033	072	037*
Marital Status	074	003	079	053	089	027	057	000	090	019
Maternal Work Status	074	000					124*	067***	096	006
Social Support:										
Network Size							159**	035*	096	000
Number of People Who Provide Support							162*	004	104	008
Willingness to Help							166*	004	104	000
PRS Intrafamily Support	127*	053**								
MSI Intrafamily Support			086	007	111	023				
MSI Informal Support			161	075*	181	070*				
FSS Informal Support			183	022	219	037				
SFS Functional Support	178*	051**					177**	011	117	013
PRS Support Satisfaction	206**	028*								
Support Satisfaction							181*	004	119	002
Child Characteristics:										
Child Age	210**	003	205	023	219	001	187*	006	124	005
Child Development Quotient (DQ)	260****	051**	277*	071*	296	077*	223**	036*	151	027
Child Diagnosis (MR/PI vs. AR)[b]	268****	008	300*	021	298*	001	229**	006	154	003
Child Diagnosis (PI vs. MR)[b]	271****	004	336*	038	372*	075*	235*	007	160	007

NOTE. Decimal points have been omitted. All the support scales have been scored so that higher scores mean more support. PRS = Parent Role Scale, MSI = Maternal Social Support Index, FSS = Family Support Scale, and SFS = Support Functions Scale. Network Size was the number of persons named by the respondent as members of their support network, Number of People Who Provided Support was the number of persons in the respondent's network who provided different types of support, and Willingness to Help was a rating made by the respondent regarding network members willingness to provide different types of aid and assistance.

[b]MR = Mentally retarded, PI = Physically impaired, and AR = At-Risk for poor developmental outcomes. The contrasts that were assessed included MR (= 1) + PI (= 1) vs. AR (= 2) and PI (= 1) vs. MR (= 2).

*p < .05, **p < .01, ***p < .005, ****p < .001.

functioning. Better family functioning was generally found in households of at-risk (compared to retarded or physically impaired) children and physically impaired (compared to retarded) children.

In every instance except one, social support was related to family functioning, and in every case well-being and time demands were related to family functioning. Moreover, the relationships were as expected based on our social systems model. Increased provision of support and enhanced well-being were related to better family functioning, whereas increased time demands had negative effects on the respondent's assessment of the integrity of their family unit. Close inspection of the zero-order correlations between social support and family functioning showed that availability of support (network size), frequency of contacts with network members (structural support), and satisfaction with support were consistently related to family integrity. The results, taken together, are consistent with the findings from studies by other investigators examining the relationships between intrapersonal and intrafamily characteristics and family well-being (Cobb & Kasl, 1977; Embry, 1980; Gore, 1978; Kasl & Cobb, 1979; Patterson & McCubbin, 1983).

Caregiver interactional behavior.   The role that social support, well-being, time demands, and family functioning played in affecting caregiver interactional behavior was assessed in four studies. The independent variables were parent and family characteristics (mother's and father's ages and educational level, family SES and income, and marital status), social support, well-being, time demands, and family functioning, and child age, DQ, and diagnosis. The dependent variables used in the four studies included the frequency of occurrence of different parent–child "games" (Dunst, 1986c) (Study 1), ratings of the amount, quality, and appropriateness of caregiver interactional behavior (Farran et al., 1983) (Study 3), and the frequency and duration of several different styles of caregiver interactional behavior (Dunst, 1986d) (Studies 4 & 6). The data in all four studies were analyzed by canonical correlation analysis. Collectively, the findings from our four studies demonstrated that there are multiple determinants of parental interactive behavior (see Table 3). The results showed that parent education and family SES, and child DQ and diagnosis were consistently related to most interactive measures. Nothing more will be said about these results except to note that they generally replicate those reported by other investigators examining parent–child relations to dyads including at-risk (see Trivette & Dunst, 1987) and nonrisk (see Lamb, 1982; Lamb & Easterbrooks, 1981; Sherrod, Vietze, & Friedman, 1978; Vietze & Anderson, 1981) children.

The relationships between support, well-being, family functioning, and caregiver interactive behavior generally supported predictions generated from our social systems model. With respect to the influences of social support, the most noteworthy finding concerned the relationship between intrafamily support (role sharing) and the display of different caregiver interactive behavior. Lack of intrafamily support was associated with a lower occurrence of pretend, verbal,

Table 2. Structure Coefficients and Multiple Rs for the Canonical Correlation Analysis of the Family Functioning Data

Independent Variables	Study 1 (N = 129) Family Integrity	Study 2 (N = 51) Family Relations	Study 3 (N = 63) Family Integrity	Study 4 (N = 100) Family Relations	Study 5 (N = 117) Family Well-Being
Parent/Family Characteristics:					
Mother Age	259***	223*	-057	-080	160
Father Age	194*	109		024	-346***
Family SES	275***	522***	191*	148	360***
Family Income	384***	491***	063	201*	427***
Marital Status	-117	-227*	-144	086	-387***
Maternal Work Status	102	387***	250**	-024	-007
Social Support:					
PRS Intrafamily Support	297***				
MSI Intrafamily Support		281***	301***	053	
MSI Informal Support		553***	557***	641****	
SFS Functional Support					364***
FSS Informal Support	293***	356***	499***		
PRS Support Satisfaction	546***				
Child Characteristics:					
Child Age	-060	-381***	-072	172*	058
Child DQ	420***	191*	490***	132	-008
Child Diagnosis (MR/PI vs. AR)	246**	-450***	-078	107	309***
Child Diagnosis (PI vs. MR)	-148	-411***	257***	-186*	-180*

148

Well-Being/Time Demands[b]:					
QRS Emotional and Physical	814****	508***	849****	479***	
PWI Well-Being		612***		561***	
WBI Well-Being (Child)					658****
WBI Well-Being (Parent)					816****
QRS Time Demands	−747****		−870****		
PTC Time Commitment (Child)					−356***
PTC Time Commitment (Parent)					−520***
Family Functioning:					
QRS Family Integration	887****		914****		
QRS Family Opportunity	850****				
SFN Family Impact			773****		
FFS Family Relationships		306****		483***	
FES Systems Maintenance		953****		905****	
FRM Family Well-Being		412****		−124	845****
Family Integration					788****
Multiple R	713****	828****	794****	681****	682****

NOTES. Decimal points have been omitted. All support, well-being, and family functioning scales are scored so that higher scores mean more positive functioning.

[a]See Table 1 for a description of the support scales.

[b]QRS = Questionnaire on Resources and Stress, PWI = Psychological Well-Being Index, WBI = Personal Well-Being Index, PTC = Personal Time Commitment Scale, SFN = Survey of Family Needs, FES = Family Environmental Scale, and FRM = Family Inventory of Resources and Management.

*p < .05, **p < .01, ***p < .005, ****p < .001.

Table 3. Structure Coefficients and Multiple Rs for the Canonical Correlation Analysis of the Parent-Child Interaction Data

Independent Variables	Study 1 (N = 136)			Study 3 (N = 65)		Study 4 (N = 100)				Study 6 (N = 59)			
	Responsive Play/Lap Games	Mastery/Pretend Play	Verbal/Discovery Play	First Solution	Second Solution	Passive	Responsive	Engaging/Elaboration	Imposing	Passive	Responsive	Engaging/Elaboration	Imposing
Parent/Family Characteristics:													
Parent Age	053	297****	043	-095	-129	173*	008	-101	-060	283*	-214	-186	-188
Parent Educational Level	560****	336****	547****	655****	415****	160	306****	618****	297****	-280*	-139	454****	-460****
Family SES	334****	481****	318****	693****	477****	135	211*	354****	-306****	-350***	049	197	-220*
Marital Status	-118	101	334****	015	-567****	062	-146	-060	076	143	-309**	212	-194
Social Support:													
PRS Intrafamily Support	103			102									
MSI Intrafamily Support		-326****	-291****	379****	100	-209*	-358****	-258***	-120	-212	-088	037	-252*
MSI Informal Support						099	254***	124	-079	-228*	260*	-088	018
SFS Functional Support					379***								
FSS Informal Support	315****	403****	347****	088									
PRS Support Satisfaction	124	-134	-147*										
Child Characteristics:													
Child Age	-512****	089	-022	-298*	-172	394****	423****	492****	-364****	210	-366***	455****	-343***
Child DQ	-148	499****	628****	094	132	620****	392****	145	-493****	544****	-690****	238*	-411****
Child Diagnosis (MR/PI vs. AR)	-249***	220*	331****	-527****	228*	338****	037	-178*	007	295*	-324**	-082	141
Child Diagnosis (PI vs. MR)	-063	-113	-317****	-282*	-018	-417****	-468****	-272***	231**	255*	-149	-171	172

Measure													
Well-Being/Time Demands:													
QRS Emotional and Physical Health	173*	-034	213**	154	062	008	220*	021	-447****	079	-074	174	-413****
PWI Well-Being						-100	016	-126	-157	-055	109	-079	-025
WBI Well-Being (Child)													
WBI Well-Being (Parent)													
QRS Time Demands	054	024	-087	-061	049								
Time Commitment (Child)										029	-328**	-245*	-105
Time Commitment (Parent)										-125	076	081	153
Family Functioning:													
QRS Family Integration	495****	243***	472****	170	048	172*	356****	109	-059	-159	-047	422****	-402****
QRS Family Opportunity													
FES Family Functioning													
FRM Family Well-Being													
Caregiver Behavior[a]:													
Frequency (1)	966****	084	993****	880****	383****	987****	868****	445****	998****	974****	-057	182	864****
Duration (1)						785****	-445****	492****		958****	931****	171	117
Frequency (2)	796****	864****	494****	961****	076			759****				752****	
Duration (2)				986****				823****				722****	
Frequency (3)					-148								
Multiple R	501****	423****	582****	663****	572****	566****	605****	615****	515****	670*	779****	784****	681*

NOTES. Decimal points have been omitted. The support, well-being, and family functioning scales are all scored so higher scores mean better functioning.

[a] The numbers in parentheses correspond to order of the caregiver behaviors shown above for Studies 1, 4, and 6 (e.g., for Study 1, (1) corresponds to the frequency of responsive play and (2) corresponds to the frequency of play of lap games). The order for the measures employed in Study 3 are: (1) = amount, (2) = quality, and (3) = appropriateness of caregiver interactive behavior.

*p < .05, **p < .01, ***p < .005, ****p < .001.

and discovery play (Study 1), a minimal amount of interactive behaviors displayed during parent–child play episodes (Study 3), and displays of less responsive, engaging, and elaborative interactive styles (Study 4). There is at least one parsimonious explanation of these sets of findings. It appears that lack of intrafamily support (i.e., role sharing) decreased the sheer amount and number of caregiver opportunities to participate in interactions with their child, which, in turn, presumably provided fewer opportunities to acquire parenting experiences. If this interpretation is correct, then at least a portion of variance in caregiver interactive behavior seems to be affected by the broader-based social context of the family (values, expectations, etc.) beyond that associated with parent education and family SES.

Whereas lack of intrafamily support had negative effects on caregiver behavior, provision of support from members of the respondents' informal networks appeared to have positive influences. The frequency of occurrence of different types of play (Study 1), as well as the amount, quality, and appropriateness of interactions (Study 3), were related to the provision and satisfaction with informal support. The increased use of responsive styles of interaction (Studies 4 & 6) was associated with adequacy of informal support, and to a lesser degree provision of support was related to decreased passive and imposing interactive behavior (Study 6). These sets of findings provide support for Cochran and Brassard's (1979) contention that caregiver's personal social networks influence parent–child interactions, although the exact manner in which support causes or mediates certain forms of behavior is at this time unclear.

In addition to the effects social support had on interactive behavior, personal and familial well-being had significant and independent influences on parent–child relations, although the data clearly show that family functioning had an appreciably greater effect on caregiver interactive behavior compared to personal well-being. Respondents who reported better family functioning were more likely to engage in different types of play with their children (Study 1), were more likely to display responsive (Study 4) and elaborative (Study 6) styles, and were less likely to be imposing during interactive episodes (Study 6). The results from Study 4 are of particular relevance because the family functioning scale used in this investigation (McCubbin et al., 1981) measures primarily familial emotional and physical well-being, and thus suggest that well-being rather than family functioning per se may be the most important determinant of at least the types of interactive styles examined in Study 6. These findings together with those found in terms of intrafamily support point to the powerful influences that intrafamily functioning plays in affecting interactive behavior.

Close inspection of the personal well-being results shows a particularly interesting set of findings. In Studies 4 and 6, several general well-being measures were employed, none of which were related to any of the interactive measures. In contrast, all the child-related well-being measures (except in Study 3) were significantly related to a number of aspects of caregiver interactive behavior.

Most notably, depressed well-being was associated with a higher frequency of the imposing style (Studies 4 & 6). The influences of child-related well-being on positive interactions were less powerful, but still significant. Both sets of well-being findings suggest that the way one feels both emotionally and physically is likely to influence the ways in which caregivers interact with their children.

Child behavior characteristics. The extent to which support, well-being, time demands, and family functioning were related to child behavior and development was assessed in two studies. The independent variables included parent and family characteristics (mother's and father's age, family SES and income, marital status, and maternal work status), social support, well-being, time demands, family functioning, and child age, DQ, and diagnosis. The dependent measures included parent ratings of both child behavior problems and community acceptance of his or her child (Holroyd, 1974, 1985), and independent ratings of child behavior characteristics. The latter were measured using The Carolina Record of Individual Behavior (CRB). The CRB includes three major categories of items that assess a number of dimensions of behavior functioning. Both factor analysis and cluster analysis by inspection were used to identify CRB items that compromised conceptually coherent categories, and scores for the items within categories used as the dependent measures. Six major categories of items were generated that measured child temperament (I: motivation, endurance, & participation; and II: goal directedness, frustration level, & attention span), responsivity (activity level, reactivity, and responsiveness to the child's caregiver and early intervention worker), behavior competence (receptive and expressive language, and social and object orientation), and affective style (I: laughing & smiling, II: avoidance, wariness, & "clinging" to the caregiver). The data were analyzed by canonical correlation analysis.

Table 4 displays the findings from the various analyses. The results from the first study showed that parent ratings of their children's behavior characteristics were significantly related to family SES and income, child DQ and diagnostic group, informal support from social network members, well-being, time demands, and family functioning. Generally, the findings were consistent with predictions generated from our social system model. Adequacy of support, enhanced well-being, and better family functioning affected the parent's assessment of positive child functioning, whereas increased time demands produced a more negative image of the child by his or her parents. Our results are consistent with those of other investigators who found that parent assessment of child behavior was influenced by support and well-being (Affleck et al., 1986; Dunst, 1985; Dunst & Trivette, 1984; Dunst et al., 1986a, 1986b; Lazar & Darlington, 1982; Trivette & Dunst, in press b).

The results of the analyses of the independent assessment of child behavior characteristics data, shown in Table 4, produced interesting and highly suggestive results, although the findings must be considered tentative considering the small sample size (N = 40) and the exploratory nature of the study. The analyses

Table 4. Structure Coefficients and Multiple Rs for the Canonical Correlation of the Child Functioning Data

Independent Variables	Study 1 (N = 130) Child Functioning	Study 3 (N = 40) Child Temperament (I)	Behavior Competence	Child Temperament (II)	Responsivity	Positive Affect	Negative Affect
Parent/Family Characteristics:							
Mother Age	109	236	255*	−018	−114	−272*	249
Father Age	079						
Family SES	193*	−230	−057	026	003	302*	161
Family Income	187*	−439***	−086	−234	026	−005	109
Marital Status	127	263*	089	219	019	−084	−042
Maternal Work Status	−007	079	151	224	003	325*	421***
Social Support:							
PRS Intrafamily Support	072	189	−073	−226	097	050	336*
MSI Intrafamily Support		−208	−026	−135	−074	204	492***
MSI Informal Support		−103	027	208	−239	263*	−028
FSS Informal Support	399*						
PRS Support Satisfaction	113						
Child Characteristics:							
Child Age	−074	−213	328*	130	686	−484**	085
Child DQ	613	651****	732****	536***	035	363**	440***
Child Diagnosis (MR/PI vs. AR)	231*	181	169	024	−203	−182	214
Child Diagnosis (PI vs. MR)	−320*	−328*	−323*	−048	060	215	−397**
Well-Being/Time Demands/Family Functioning:							
QRS Emotional and Physical Health	725	390**	146	500***	212	029	427***
QRS Time Demands	−746	−290*	−258	−603****	−068	−072	−241
QRS Family Functioning	480**	108	457***	358**	396	123	073

Child Behavior Characteristics:

	C1	C2	C3	C4	C5	C6	C7
QRS Behavior Problems	986****						
QRS Social Acceptance	595***						
CRB Motivation		815****					
CRB Endurance		964****					
CRB Participation		835****					
CRB Expressive Communication			875****				
CRB Receptive Communication			757****				
CRB Object Orientation			895****				
CRB Social Orientation			640****				
CRB Goal Directiveness				606****			
CRB Frustation Level				412***			
CRB Attention Span				885****			
CRB Activity Level					527		
CRB Reactivity					976		
CRB Responsiveness to Caregiver					355		
CRB Responsiveness to Intervention Staff					398		

Child Behavior Characteristics:

	C1	C2	C3	C4	C5	C6	C7
CRB Laughing						093	
CRB Smiling						917****	
CRB Avoidance							
CRB Wariness							−982****
CRB Clinging							−701****
Multiple R	743****	773*	920****	852**	660	834****	772*

$*p < .05$, $**p < .01$, $***p < .005$, $****p < .001$.

155

produced significant multiple Rs in all but one analysis. Because of the complexity of the findings, we limit our discussion to the results pertaining to the effects of support, well-being, time demands, and family functioning on child behavior. Generally, however, only child DQ was consistently related to child behavior: children with higher DQs tended to display greater amounts of positive and less negative behavior characteristics.

As can be seen from Table 4, social support was related to both positive and negative child affect. Increased provision of support from personal network members was associated with greater displays of smiling and less negative behavior, whereas lack of intrafamily support was related to increased displays of negative affect. The findings suggest that the respondents' contacts with social network members, which presumably included their children on some occasions, directly provided opportunities for the children to interact with others which enhanced positive affective behavior and decreased the likelihood of displays of separation and stranger anxiety (Cochran & Brassard, 1979). The results also suggest that social support indirectly influenced child behavior by creating opportunities for the parents to interact with network members either alone or with other adults, which in turn provided the child the opportunity to learn social contingencies and expectations that promoted positive and decreased negative forms of behavior (Lamb, 1982).

Both well-being and time demands were related to all the items comprising the two temperament clusters. Respondents reporting enhanced well-being were more likely to have children who displayed "positive" temperament styles whereas parents who reported that their children placed excessive time demands upon them had offspring who displayed "negative" temperament styles. Inasmuch as support was found to affect both well-being and time demands (see above), but was unrelated to child temperament, the findings suggest that social support indirectly influenced child behavioral style. Presumably, support promoted well-being and lessened time demands, which in turn provided the parents the emotional and physical energy to interact with and encourage their children's development, which then affected the behavior characteristics of their offspring.

Family functioning was significantly related to one temperament cluster and the behavior competence cluster. Respondents reporting better family functioning had children who displayed both a greater typography of competencies and a more "positive" temperament style. The results again suggest indirect effects of social support, inasmuch as support was found related to family functioning but unrelated to behavior competence or temperament. The influences of familial well-being would seem to be the same as those just described for personal well-being. The order of effects on behavior competence would seem to be somewhat different. Support affected familial well-being, which in turn influenced communication and interactive exchanges between family members, including those with the respondent's child, which then promoted communicative competence and the orientation of the youngster.

Taken together, the findings from the CRB data analyses suggest that there are both second and higher-order effects of extrafamily influences on a number of dimensions of child behavior characteristics. The results provide support for contentions by Bronfenbrenner (1979) and Cochran and Brassard (1979) regarding the influence of informal support on child functioning, and extend our knowledge regarding the direct and indirect influences of extrafamily experiences on behav-. ior and development. Our findings are consistent with results reported by others (Crnic et al., 1983b, 1984, 1986; Crockenberg, 1981; Dunst & Trivette, 1984; Dunst et al., 1986a, 1986b; Furstenberg & Crawford, 1978; Trivette & Dunst, in press b), although replicating the study as well as documenting the effects of support on other areas of functioning are clearly needed in order to draw more than just tentative conclusions about the broader-based context of social systems influences on child behavior.

General Discussion   Collectively, the findings from our eight studies generally are consistent with the predicted direct and indirect influences of social support depicted in Figure 1 above. Support had its most influential direct impact on personal and familial well-being, but appeared to have less direct influences on caregiver interactional behavior and child behavior and development. Tentatively, the direction of the relationships seems to be as follows: Support affects well-being, which in turn affects interactional styles, which in turn influences child behavior. We stress the tentative nature of this conclusion given the fact that the research reported herein was cross-sectional in design, although preliminary analyses of our longitudinal data indicate that these relationships hold true with regard to the predicted causal and mediational pathways.

Several themes have emerged from our research on social support that are not readily apparent despite the fact that they are perhaps the most important from an intervention perspective. The first concerns the relationship between a family's perceived need for support and the type of aid and assistance that is provided or offered. The second concerns the manner in which help is provided. It has become increasingly obvious as our research program has progressed that support is most beneficial if it matches the need for aid and assistance as identified by a family. Indeed, we would go so far as to say that attempts to be helpful (supportive) are most likely to have positive consequences only in situations where there is congruence between what is needed and what is offered. This recurring theme has been used as a basis for proposing a needs-based model of assessment and intervention. It has also become obvious that it is not simply the provision of aid and assistance that is helpful, but the manner in which it is offered or provided that has either positive or negative consequences. Help is most likely to be beneficial if it promotes the acquisition of self-sustaining and adaptive behavior that makes a family better able to meet needs and achieve desired goals. This recurring theme has been used as a basis for proposing an empowerment approach to working with families. Both of these are described in more detail below.

One goal of our research program has been to disentangle the complexities of factors affecting family functioning in order to be able to effectively intervene to promote parental, family, and child development. The social system model that has evolved from our work emphasizes the role social support plays in influencing parent and familial well-being, parent–child relations, and child functioning, because social support constitutes a construct that can easily be operationalized as a distinct set of interventions. Although our research model has appreciably helped us learn about the complexities of the relationships between social support and family functioning, it is not a model that can directly be used for practice. The model and data generated from it, however, have strongly influenced how we intervene with families. We now turn to a description of how our social systems model of family functioning is translated into both practical and operative features.

FROM THEORY AND RESEARCH TO PRACTICE

The data presented above as well as evidence reviewed elsewhere (Dunst, 1986b; Dunst & Trivette, in press a) have served as a foundation for rethinking early intervention practices and structuring the manner in which intervention trials are conducted. We have attempted to reduce the complexities of family functioning to a number of operative features that guide provision and mediation of support to families served by our program. In this section we describe a number of the operative features of the FIPP family systems approach to early intervention as well as briefly describe the findings from several additional studies designed to test certain assumptions of our intervention model. The major operative features include a social systems definition of early intervention, a philosophical orientation that emphasizes family enablement and empowerment, and a needs-based approach to assessment and intervention, all of which have evolved from our social systems research and clinical experience.

A SOCIAL SYSTEMS DEFINITION OF EARLY INTERVENTION

Our efforts to develop and test the usefulness of our social systems model for both research and intervention purposes have led us to a redefinition of early intervention. Early intervention has generally been defined either at the level of program involvement (i.e., involved vs. not involved) or in terms of the provision of a specific therapeutic or educational treatment (see Bricker, Bailey, & Bruder, 1984, for a detailed description of definitions of early intervention). This narrowly oriented perspective of early intervention is overly constricted because it both fails to recognize the potential effects of other forms of support, and has limited our understanding of how to effectively promote and strengthen families of developmentally at-risk children. Based on the social systems model and analyses described above, Dunst (1985) has proposed a broader-based definition of early intervention as

> the provision of support to families of infants and young children from members of informal and formal social support networks that impact both *directly* and *indirectly* upon parent, family, and child functioning. (p. 179).

Stated differently, early intervention can be conceptualized as the aggregation of the many different types of help, assistance, services, etc. that individuals and groups provide to families of very young children. Involvement in a preschool special education program is one type of early intervention, but so is compassion from a friend, advice from a physician, child care, counseling by a minister, role sharing between a husband and wife, and so on. Because our research indicates that informal support is likely to have discernible effects on parent, family, and child functioning, the need to consider informal support as one type of intervention is strongly indicated.

Evidence For a Social Systems Definition of Early Intervention

The difference between a traditional and a social systems definition of early intervention can be conceptually illustrated in terms of a variance interpretation of the effects of the treatment (intervention) variable. The implicit assumption of a traditional perspective of early intervention is that the major portion of the variance accounted for in the dependent variable is attributable to the early intervention program or its program components, and that the remaining variability not accounted for in the dependent variable is substantially error variance. In contrast, a social systems perspective of early intervention assumes that beyond the variance accounted for by early intervention, significant amounts of variance are attributable to other sources of support as well as other explanatory variables.

Dunst (1985) tested the validity of these contrasting views of intervention by assessing the degree to which parent, family, and child functioning was related to six sources of support: intrafamily (e.g., spouse or mate), formal kinship (e.g., own relatives, spouse's relatives), informal support (e.g., own friends, spouse's friends), social groups (e.g., social clubs, parent groups), early intervention (e.g., therapists, early intervention program staff), and other professionals (e.g., agencies, family physician). Of the 10 dependent measures that were employed in this study, early intervention accounted for a significant amount of variance in only one outcome variable (family opportunities; Holroyd, 1985). In contrast, informal support accounted for significant proportions of variance in nine of the outcome measures (parent well-being and time demands, family integration, child behavior difficulties and social acceptance [Holroyd, 1985], parent expectations for the future of the child [Dunst & Trivette, 1986b], and number and frequency of parent–child play opportunities [Dunst, 1986c]). Intrafamily support was significantly related to five dependent measures (well-being, time demands, family integration, parent perceptions of child physical abilities, and number of parent–child play opportunities).

The findings from the Dunst (1985) study were subsequently replicated in a larger study involving 224 parents of retarded, handicapped, and developmentally at-risk preschoolers. The subjects were administered the Family Support Scale (FSS; Dunst et al., 1984) and completed the Parent-Child Play Scale (Dunst, 1986c) and selected subscales on the Questionnaire on Resources and Stress (Holroyd, 1985). The items on the FSS were grouped into four support categories: kinship support (spouse or mate, relatives, etc.), informal support (own friends, spouse's friends, other parents, church members), social groups (clubs, parent groups, etc.), and early intervention (therapists, teachers, school/daycare center staff, early intervention program staff), and aggregated scores for each category correlated with the dependent measures. Kinship support was significantly related to parent well-being ($r = .28$, $p < .01$), time demands placed upon the parents by their handicapped children ($r = -.24$, $p < .01$), and family integration ($r = .27$, $p < .01$). Informal support was related to well-being ($r = .26$, $p < .05$), time demands ($r = -.23$, $p < .01$), and both number ($r = .25$, $p < .01$) and frequency ($r = .22$, $p < .05$) of parent–child play opportunities. Social group support was related to frequency of parent–child play ($r = .18$, $p < .05$). The early intervention category was not related to any of the outcome measures.

Taken together, the findings from both the Dunst (1985) investigation and the replication study briefly described here question the assumptions implicit in a traditional perspective of early intervention (see especially Dunst, 1986a), and provide support for the broad-based social system definition of early intervention presented above.

PROACTIVE EMPOWERMENT THROUGH PARTNERSHIPS

The methods and approaches used by FIPP for supporting families are guided by a philosophy that is called Proactive Empowerment through Partnerships (PEP). The PEP model places major emphasis on (a) identifying and strengthening child and family capabilities using a proactive rather than a deficit approach; (b) enabling and empowering parents with the necessary knowledge, skills, and resources needed to perform family and parenting functions in a competent manner; and (c) by using partnerships between parents and professionals as the means to strengthen, enable, and empower families.

Our program is proactive in the sense that we take a positive stance toward children and their families. A proactive approach focuses on the child's and family's strengths and not their weaknesses, and promotes positive functioning by supporting families (Zigler & Berman, 1983). As Stoneman (1985) pointed out,

"Every family has strengths and, if the emphasis is on supporting strengths rather than rectifying weaknesses, chances for making a difference in the lives of children and families are vastly increased" (p. 462).

Our program enables and empowers families by creating opportunities that permit greater understanding and control over resources and decision making. Rappaport (1981) stated this in the following manner:

> Empowerment implies that many competencies are already present or at least possible. . . . Empowerment implies that what you see as poor functioning is a result of social structure and lack of resources which make it impossible for the existing competencies to operate. It implies that in those cases where new competencies need to be learned, they are best learned in a context of living life rather than in artificial programs where everyone, including the person learning, knows that it is really the expert who is in charge. (p. 16)

This set of assertions includes those conditions that we believe reflects the way in which we need to think about helping relationships and empowerment. First, it states that people are already competent or that they have the capacity to become competent. This is what we refer to as a *proactive* stance toward helping relationships. Second, it states that the failure to display competence is not due to deficits within the person but rather the failure of social systems to create opportunities for competencies to be displayed. Creating opportunities for competence to be displayed is what we refer to as *enabling* experiences. Third, it implicitly states that the person who is the learner, client, etc. must attribute behavior change to his or her own actions if one is to acquire a sense of control. This is what we mean when we say a person is *empowered*. Collectively, these three assertions provide a basis for viewing empowerment from a broader-based social systems perspective. An individual or social unit (e.g., family) that is empowered knows what physical and psychological resources they have, how to go about getting resources they don't have, and understands that they played a major role in gaining access and control over those resources (Bandura, 1977).

Our program enhances a sense of empowerment within the context of partnerships between families and professionals that avoids the paternalism characteristic of most client–professional relationships. Enabling and empowering families "requires a breakdown of the typical role relationship between professionals and community people" (Rappaport, 1981, p. 19). Partnerships imply that partners are capable individuals who become more capable by sharing knowledge, skills, and resources in a manner that leaves each person better off after entering into the cooperative endeavor.

Helping Relationships and the PEP Philosophy

The PEP philosophy suggests unique ways of engaging in help-giving exchanges. We have reviewed elsewhere the evidence concerning the types of help-giver behavior that is consistent with our PEP philosophy and is likely to have positive influences on help seekers (Dunst, 1986b; Dunst & Trivette, in press a). Our review and synthesis of the literature suggested 12 principles (Dunst & Trivette, in press d) that we try to put into practice as part of the provision and mediation of support. These principles are:

1. People respond better to help when donor characteristics are positive and proactive (Fisher, 1983). Help givers who display a sincere sense of caring, warmth, and encouragement when offering or responding to requests for help are more likely to have health promoting and competency producing influences on the help seeker. "When positive donor motives are attributed (e.g., the donor is perceived to act out of kindness or generosity), aid is more supportive and results in more favorable reactions" (Fisher, Nadler, & Whitcher-Alagna, 1983, p. 73).

2. Help is more likely to be favorably received if it is offered rather than requested (Fisher et al., 1983). Help seeking may be implicit or explicit, and the help giver's sensitivity to verbal, nonverbal, and paraverbal messages displayed by the help seeker is a key to being able to read a person's behavior and respond appropriately. Help givers are viewed as more positive by help seekers when they offer help *in response* to client identified needs (Gross, Wallston, & Piliavin, 1979).

3. Help is more likely to be beneficial when the locus of decision making clearly rests with the help seeker, including decisions about the need or goal, the options for carrying out the intentions, and whether or not to accept or reject help that is offered (Fisher et al., 1983). To be maximally effective, the ability to refuse help must be explicitly recognized by the donor, the decision sanctioned, and the opportunity for future exchanges left often as an option for the help seeker to use. Aid that implies few lost freedoms is most likely to have positive effects in response to help giving.

4. Help is more likely to be beneficial when aid and assistance are normative in terms of the clients own culture (Fisher et al., 1983). Nonnormative help is oftentimes demeaning and conveys a sense that the client has an inferior status or is incompetent (Hobbs et al., 1984). Help is maximally effective if it does not infer deviance or undue variation with respect to how other members of the client's culture or social network would deal with the same problem or need (Gross & McMullen, 1983).

5. Help is maximally effective when the aid and assistance is congruent with the help seeker's appraisal of his or her problem or need (Fisher, 1983). Positive reactions to help giving is more likely to occur when aid and assistance is appropriate, and matches one's appraisal of problems or needs.

6. People are more likely to accept aid and assistance when the response costs of seeking and accepting help do not outweigh the benefits (Gross & McMullen, 1983). Help giving that reduces threats to self-esteem, moderates obligations to pay, protects behavior freedoms (decision making), and promotes competence and a sense of adequacy, are more likely to be seen as personally cost effective.

7. Help is more likely to be favorably received if it can be reciprocated and the possibility of "repaying" the help giver is sanctioned (Fisher et al., 1983). "Reciprocity is (most) likely to be the preferred mode of reducing indebtedness to the extent that recipients are made aware of this option and they perceive that the opportunity to reciprocate exists" (Greenberg & Westcott, 1983, p. 95). A help giver who provides aid and assistance and accepts aid and assistance makes the exchanges fair and equitable, which in turn bolsters the help seekers sense that he or she has as much to give as to take.

8. Help is more likely to be beneficial if the donor bolsters the self-esteem of the recipient, and helps the individual experience immediate success in solving a problem or meeting a need (Nadler & Mayseless, 1983). Bolstering self-esteem is accomplished by using a person's strengths in other areas as a basis for helping the person solve small problems and experience immediate success before tackling more difficult problems and needs. "If help is given after efforts toward self-esteem enhancement have been successful, it is more likely to precipitate adaptive behaviors (e.g., self-help efforts and subsequent improved performance) than if given before such efforts are attempted" (Nadler & Mayseless, 1983, p. 178).

9. Help is more likely to be beneficial if the donor promotes the family's use of natural support networks and neither replaces nor supplants them with professional services (Hobbs, 1975; Hobbs et al., 1984). According to Hobbs (1975), help giving efforts are empowering if they strengthen normal socializing agents (relatives, neighbors, the church, etc.), and enhance a sense of community that emphasizes the promotion of the competence and well-being of all members in the family's social network.

10. Helping relationships are more likely to promote positive responses when the donor conveys a sense of cooperation and joint responsibility (partnership) for meeting needs and solving problems (Hobbs et al., 1984). Donor–recipient exchanges that promote participatory decision making and shared responsibility among the help seeker and help giver set the occasion for the help seeker to feel valued, important, and an "equal."

11. Help is more likely to be beneficial when it promotes the acquisition of effective behavior that decreases the need for help, thus making the person more capable and competent (Skinner, 1978). This type of help "enables the recipient to become more self-sustaining and less in need of

future help'' (Brickman et al., 1983, p. 19), thus promoting independence (Fisher et al., 1983) and problem-solving capabilities (DePaulo et al., 1983).

12. Help is more likely to be beneficial if the donor helps the recipient not only to see that problems have been solved or needs have been met, but that the client functioned as an active, responsible agent who played a significant role in improving his or her own life (Bandura, 1977). It is the ''recipient's own belief in (him or herself) as a causal agent that determines whether the gains made will last or disappear'' (Brickman et al., 1983, p. 32). Recipients must therefore perceive improvement, see themselves as no longer in need of help, and see themselves as both responsible for producing the observed changes and maintenance of these changes, if donor–recipient exchanges are to be effective (Bandura, 1977). This sense of intra- and interpersonal control is most likely to be acquired as a function of learning effective, instrumental behavior.

Taken together, our PEP philosophy, and enablement and empowerment principles, provide the necessary conceptual framework for setting the occasion for maximally efficacious help-seeker–help-giver exchanges. We next describe the manner in which these notions are operationalized.

NEEDS-BASED ASSESSMENT AND INTERVENTION

Both the provision and mediation of support to families is accomplished using a needs-based assessment and intervention strategy. Our assessment/intervention model includes four major components: specification of family needs, mobilization of intrafamily resources and capabilities, mobilization of extrafamily sources of support and resources to meet needs, and staff roles in helping families access resources from their support networks (Dunst, Trivette, & Deal, in press b). Family concerns, issues, and priorities are first identified using a number of needs-based assessment procedures and strategies. Once needs have been identified, the parents and staff together ''map'' the family's resources in terms of both existing sources of support and untapped, but potential sources of aid and assistance, including both intrafamily and extrafamily sources. After needs and both sources of support and resources have been identified, staff function in a number of different capacities to enable and empower families in order that they may become more competent in being able to get needs met and achieve desired goals (Dunst, 1986b; Dunst & Trivette, in press a). This process was stated in the following manner by Hobbs, Dokecki, Hoover-Dempsey, Moroney, Shayne, and Weeks (1984) in terms of the goal of assessment and intervention from a family systems perspective: ''The goal . . . is to identify family needs, locate the informal and formal resources for meeting those needs, and help link families with the identified resources'' (p. 50). To do so both enables and empowers families in a way that makes them more competent and better able to mobilize their resources in a manner that promotes child, parent, and family functioning (see especially Dunst, 1986b).

Needs and Needs Hierarchies

All our intervention efforts revolve around the ability to identify and meet family members' needs. The notion of needs is a relative phenomenon, and may be defined as an individual's perception of the discrepancy between actual states or conditions and what is considered normative or valued *from the help-seeker's and not the help-giver's perspective*. Our approach to intervention emphasizes identification of what individual families view as important, and in all cases family-identified needs take precedence over professional-identified needs as targets of intervention.

Although "the term 'need' undoubtedly (must) be viewed in relative terms" (Hartman & Laird, 1983, p. 164), it is nonetheless possible to specify major categories of needs as well as order needs along a continuum from the most to the least basic (Dunst & Leet, 1987a; Hartman & Laird, 1983; Trivette et al., in press). The major categories of needs include at least the following: financial adequacy, food and shelter, health and protection, communication and mobility, vocational opportunities, availability of time, education and enrichment, emotional stability, and cultural/social involvement.

The notion of *environmental press* is central to understanding how needs influence behavior. Garbarino (1983) defined environmental press as:

> the combined influence of forces working in an environment to shape the behavior and development of individuals in that setting. It arises from the circumstances confronting and surrounding an individual that generate (needs and) psychosocial momentum, which tend to guide that individual in a particular direction. (p. 8)

This set of conditions suggest that those "forces" that are strongest will take precedence, and steer behavior in certain directions. Thus, a person's perception of what constitutes the most important needs at a particular point in time will likely assume priority status, and guide the person's behavior.

The proposition that individual and family needs are one set of forces that affect behavior is fundamental to family systems theory (Hartman & Laird, 1983). Moreover, because needs can be roughly ordered in a hierarchy from the most to least basic, emphasis is likely to be placed on meeting unmet needs that are at the top of the hierarchy (i.e., those that are most basic). When embedded within our social systems perspective, the notions of needs and need hierarchies take on new meaning, especially in terms of assessment and intervention practices. For example, in our work with families served by our program, we have increasingly come to the realization that unmet needs due to inadequacies in basic family resources (nutrition, shelter, safety, health care, etc.) negatively affect health and well-being and decrease the probability that professionally prescribed, child-level interventions will be carried out by the child's caregivers. When basic needs are unmet, this set of conditions acts as a force that "presses" one to invest emotional and physical energy to meet these needs. This in turn takes its toll on personal well-being and health, and makes attention to professional-prescribed regimens a low priority. The latter is most likely to occur when professional recommendations do not involve actions designed to meet basic needs. Thus, a family who fails to adhere to a professionally-prescribed regimen may do so not because its members are resistant, uncooperative, or noncompliant, but because the family's circumstances steer behavior in other directions.

Empirical evidence. The extent to which unmet needs affect well-being and interfere with implementation of professionally-prescribed regimens has been tested in three studies conducted in our program (Dunst & Leet, 1987; Dunst, Vance, & Cooper, 1986; Trivette & Dunst, in preparation). The subjects were parents of handicapped, retarded, and developmentally at-risk children in two of the studies and teenage mothers in the other investigation. In each study, the parents completed either the Family Resource Scale (Dunst, Leet, & Trivette, in press) or Support Function Scale (Dunst & Trivette, 1985a), both of which assess the extent to which the respondents indicated a need for different types of resources and support. In each of the studies, the parents completed well-being measures that assessed both physical and emotional health. In two of the studies, the parents also were asked to indicate the extent to which they had the time, energy, and personal investment (commitment) to carry out child-level educational and therapeutic interventions.

The results from all three studies confirmed our expectations. Dunst and Leet (1987b) found a correlation of 0.56 (p < .001), Dunst et al. (1986c) a correlation of 0.45 (p < .05), and Trivette and Dunst (in preparation) a correlation of 0.34 (p < .001) between parental assessment of needs and personal well-being. The greater the number of unmet needs, the greater the number of emotional and physical problems reported by the parents. With respect to commitment to child-level interventions, Dunst and Leet (1987) found a correlation of 0.53 (p < .001), and Dunst et al. (1986c) a correlation of 0.54 (p < .01), between needs scores and the commitment measures. The greater the number of unmet needs, the greater the probability that the parents would indicate they did not have the time, energy, and personal investment to carry out child-level interventions.

A needs hierarchy perspective of environmental press has one major implication for working with families. The relationships between family resources, well-being, and adherence to prescribed regimens would indicate that, before parents are asked to carryout child-level interventions, efforts to meet more basic family needs must be made in order for parents to have the time, energy, and personal investment to work with their own children in an educational or therapeutic capacity. This is a fundamental operative feature of our program.

Family Functioning Style and Intrafamily Resources

The ways in which families cope with life events, go about meeting needs, and promote the growth and development of family members is partly dependent upon family strengths, capabilities, and other intrafamily resources. According to Williams, Lingren, Rowe, Van Zandt, and Stinnett (1985), family strengths refer to those relationship patterns, *interpersonal skills and competencies, and social and psychological characteristics* which create a sense of positive family identity, promote satisfying and fulfilling interactions among family members, encourage the development of the potential of the family group and individual family members, and contribute to the family's ability to deal effectively with stress and crisis (Preface; emphasis added).

The most ambitious work to date on family strengths has been conducted by Stinnett and his colleagues (Stinnett, 1979, 1983, 1985a; Stinnett, Knorr, DeFrain, & Rowe, 1981; Stinnett & DeFrain, 1985; Stinnett, Lynn, Kimmons, Fuenning, & DeFrain, 1984), who have extensively obtained information from families about what they indicated are the characteristics that define strong families. The work of Stinnett as well as others (e.g., Curran, 1983; Hill, 1971; Lewis, Beavers, Gossett, & Phillips, 1986; Otto, 1975; Satir, 1972) suggest that there are about eight major, nonmutually exclusive qualities of strong families. Before listing these characteristics, however, it should be made explicitly clear that not all "strong" families are characterized by the presence of all eight qualities. A combination of qualities appears to define strong families, with certain combinations defining different *family functioning styles*. As the work of Lewis et al. (1976) demonstrated, "optimally functioning or competent families appears to be (due to) the presence and interrelationship of a number of variables" (p. 205). With this caveat, the eight qualities include: (a) a belief and sense of *commitment* toward promoting the wellness and growth of individual family members as well as that of the family unit; (b) *appreciation* for the small and large things that individual family members do well and encouragement to be better; (c) the ability to *communicate* with one another in a way that emphasizes positive interactions; (d) concentrated effort to spend *time* and do things together, no matter how formal or informal the activity or event; (e) a *sense of purpose* that permeates the reasons and basis for "going on" in both bad and good times; (f) a varied repertoire of *coping strategies*, and the ability to see crisis and problems as an opportunity to learn and grow; (g) a clear set of family *rules, values,* and *beliefs* that establish expectations about acceptable and desired behavior; and (h) a *balance* between the use of internal and external family resources for coping and adapting to life events and planning for the future.

An examination of the literature upon which these eight qualities emerge finds several themes that seem to be the defining characteristics of strong families in terms of the ability to muster the time, energy, and resources to meet needs. Strong families tend to:

1. Be *positive* and see the positive in almost all aspects of their lives, even during crises and tramatic life experiences.
2. Convey a sense of *congruence* among family members regarding the importance and value of assigning time and energy to meet needs.
3. Include family members who are *flexible* and *adaptable* in the roles necessary to procure resources to meet needs.
4. Have at their disposal a variety of ways of mobilizing resources that vary depending upon the situation and context that define needs. There is reason to believe that these four characteristics increase the likelihood that families will be able to achieve desired goals, and the extent to which the qualities are present as part of a family's attempt to meet needs is assessed as part of our intervention process.

The ability to recognize family strengths and use them as part of promoting family functioning is an important part of work with families. However, we believe there is danger in using the word *strength* to refer to family capabilities, because the term implies a continuum with weaknesses being at the opposite end. We prefer the term family functioning style because it implies *unique* ways of dealing with life events and promoting growth and development. There are no right or wrong family functioning styles, but rather differentially effective styles that are likely to be employed in response to different events and situations. The work of Pearlin and Schooler (1978) and Folkman and her colleagues (Folkman, 1984; Folkman & Lazarus, 1980, 1985; Folkman, Lazarus, Dunkel-Shetter, DeLongis, & Gruen, 1986) on the structure and utilization of coping mechanisms support this contention. These investigators found that persons employ different coping behaviors in response to different life events, and that the behaviors that a person has available to himself or herself defines coping style. We would suggest that families as well have various types of strengths and competencies that collectively define their unique family functioning styles, and that these styles reflect the ways in which families cope and grow. Indeed, the presence and combination of different psychological characteristics are the defining features of unique functioning styles (Lewis et al., 1976; Pearlin & Schooler, 1978).

Social Networks As Sources of Support and Extrafamily Resources

In our intervention model, social networks are considered a primary source of support and resources for meeting needs. *Social support* is defined as "the resources provided by other persons . . . (and) differs in type and function . . . at different periods of life" (Cohen & Syme, 1985, p. 4). *Resources* are defined as "something that lies ready for use or that can be drawn upon for aid or to take care of . . . in time of a need or emergency" (Webster's New World Dictionary, 1974, p. 1211). Resources and social support include the emotional, physical, informational, instrumental, and material aid and assistance provided by others that promotes parent, family, and child functioning.

Operationally, sources of support and resources are thought of as varying along a continuum beginning with the family unit and moving outward and progressively more distant from individual family members. According to Bronfenbrenner (1979), ecological units, or social networks, may be conceived topologically as a nested arrangement of concentric structures each embedded within one another. In our work on explicating the major sources of support potentially available to families, we have been able to discern seven major social units and groups (Dunst, 1985). These are the nuclear family (children, parents, other household members), formal kinship (blood and marriage relatives), informal kinship (friends, neighbors, co-workers, etc.), social organizations (church, clubs, etc.), generic professionals and agencies (family/child's physician, health department, public schools, day care centers, etc.), specialized professional services (early intervention program, specialized clinics, therapists, clinicians, etc.), and policy makers (local and county governments, school boards, etc.). With respect to mediation and provision of support, *the focus of all intervention efforts is the mobilization of informal support networks at the level closest to the family* to the extent that individuals or groups have or can generate the resources necessary to meet individual family needs (Attneave, 1976; Hobbs, 1975). That is, once needs are identified, efforts are made to design and implement interventions that use persons who are members of the family's informal support network rather than relying on members of more remote networks to always provide supportive services. This strategy insures that our program does not replace or supplant normal socializing agents but rather strengthens them through establishment of linkages that permit needs to be met (Hobbs, 1975). Consequently, we strive to provide only those supportive services that cannot be provided by normal socializing agents.

A rule-of-thumb that we follow in working with families is never to provide a professional resource or service that can be provided by members of the families' informal social networks. Moreover, to the extent possible, provision of help or assistance is made contingent upon families playing an active role in carrying out jointly agreed upon interventions. Noncontingent helping only postpones the acquisition of effective behavior and increases the probability of creating a dependency on professionals (Brickman et al., 1982, 1983).

Professional Roles in Mobilizing and Strengthening Informal Support Networks

The needs-based assessment/intervention model for mobilizing and strengthening informal support networks require rather unique professional roles in providing and mediating support and resources to families. This is the case because different needs dictate different types of interventions. Consequently, truly individualized interventions tailor treatments to the needs of family members rather than making families fit into predetermined treatment programs. Our program is best conceptualized as a distinct set of help-giving styles rather than a specific set of programmatic activities and services.

The twelve principles described above provide a set of guidelines regarding the characteristics of help-giver behavior and helping relationships that are most likely to enable, empower, and strengthen families as well as promote acquisition of the types of competencies necessary for meeting needs (Dunst, 1986b; Dunst & Trivette, 1987, in press a). These principles suggest new and expanded roles that professionals must assume in order to truly be responsive to a family's needs (see especially Slater & Wikler, 1986; Trivette et al., in press; Solomon, 1985).

Our experiences in implementing a needs-based social systems approach to assessment and intervention have taught us a number of things about the logistics of doing family-level work. First, we have learned that one cannot emphasize enough the importance of identifying family-level needs and goals, and basing all intervention efforts around these needs. Not doing so will almost certainly reduce the probability that families will show interest in participating in intervention services (e.g., parent support groups). Second, the ability to meet needs and assist families in attaining goals they have set for themselves is best accomplished by (a) utilizing their informal support network to the extent possible, and (b) enabling families to take an active role in accessing resources and support. There is a tendency for professional "helpers" to do everything for families where families become passive recipients of aid and assistance. To do so supplants the family's natural support network and oftentimes has harmful consequences, including attenuation of self-esteem, creation of dependencies, and promotion of helplessness (see especially Dunst & Trivette, in press a). Third, we find that asking professionals to assume more varied roles in working with families oftentimes elicits the response that to do so means added responsibilities to their already taxing jobs. The fact of the matter is, the broader-based orientation we have often makes the professional's job a lot easier. This is the case because major emphasis is placed on promoting families' acquisition of competencies that permit them to become more independent and self-sustaining in meeting most day-to-day needs rather than the professional assuming responsibility for doing so. Thus, to the extent that professionals can enable and empower families in a manner that promotes their acquisition of self-sustaining competencies, the family is much more likely to be able to independently mobilize a resource for meeting needs.

Several Illustrative Examples

The types of programmatic activities that are used to conduct needs-based assessments and interventions are quite varied (see Dunst & Trivette, in press c, for a detailed description of the major activities within FIPP components). Several examples are briefly described here to illustrate the contexts in which interventions are conducted.

The majority of families served by FIPP are seen as part of home-based visits conducted either weekly or every other week. These home visits are used for assessing child and family needs, exploring options for meeting needs, developing strategies for implementing interventions, and continually revising and updating intervention plans as needs are met and new needs arise. Home visits provide a unique opportunity to establish partnerships between families and FIPP staff, and this service-delivery option has proved especially effective for gaining a better understanding of family functioning and the life styles and belief systems that influence family priorities and goals.

Home visiting is an integral part of a number of FIPP activities and projects, including our transdisciplinary child and family intervention teams, Project HAPPEN (Helping Agencies Promote Parent Empowerment Through Networking), and Project ASSIST (Accessing Social Support Interventions and Services by Teenagers). A particularly interesting part of Project HAPPEN involves an attempt to isolate the conditions that promote or impede efforts to empower parents. As part of the particular needs-based assessment/intervention strategies employed by this project, the context in which needs are addressed is taken into consideration. This involves classifying needs according to whether they are generated as a result of some normative or nonnormative *crisis*, or *coping* with day-to-day demands and stresses, or are related to *growth* oriented needs. The initial reading of our experiences tells us that the ability to empower families is increased appreciably as needs are generated toward the coping and growing end of the needs continuum.

A number of community-level activities and projects, including community clusters and the HOPE Network (Helping Other Parents Through Empathy), are specifically designed to establish support systems for meeting needs that otherwise would likely go unmet. Community clusters are comprised of families of handicapped, retarded, and at-risk children residing in the same community who meet either bimonthly or monthly to discuss issues of concern to them, advocate for services for their children and themselves, and deal with any other topics related to group identified needs. FIPP staff mediate the establishment of clusters but individual family participants take operational control of the groups as they are enabled and empowered to generate options for meeting needs and acting on the options. Similarly, the HOPE Network is a parent-to-parent project comprised of approximately 240 parents of retarded and handicapped children residing in various locations throughout our program catchment area who are available to talk to other families about any topic related to the birth and rearing of a disabled child. The HOPE Network was specifically established in response to the repeated requests from parents to have the opportunity to talk to other parents of disabled children. This project establishes supportive linkage that creates opportunities for mutual exchange of different types of support.

Project SHARE (Sources of Help Received and Exchanged) is one of the most unique and successful projects we have ever operated, because it puts into practice nearly all our enabling and empowering principles as part of service-delivery efforts. The project consists of a SHARE Network of individuals ranging from teenagers to the elderly, lower to upper SES background families, single and married persons, parents and nonparents, etc. The common thread that holds the group together is their individual needs and strengths. SHARE members engage in exchanges of services and products in order to get needs met (e.g., providing babysitting in exchange for canned or cooked food). The project is based on the premise that each and every individual has capabilities and strengths that can be of benefit to others, and that, by creating opportunities for persons to utilize their strengths, the person is empowered par excellence (Rappaport, 1981).

The above are just a few examples of the manner in which FIPP activities function as the context of empowering families. By no means would we want to lead the reader to believe that all staff roles and all programmatic activities are conducted as described throughout this section. The manner in which we described our philosophy and needs-based model are goals that we strive to achieve, and we believe that as a program we have made considerable strides toward attainment of this goal.

RETROSPECT AND PROSPECT

We conclude our chapter with a few remarks about what we have learned thus far about our research and programmatic efforts and what we believe to be future directions for our work. The evolution of the social systems model of functioning described in this chapter has not only, in our opinion, provided the type of framework for testing hypotheses about factors affecting family functioning, but also served as a model for generating guidelines about intervention practices. Because of its emphasis on intervention variables, the model provides a basis for directly linking research and practice vis-a-vis substantive principles and intervention operatives.

Perhaps the most important thing we have learned from our research findings is the importance of informal social support with respect to its relationship to parent, family, and child functioning. Indeed, the influences of support from personal social network members are so great that the impact of social support as a form of intervention is not only suggested but highly indicated.

When we began our family-level research program some 6 years ago, we anticipated that our research findings would have direct implications for intervention practices, and would be able to be directly translated into intervention techniques and strategies. However, as our research program has evolved, and as the complexities of family functioning have unfolded, we now believe there may not nor should there be a direct link between research and practice. As already indicated, we are now of the opinion that research findings should suggest guidelines and operatives, and that operatives are the missing link between research and practice. To be of value to practitioners, the complexities of family functioning must be reduced to a manageable number of operatives that can be easily mastered and applied, and, when used clinically, reflect what we know about family functioning and those factors promoting growth and development in all family members. Our PEP philosophy, needs-based assessment and intervention model, and enabling and empowering principles represent our initial attempt to generate programmatic operations. A major emphasis of future work will be the study of the usefulness of those operatives for intervention purposes.

A major direction of future research and programmatic efforts include increased attention to help giver behavior as part of the provision and mediation of support. We are coming to the realization that it is not just support per se that is likely to have positive influences, but that the manner in which it is provided may be a major determinant of whether it has positive effects. This is a topic that we have begun to consider systematically (Dunst, 1986b; Dunst & Trivette, in press a, d), and will begin to include as a factor influencing parent, family, and child functioning as a part of our research program. To the extent that we can isolate help-giver behaviors that have the greatest positive impact on help-receivers, programmatic operatives are strongly suggested.

The evolution of our research and programmatic efforts has been challenging, at times frustrating, but always enlightening. The approach we have taken for learning about family functioning has, in our opinion, not only significantly increased our knowledge about families but has also improved our ability to effectively intervene to promote optimal parent, family, and child development.

REFERENCES

Affleck, G., Tennen, H., Allen, D. A., & Gershman, K. (1986). Perceived social support and maternal adaptation during the transition from hospital to home care of high-risk infants. *Infant Mental Health Journal, 7,* 6–18.

Attneave, C. (1976). Social networks as the unit of intervention. In P. Guerin (Ed.), *Family therapy: Theory and practice* (pp. 220–232). New York: Gardner Press.

Bandura, A. (1977). Self-efficacy: Toward a unifying theory of behavioral change. *Psychological Review, 84,* 191–215.

Bradburn, N. M., & Caplovitz, D. (1965). *Reports on happiness.* Chicago, IL: Aldine Press.

Brandtstadter, J. (1980). Relationships between life-span developmental theory, research, and intervention: A revision of some stereotypes. In R. R. Turner & H. W. Reese (Eds.), *Life-span developmental psychology: Intervention* (pp. 3–28). New York: Academic Press.

Bricker, D., Bailey, E., & Bruder, M. B. (1984). The efficacy of early intervention and the handicapped infant: A wise or wasted resource. In M. Wolraich & D. K. Routh (Eds.), *Advances in developmental and behavioral pediatrics* (Vol. 5, pp. 373–423). Greenwich, CT: Jai Press.

Brickman, P., Kidder, L. H., Coates, D., Rabinowitz, V., Cohn, E., & Karuza, J. (1983). The dilemmas of helping: Making aid fair and effective. In J. D. Fisher, A. Nadler, & B. M. DePaulo (Eds.), *New directions in helping: Vol. 1. Recipient reactions to aid* (pp. 18–51). New York: Academic Press.

Brickman, P., Rabinowitz, V., Karuza, J., Coates, D., Cohn, E., & Kidder, L. (1982). Models of helping and coping. *American Psychologist, 37,* 368–384.

Bronfenbrenner, U. (1979). *The ecology of human development: Experiments by nature and design.* Cambridge, MA: Harvard University Press.

Bronfenbrenner, U. (1986). Ecology of the family as a context for human development: Research perspectives. *Developmental Psychology, 22,* 723–742.

Bunge, M. (1967). *Scientific research II: The search for truth.* Berlin: Springer.

Cobb, S., & Kasl, S. (1977). *Termination: The consequences of job loss.* Cincinnati, OH: DHEW (H10SH) Publication No. 77-224.

Cochran, M., & Brassard, J. (1979). Child development and personal social networks. *Child Development, 50,* 601–616.

Cohen, J., & Cohen, P. 1983). *Applied multiple regressions/correlation analysis for behavioral sciences* (2nd ed.). Hillsdale, NJ: Erlbaum.

Cohen, S., & Syme, S. L. (Eds.). (1985). *Social support and health.* New York: Academic Press.

Colletta, N. (1981). Social support and the risk of maternal rejection by adolescent mothers. *The Journal of Psychology, 109,* 191-197.

Crnic, K., Friedrich, W., & Greenberg, M. (1983a). Adaptation of families with mentally retarded children: A model of stress, coping and family ecology. *American Journal of Mental Deficiency, 88,* 125–138.

Crnic, A., Greenberg, M., Ragozin, A., Robinson, N., & Basham, R. (1983b). Effects of stress and social support on mothers of premature and full-term infants. *Child Development, 54,* 209–217.

Crnic, K. A., Greenberg, M. T., Robinson, N. M., & Ragozin, A. S. (1984). Maternal stress and social support: Effects on the mother-infant relationship from birth to eighteen months. *American Journal of Orthopsychiatry, 54,* 224–235.

Crnic, K. A., Greenberg, M. T., & Slough, N. M. (1986). Early stress and social support influences on mothers' and high-risk infants' functioning in late infancy. *Infant Mental Health Journal, 7,* 19–48.

Crockenberg, S. B. (1981). Infant irritability, mother responsiveness and social influences on the security of infant-mother attachment. *Child Development, 52,* 857–865.

Curran, D. (1983). *Traits of a healthy family.* Minneapolis, MN: Winston Press.

DePaulo, B., Nadler, A., & Fisher, J. (Eds.). (1983). *New directions in helping: Vol. 2. Help-seeking.* New York: Academic Press.

Duncan, O. D., Featherman, D. L., & Duncan, B. (1972). *Socioeconomic background and achievement.* New York: Seminar.

Dunst, C. J. (1982, November). *Early intervention, social support, and institutional avoidance.* Paper presented at the annual meeting of the Southeastern American Association on Mental Deficiency, Louisville, KY.

Dunst, C. J. (1983). Emerging trends and advances in early intervention programs. *New Jersey Journal of School Psychology, 2,* 26–40.

Dunst, C. J. (1985). Rethinking early intervention. *Analysis and Intervention in Developmental Disabilities, 5,* 165–201.

Dunst, C. J. (1986a). *A Rating Scale for Assessing Parent–Child Play Opportunities.* Unpublished scale, Family, Infant and Preschool Program, Western Carolina Center, Morganton, NC.

Dunst, C. J. (1986b). *Caregiver Styles of Interaction Scales.* Unpublished scale, Family, Infant and Preschool Program, Western Carolina Center, Morganton, NC.

Dunst, C. J. (1986c, October). *Helping relationships and enabling and empowering families.* Paper presented at the 11th Annual Regional Intervention Program Expansion Conference, Cleveland, OH.

Dunst, C. J. (1986d). Overview of the efficacy of early intervention programs. In L. Brickman & D. Weatherford (Eds.), *Evaluating early intervention programs for severely handicapped children and their families* (pp. 79–147). Austin, TX: PRO-ED.

Dunst, C. J., Cooper, C. S., & Bolick, F. A. (1987). Supporting families of handicapped children: Issues for families. In J. Garbarino & K. Authier (Eds.), *Special children, special risks: The maltreatment of children with disabilities* (pp. 17–46). New York: Aldine Press.

Dunst, C. J., Jenkins, V., & Trivette, C. M. (1984). The Family Support Scale: Reliability and validity. *Journal of Individual, Family, and Community Wellness, 1*, 45–52.

Dunst, C. J., Leet, H. E., & Trivette, C. (in press). Family resources, personal well-being and early intervention. *Journal of Special Education.*

Dunst, C. J., & Leet, H. E. (1987). Measuring the adequacy of resources in households with young children. *Child: Care, Health and Development, 17*, 111–125.

Dunst, C. J., & Trivette, C. M. (1984, August). *Differential influences of social support on mentally retarded children and their families.* Paper presented at the annual meeting of the American Psychological Association, Toronto, Canada.

Dunst, C. J., & Trivette, C. M. (1985a). *Personal Time Commitment Scale.* Unpublished scale, Family, Infant and Preschool Program, Western Carolina Center, Morganton, NC.

Dunst, C. J., & Trivette, C. M. (1985b). *Support Functions Scale.* Unpublished scale, Family, Infant and Preschool Program, Western Carolina Center, Morganton, NC.

Dunst, C. J., & Trivette, C. M. (1986a). *Child Expectation Scale: Reliability and validity.* Unpublished scale, Family, Infant and Preschool Program, Western Carolina Center, Morganton, NC.

Dunst, C. J., & Trivette, C. M. (1986b). Looking beyond the parent–child dyad for the determinants of maternal styles of interaction. *Infant Mental Health Journal, 7*, 69–80.

Dunst, C. J., & Trivette, C. M. (1987). Enabling and empowering families: Conceptual and intervention issues. *School Psychology Review, 16*,(4), 443-456.

Dunst, C. J., & Trivette, C. M. (in press a). Determinants of caregiver styles of interaction used with developmentally at-risk children. In K. Marfo (Ed.), *Mental handicap and parent–child interactions.* New York: Praeger Press.

Dunst, C. J., & Trivette, C. M. (in press b). Enabling and empowering families: Conceptual and intervention issues. *School Psychology Review, 16*(4).

Dunst, C. J., & Trivette, C. M. (in press c). Helping, helplessness and harm. In J. Witt, S. Elliott, & F. Gresham (Eds.), *Handbook of behavior therapy in education.* New York: Plenum Press.

Dunst, C. J., & Trivette, C. M. (in press d). Toward experimental evaluations of the Family, Infant and Preschool Program. In H. Weiss & F. Jacobs (Eds.), *Evaluating family programs.* New York: Aldine Press.

Dunst, C. J., Trivette, C. M., & Cross, A. H. (1986a). Mediating influences of social support: Personal, family, and child outcomes. *American Journal of Mental Deficiency, 90*, 403–417.

Dunst, C. J., Trivette, C. M., & Cross, A. H. (1986b). Roles and support networks of mothers of handicapped children. In R. Fewell & P. Vadasy (Eds.), *Families of handicapped children: Needs and support across the lifespan* (pp. 167–192). Austin, TX: PRO-ED.

Dunst, C. J., Trivette, C. M., & Cross, A. H. (in press a). Social support networks of Appalachian and nonAppalachian families with handicapped children: Relationship to personal and family well-being. In S. Keefe (Ed.), *Mental Health in Appalachia.* Lexington, KY: University of Kentucky Press.

Dunst, C. J., Trivette, C. M., & Deal, A. (in press b). *Enabling and empowering families: Principles and guidelines for practice.* Cambridge, MA: Brookline Books.

Dunst, C. J., Vance, S. D., & Cooper, C. S. (1986). A social systems perspective of adolescent pregnancy: Determinants of parent and parent–child behavior. *Infant Mental Health Journal, 7*, 34–48.

Embry, L. (1980). Family support for handicapped preschool children at risk for abuse. *New Directions for Exceptional Children, 4*, 29–58.

Farran, D., Kasari, C., & Jay, S. (1983). *Parent Child Interaction Scale.* Unpublished scale, Frank Porter Graham Child Development Center, University of North Carolina, Chapel Hill, NC.

Fisher, J. D. (1983). Recipient reactions to aid: The parameters of the field. In J. D. Fisher, A.

Nadler, & B. M. DePaulo (Eds.), *New directions in helping: Vol. 1. Recipient reactions to aid* (pp. 3–14). New York: Academic Press.

Fisher, J. D., Nadler, A., & Whitcher-Alagna, S. (1983). Four theoretical approaches for conceptualizing reactions to aid. In J. D. Fisher, A. Nadler, & B. M. DePaulo (Eds.), *New directions in helping: Vol. 1. Recipient reactions to aid* (pp. 51–84). New York: Academic Press.

Folkman, S. (1984). Personal control and stress and coping processes: A theoretical analysis. *Journal of Personality and Social Psychology, 46,* 839–852.

Folkman, S., & Lazarus, R. S. (1980). An analysis of coping in a middle-aged community sample. *Journal of Health and Social Behavior, 21,* 219–239.

Folkman, S., & Lazarus, R. S. (1985). If it changes it must be a process: Study of emotion and coping during three stages of a college examination. *Journal of Personality and Social Psychology, 18,* 150–170.

Folkman, S., Lazarus, R. S., Dunkel-Shetter, C., DeLongis, A., & Gruen, R. J. (1986). The dynamics of a stressful encounter: Cognitive appraisal, coping, and encounter outcomes. *Journal of Personality and Social Psychology, 50,* 992–1003.

Foster, M., Berger, M., & McLean, M. (1981). Rethinking a good idea: A reassessment of parent involvement. *Topics in Early Childhood Special Education, 1*(3), 55–65.

Furstenberg, F., & Crawford, A. (1978). Family support: Helping teenage mothers to cope. *Family Planning Perspectives, 10,* 322–333.

Gallagher, J. J., Cross, A. H., & Scharfman, W. (1981). *Parent Role Scale.* Unpublished scale, University of North Carolina, Frank Porter Graham Child Development Center, Chapel Hill, NC.

Garbarino, J. (1983). Social support networks: RX for the helping professionals. In J. Whittaker & J. Garbarino (Eds.), *Social support networks: Informal helping in the human services* (pp. 3–28). New York: Aldine Press.

Gore, S. (1978). The effect of social support in moderating the health consequences of unemployment. *Journal of Health and Social Behavior, 19,* 157–165.

Gore, S. (1985). Social support and styles of coping with stress. In S. Cohen & S. L. Syme (Eds.), *Social support and health* (pp. 263–278). New York: Academic Press.

Gottlieb, B. H. (1981). Social networks and social support in community mental health. In B. H. Gottlieb (Ed.), *Social networks and social support* (pp. 11–42). Beverly Hills, CA: Sage Publications.

Greenberg, M. S., & Westcott, D. R. (1983). Indebtedness as a mediator of reactions to aid. In J. D. Fisher, A. Nadler, & B. M. DePaulo (Eds.), *New directions in helping: Vol. 1. Recipient reactions to aid* (pp. 85–112). New York: Academic Press.

Gross, A. E., & McMullen, P. A. (1983). Models of the help-seeking process. In B. DePaulo, A. Nadler, & J. Fisher (Eds.), *New directions in helping: Vol. 2. Help-seeking* (pp. 45–70). New York: Academic Press.

Gross, A. E., Wallston, B. S., & Piliavin, I. (1979). Reactance attribution, equity, and the help recipient. *Journal of Applied Social Psychology, 9,* 297–313.

Hall, A., & Wellman, B. (1985). Social networks and social support. In S. Cohen & S. L. Syme (Eds.), *Social support and health* (pp. 23-42). New York: Academic Press.

Hartman, A., & Laird, J. (1983). *Family-centered social work practice.* New York: Free Press.

Heller, W., Amaral, T., & Procidano, M. (1978, August). *The experimental study of social support: An approach to understanding the indigenous helper.* Paper presented at the 86th Meeting of the American Psychological Association, Toronto, Canada.

Hill, R. (1971). *The strengths of black families.* New York: Emerson Hall.

Hobbs, N. (1975). *The futures of children: Categories, labels, and their consequences.* San Francisco, CA: Jossey-Bass.

Hobbs, N., Dokecki, P. R., Hoover-Dempsey, K. V., Moroney, R. M., Shayne, M. W., & Weeks, K. H. (1984). *Strengthening families.* San Francisco, CA: Jossey-Bass.

Hollingshead, A. B. (1975). *Four factor index of social status.* Unpublished paper, Yale University, Department of Sociology, New Haven, CT.

Holahan, C. J., & Wilcox, B. L. (1978). Residential satisfaction and friendship formation in high and low rise student housing: An international analysis. *Journal of Educational Psychology, 70,* 237–241.

Holroyd, J. (1974). The Questionnaire on Resources and Stress: An instrument to measure family responses to a handicapped family member. *Journal of Community Psychology, 2,* 92–94.

Holroyd, J. (1985). *Questionnaire on Resources and Stress Manual.* Unpublished scale, Neuropsychiatric Institute, Department of Psychiatric and Biobehavioral Sciences, University of California, Los Angeles.

House, J. S., & Kahn, R. L. (1985). Measures and concepts of social support. In S. Cohen & S. L. Syme (Eds.), *Social support and health* (pp. 83–108). New York: Academic Press.

Kasl, S. V., & Cobb, S. (1979). Some mental health consequences of plant closing and job loss. In L. A. Ferman & J. P. Gordus (Eds.), *Mental Health and the Economy* (pp. 255–299). Kalamazoo, MI: W. E. Upjohn Institute.

Lamb, M. E. (1982). On the familial origins of personality and social styles. In L. Laosa & I. Sigel (Eds.), *Families as learning environments for children* (pp. 179–202). New York: Plenum Press.

Lamb, M. E., & Easterbrooks, M. A. (1981). Individual differences in parental sensitivity: Origins, components, and consequences. In M. E. Lamb & L. R. Sherrod (Eds.), *Infant social cognition: Empirical and theoretical considerations* (pp. 127–153). Hillsdale, NJ: Erlbaum.

Lazar, I., & Darlington, R. (1982). Lasting effects of early education: A report from the consortium for longitudinal studies. *Monographs of the Society for Research in Child Development, 47,* (2-3, Serial No. 195).

Levine, M. S. (1977). *Canonical analysis and factor comparison.* Sage University Paper series on Quantitative Applications in the Social Sciences, 07-006. Beverly Hills & London: Sage Publications.

Lewis, J. M., Beavers, W. R., Gossett, J. T., & Phillips, V. A. (1976). *No single thread: Psychological health in family systems.* New York: Brunner/Mazel.

McCubbin, H. I., Cauble, A. E., & Patterson, J. M. (Eds.). (1982). *Family stress, coping, and social support.* Springfield, IL: Thomas.

McCubbin, H. I., Comeau, J. K., & Harkins, J. A. (1981). Family Inventory of Resources for Management. In H. I. McCubbin & J. M. Patterson (Eds.), *Systematic assessment of family stress, resources and coping* (pp. 67–69). St. Paul, MN: Family Stress and Coping Project.

McGuire, J. C., & Gottlieb, B. H. (1979). Social support groups among new parents: An experimental study in primary prevention. *Journal of Clinical Child Psychology, 8,* 111–116.

Mitchell, R. E., & Trickett, E. J. (1980). Task force report: Social networks as mediators of social support. *Community Mental Health Journal, 16,* 27–43.

Moore, J. A., Hamerlynck, L. A., Barsh, E. T., Spieker, S., & Jones, R. R. (1982). *Extending family resources.* Unpublished scale, Children's Clinic & Preschool, 1850 Boyer Ave. E., Seattle, WA.

Moos, R. H. (1974). *Family Environment Scale.* Palo Alto, CA: Consulting Psychologists Press.

Moos, R. H. (Ed.). (1986). *Coping with life crisis: An integrated approach.* New York: Plenum Press.

Nadler, A., & Mayseless, O. (1983). Recipient self-esteem and reactions to help. In J. D. Fisher, A. Nadler, & B. M. DePaulo (Eds.), *New directions in helping: Vol. 1. Recipient reactions to aid* (pp. 167-188). New York: Academic Press.

Otto, H. A. (1975). *The use of family strength concepts and methods in family life education: A handbook.* Beverly Hills, CA: The Holistic Press.

Pascoe, J. M., Loda, F. A., Jeffries, V., & Earp, J. (1981). The association between mothers' social support and provision of stimulation to their children. *Developmental and Behavioral Pediatrics, 2,* 15–19.

Patterson, J. M., & McCubbin, H. I. (1983). Chronic illness: Family stress and coping. In C. R. Figley & H. I. McCubbin (Eds.), *Stress and the family: Vol. II. Coping with catastrophe* (pp. 21-36). New York: Brunner-Mazel.

Pattison, E. M., DeFrancisco, D., Wood, P., Frazier, H., & Crowder, J. (1975). A psychosocial kinship model for family therapy. *American Journal of Psychiatry, 132,* 1246-1251.

Pearlin, L. I., & Schooler, C. (1978). The structure of coping. *Journal of Health and Social Behavior, 20,* 166-177.

Philliber, S., & Graham, E. (1981). The impact of age of mother and mother-child interaction patterns. *Journal of Marriage and Family, 43,* 109-115.

Rappaport, J. (1981). In praise of paradox: A social policy of empowerment over prevention. *American Journal of Community Psychology, 9,* 1-25.

Reese, H. W., & Overton, W. F. (1980). Models, methods, and ethics of intervention. In R. R. Turner & H. W. Reese (Eds.), *Life-span developmental psychology: Intervention* (pp. 29–47). New York: Academic Press.

Richman, J., & Flaherty, J. (1985). Coping and depression: The relative contribution of internal and external resources during a life cycle transition. *The Journal of Nervous and Mental Disease, 173,* 590–595.

Roskin, M. (1982). Coping with life changes—a preventive social work approach. *American Journal of Community Psychology, 10,* 331–340.

Salisbury, C. L. & Intagliata, J. (1986). *Respite care: Support for persons with developmental disabilities and their families.* Baltimore, MD: Paul H. Brookes.

Satir, V. (1972). *Peoplemaking.* Palo Alto, CA: Science and Behavior Books.

Sewell, W. H., & Hauser, R. M. (1975). *Education, occupation, and earnings: Achievement in the early career.* New York: Academic Press.

Shapiro, J. (1983). Family reactions and coping strategies in response to the physically ill or handicapped child: A review. *Social Science Medicine, 17,* 913–931.

Sherrod, K., Vietze, P., & Friedman, S. (1978). *Infancy.* Monterey, CA: Brooks/Cole Publishing.

Simeonsson, R. J. (1979). *Carolina Record of Individual Behavior.* Unpublished scale, Carolina Institute for Research on Early Education of the Handicapped, University of North Carolina, Chapel Hill, NC.

Skinner, B. F. (1978). The ethics of helping people. In L. Wispe (Ed.), *Sympathy, altruism, and helping behavior* (pp. 249-262). New York: Academic Press.

Slater, M. A. & Wikler, L. (1986). "Normalized" family resources for families with a developmentally disabled child. *Social Work, 31,* 385–390.

Solomon, B. B. (1985). How do we really empower families? New strategies for social work practitioners. *Family Resource Coalition Report,* No. 3, 2-3.

Stinnett, N. (1979). In search of strong families. In N. Stinnett, B. Chesser, & J. DeFrain (Eds.), *Building family strength: Blueprints for action* Lincoln, NE: University of Nebraska Press.

Stinnett, N. (1983). Strong families: A portrait. In D. Mace (Ed.), *Prevention in family services: Approaches to family wellness* (pp. 27-38). Beverly Hills, CA: Sage.

Stinnett, N. (1985). Research on strong families. In G. A. Rekers (Ed.), *National leadership forum on strong families.* Ventura, CA: Regal Books.

Stinnett, N., & DeFrain, J. (1985). *Secrets of strong families.* Boston, MA: Little, Brown & Co.

Stinnett, N., Knorr, B., DeFrain, J., & Rowe, G. (1981). How strong families cope with crisis. *Family Perspective, 15*(4), 159-166.

Stinnett, N., Lynn D., Kimmons, L., Fuenning, S., & DeFrain, J. (1984). Family strengths and personal wellness. *Wellness Perspectives 1,* 25-31.

Stoneman, Z. (1985). Family involvement in early childhood special education programs. In N. H. Fallen & W. Umansky (Eds.), *Young children with special needs* (2nd ed.) (pp. 442-469). Columbus, OH: Charles E. Merrill.

Thompson, B. (1984). *Canonical correlation analysis: Uses and interpretation.* Sage University Paper series on Quantitative Application in the Social Sciences, 07-047. Beverly Hills & London: Sage Publications.

Tolsdorf, C. C. (1976). Social networks, support, and coping: An exploratory study. *Family Process, 15*, 407–417.

Trivette, C. M., Deal, A., & Dunst, C. J. (in press). Family needs, sources of support, and professional roles: Critical elements of family systems assessment and intervention. *Diagnostique*.

Trivette, C. M., & Dunst, C. J. (1985). *Personal Well-Being Index*. Unpublished scale, Family, Infant and Preschool Program, Western Carolina Center, Morganton, NC.

Trivette, C. M., & Dunst, C. J. (1987). *Caregiver styles of interaction: Child, parent, family, and extrafamily influences*. Unpublished paper, Family, Infant and Preschool Program, Western Carolina Center, Morganton, NC.

Trivette, C. M., & Dunst, C. J. (in press a). Characteristics and influences of role division and social support among mothers of handicapped preschoolers. *Parenting Studies*.

Trivette, C. M., & Dunst, C. J. (in press b). Proactive influences of support on children and their families. In H. G. Lingren (Ed.), *Family Strengths: Vol. 8. Positive and preventive measures*. Lincoln, NE: University of Nebraska Press.

Trivette, C. M., & Dunst, C. J. (in preparation). *Notions of constitutional support and its relationship to maternal well-being*.

Vietze, P. M., & Anderson, B. S. (1981). Styles of parent–child interaction. In M. J. Begab, H. C. Haywood, & H. L. Garber (Eds.), *Psychosocial influences in retarded performance: Issues and theories in development* (pp. 255-283). Baltimore, MD: University Park Press.

Wilcox, B. L., & Birkel, R. C. (1983). Social networks and the help-seeking process: A structural perspective. In A. Nadler, J. D. Fisher, & B. M. DePaulo (Eds.), *New directions in helping: Vol. 3. Applied perspectives on help-seeking and -receiving* (pp. 235-253). New York: Academic Press.

Williams, R., Lingren, H., Rowe, G., Van Zandt, S., & Stinnett, N. (Eds.) (1985). *Family strengths 6: Enhancement of interaction*. Lincoln, NE: Department of Human Development and the Family, University of Nebraska.

Zigler, E., & Berman, W. (1983). Discerning the future of early childhood intervention. *American Psychologist, 38*, 894-906.

Chapter 8
The Design of Family Support Programs in High Risk Communities: Lessons from the Child Survival/Fair Start Initiative*

Robert Halpern
Erikson Institute

Mary Larner
High/Scope Educational Research Foundation

INTRODUCTION

Poverty among young families, while invariably harmful, is not a monolithic phenomenon, in cause, manifestation, or effect. High risk young families and communities in the United States differ in a number of ways that are relevant to the design of family support programs. In this chapter we examine how the characteristics of families, program staff, sponsoring agencies, and communities shape the development of family support programs for young, low income families. The example we will use is the Ford Foundation's Child Survival/Fair Start (CS/FS) Initiative, with which we have been affiliated for the past four years.

Our main thesis is that family support programs develop through negotiations among key participants (administrators, staff, target families) who often hold competing views of family needs, and contrasting beliefs about the service strategies that can best address those needs. Initially, the most important parties to the negotiation process are the program developers, sponsoring agency administrators, and funders. Later, their voices are joined by those of program staff (supervisors and front-line workers), families receiving the service, and interested community members. Because these individuals play different roles in the developing program, they have different perspectives on what the program is and ought to be.

When the family support program is first proposed, the problem formulation and goals reflect the program developers' general understanding of how environ-

* The authors wish to thank their colleagues in the Child Survival/Fair Start Initiative, especially the staffs of the home visiting programs directed by Emily Vargas Adams, Barbara Clinton, Sandral Hullett, Beverly Hunt, and Susan Widmayer for their generosity in sharing observations, experiences, and understanding gleaned while mounting demonstration programs in difficult field conditions. Their work made this chapter possible. Wanda Newell, Shelby Miller, and Lupe Mandujano-Garcia also contributed valuable insights. We are all indebted to the Ford Foundation and to program officers Oscar Harkavy, Marsha Hunter, and Marge Koblinsky for their support and intellectual vision.

mental conditions and caregiving behaviors influence child health and development; and their specific analysis of how local environmental conditions, target population beliefs and behaviors are influencing child health and development. Proposed emphases and activities are shaped also by the sponsoring agency's mandate and philosophy, and by the interests of the funders. Once the program begins to take shape in the field, its contours are altered by the characteristics and strengths of staff members (both supervisors and family workers), by the interests and needs of the families, and by the surrounding landscape of human services.

The negotiation process is usually most active during the year or two in which the program-in-theory is becoming operational. It occurs in dozens of decisions about recruitment of staff, training, curriculum development, and so forth; in the early interactions between program staff and families; and in exchanges between program and sponsoring agency, and between program and other community agencies. The negotiation process continues as lessons from early experience are used to revise strategies in domains ranging from whom to recruit as front-line workers to what to emphasize in work with families.

A secondary thesis of this chapter is that, as a result of the interplay of forces described above, a certain amount of re-invention is necessary with each new program initiative, even when the initiative is based on replication of a well-developed model. When problem-solving strategies that have proven successful elsewhere are adopted, they must be altered to fit the relatively specific local causes of the problems being addressed. For example, home visitors in many programs encourage pregnant women to seek early prenatal care, but they are battling different barriers in different communities. In one program, success might come from providing transportation to a distant public health department, in another from helping decipher the Medicaid eligibility form, or from convincing a teenager that it is time to acknowledge her pregnancy and seek health care.

Not only must program approaches fit local needs, the process of negotiation that guides program development will itself take a unique shape that reflects local conditions. The practical knowledge acquired by others who have worked with similar programs can sensitize program developers to common difficulties and options, but cannot serve as a blueprint. Each program faces a unique configuration of challenges and opportunities, determined by the families it intends to serve, the community where it will work, the agency that will house it, and the particular talents and shortcomings of its staff. Each program must learn how to work with those local givens in its effort to become a sustainable support system for local families.

BRIEF REVIEW OF THE LITERATURE ON EARLY CHILDHOOD PROGRAM ADAPTATION

The influence of local conditions on program development, implementation, and effects has been an important theme in major multisite early childhood demonstrations. We will focus in this brief review on the evolving manner of dealing with community and population differences in demonstrations sponsored by the federal government, in particular the Administration for Children, Youth and Families (ACYF). This evolution is characterized by a shift from attempting to place fully specified program models into communities, with the expectation of uniform implementation and effects from one setting to the next, to a recognition that while funders can specify a general set of purposes and activities, the detailed program is most appropriately and inevitably shaped at the community level.

Planned Variation Head Start.   The first generation of multisite demonstrations is exemplified by Planned Variation Head Start. In this experiment a number of theoretically and substantively different curriculum models (e.g., child-directed vs. adult-directed activity, discovery vs. direct instruction) were each implemented in a number of sites. The overall analytic design called for comparisons between models within and across sites, in the hope of identifying a small number of generally superior models. In these demonstrations, community and population variables were viewed primarily as factors that confounded (and complicated) efforts to compare models. Model sponsors were encouraged to enforce as much uniformity in implementation as possible (Smith, 1975; Stebbins, St. Pierre, Proper, Anderson, & Cerra, 1977).

But the goal of identifying generally superior models proved to be inappropriate. The experience of conducting the experiment indicated that: (a) in spite of sponsor training and technical assistance, each model was implemented somewhat differently at different local sites, as it adapted to implementing agency, community and population characteristics; and (b) differences in program effects between communities implementing a particular model were often greater than differences between models implemented in similar communities (Travers & Light, 1982).

In two later multisite demonstrations, The Parent Child Development Centers (PCDC) and the Child and Family Resource Program (CFRP), local conditions were viewed as essential ingredients in program development, and in examination of program effects (Dokecki, Hargrove & Sandler, 1983; Travers, Nauta, & Irwin, 1982). Local program development teams and implementing agencies were provided an overall framework within which to work—a set of purposes, age range of children to serve, guiding theoretical assumptions, and so forth— but were encouraged to develop models suited to their unique community conditions and population characteristics.

Parent Child Development Centers.   The central goal of the Parent Child Development Center (PCDC) experiment was to develop and evaluate community-based parent education models suited to the needs of different groups of low income families with children from birth to three years of age. The experiment used existing Parent-Child Centers as a community base. It was implemented in three sites: Birmingham, serving black and white families; Houston, serving Mexican-American families; and New Orleans, serving black families (Andrews et al., 1982).

In the first phase of the experiment, each site was to develop a model that reflected the needs and priorities of the target population to be served. Each site also was responsible for designing its own evaluation, albeit within a common over-arching theoretical framework (examining the crucial mediating role of maternal behavior on infant development and accepting a commitment to measuring a common core of variables). If the models were found to be effective, they were to be replicated and carefully evaluated again, and then disseminated on a broader scale.

The program development process was managed by each local research team, in collaboration with Parent Child Development Center staff and community members. The collaborative process involved interviews and meetings with community members, and the formation of a Parent Advisory Council. The site-specific development process in fact led to three distinct models that varied in onset, intensity, duration, and activities (although all focused on parenting, child development, and community resources).

Birmingham developed a model focused on progressively greater parent responsibility, eventually including peer teaching. Families participated from infant ages 3 to 36 months. The first-year mothers spent 3 half-days at the center taking classes, and participating with their infants in a nursery, where more experienced participants, "teaching mothers," served as models. Most participants then went on to become understudies to the teaching mothers, and a majority of those went on to become teaching mothers themselves, teaching 5 half-days and participating in other center activities.

The Houston team designed a 2-year program that began at 12 months with a year of weekly home visits, in part because interviews with young parents in the target population convinced team members that it would be difficult to get women to participate in center-based activities until they and their husbands came to know and trust the program staff. The second-year mothers attended 3-hour sessions at the center, 4 days a week, with twice monthly evening meetings for both parents.

The New Orleans program went from 2 months to 3 years. It consisted of two classes a week, 3 hours each, for the full period. The program also featured a strong preventive health and health education component, because the community had particularly inadequate health care for poor families.

Child and Family Resource Programs.   The Child and Family Resource Program (CFRP) experiment was designed to be a multisite demonstration of the effects of comprehensive family support. As with the PCDCs, the Administration for Children, Youth and Families, the sponsor of the experiment, provided a general set of goals and a broad theoretical framework, but encouraged each of the 11 local sites involved "to adapt to the needs and resources of their communities. As a result, CFRP was invented 11 times" (Travers et al., 1982, p. 3).

The common core of the CFRP model was a lay home visiting program for families with infants from birth to 3 years of age, with each site also providing a range of complementary center-based social services and activities. The program was supposed to link participating children to an affiliated Head Start program and develop a preschool–school linkage component, to assure a smooth transition into school.

In 1977 a contract for evaluating 5 of the 11 CFRP programs was awarded to Abt Associates. (The sites were Las Vegas, Oklahoma City, St. Petersburg, Salem, and Jackson). The Abt team, recognizing the diversity in local populations and program models, developed both a common cross-site summative evaluation and a process/treatment study designed to examine how site-specific differences in context and implementation might be related to site-specific patterns of outcomes.

Program design and emphases were not intended to vary systematically, but the Abt team found that ACYF's mandate was indeed interpreted and worked out differently at each site. For example, the characteristics of home visitors, the frequency of home visits and the emphasis of home visiting all varied significantly. So did the relationship to the affiliated Head Start program, and as a consequence the professional supports beyond the home visitor available to families.

In a few sites home visitors were selected who had experienced the same life conditions as families to be served. For example, Las Vegas, which served single teen mothers, employed home visitors who themselves were single and had been teen mothers. In Salem, where advocacy was seen as a crucial family support need, home visitors were selected partly for their advocacy skills. In St. Petersburg, the site with the strongest child development emphasis, two of the four home visitors were college graduates, the other two were high school graduates.

While the frequency of visits averaged about three every 4 months over a 2-year period, it ranged from once a month to once every 2 months. The relative emphasis during visits on child development versus "social service" (addressing a host of other family needs) also varied significantly. One site used home visit teams, with one member focusing her visits on general family needs, the other during her visits attending to child development.

The integration between the CFRP program and its affiliated Head Start varied from total to none. In a few sites CFRP was an umbrella agency, with Head Start as one component. In others CFRP was a component of Head Start. At still others the two programs functioned independently (Travers et al., 1982, p. 4). These varying relationships were a function of whether CFRP and Head Start were under the same or different delegate agencies, and the strength and character of the local Head Start program. As a result, families at different sites received very different amounts of support services beyond home visiting.

Patterns of effects found for CFRP also reflected differences in local conditions, population attributes and deliberately chosen emphases. There were no effects found on various child development and behavior measures, and only modest effects on maternal teaching skills. But there were significant program-favoring effects on use of community resources, and likelihood of maternal employment and/or participation in job training. These tended to be consistent with local emphases.

For example, the Las Vegas program, where jobs were plentiful and program staff emphasized tangible improvement in family circumstances, had larger effects on return to employment or job training, than did the Salem program, where a strong mental health emphasis led program staff to value the program's education and personal counselling over jobs (and where women were actually counselled to leave jobs to participate in the program).

In the federally funded demonstrations described above one can see the evolution of sensitivity to the importance of local conditions in program design and development. The evaluations of the PCDC and CFRP experiments, not discussed above, were designed to account for and examine site differences: in the former case, with three independent evaluations based on a common core of variables; in the latter, with site-level implementation studies, designed to help explain site-specific patterns of effects. Together these studies of the major multisite demonstration programs in early childhood intervention have taught us to respect the significance of site-specific influences. Not only do programs naturally adapt to fit local circumstances, they often achieve their greatest impacts on families when they are tailored to their context.

The discussion in the remainder of this chapter is drawn from an ongoing study by the authors that is part of the Child Survival/Fair Start Cross-Project Evaluation. This study, involving extensive interviewing at each of the local sites, is focusing on regularities and lessons in the program development process; and on site-level factors affecting patterns of implementation. The ensuing discussion reports early findings regarding the latter focus.

OVERVIEW OF THE CHILD SURVIVAL/FAIR START INITIATIVE

Under Child Survival/Fair Start the Ford Foundation has sponsored community-based strategies to improve pregnancy outcomes, infant health and development among low-income families. The Foundation has encouraged the development of programs relying on peer-to-peer support of prospective and/or new parents in order to:

1. Promote simple health self-care practices;
2. Encourage appropriate utilization of available formal medical care;
3. Augment knowledge and skills in childrearing; and, as necessary, help strengthen the parent-infant relationship;
4. Help strengthen parental skills in coping with other aspects of family life that impinge on childrearing; and
5. Help families gain access to services and formal institutional supports.

Concerned that the demonstration programs it supported should meet the needs of the communities served, the Foundation did not specify a particular intervention model to be implemented by all but encouraged local grantees to interpret the broad goals and approaches as a framework within which to work. Specific intervention strategies would be worked out in light of implementing agency mandate, target population features and support needs, availability of other community resources, and the like. The majority of the demonstration programs developed home visiting interventions, but other efforts were also supported. One grantee organized ongoing groups of pregnant and parenting teens, another sponsored community education efforts and worked for institutional reform in a major hospital system, and a third focused on outreach efforts to locate pregnant women and enroll them in prenatal care. The authors of this chapter were given a grant to assist with program development, help local grantees design and implement their own evaluations, and conduct a variety of cross-project evaluation activities, of which this chapter is one element.

Our observations in the remainder of the chapter will be drawn from the experience of the five home visiting programs with which we have worked most closely. These local projects serve a heterogeneous group of high risk populations: migrant Mexican-American farmworker families in two farm labor camps in Florida; Haitian immigrants and refugees in Ft. Lauderdale and Immokalee, Florida; young black mothers in the three poorest counties of west Alabama; isolated black and white rural families in six Appalachian counties; and urban Mexican-Americans in Austin, Texas. The central features of each program model are outlined in Table 1.

The CS/FS programs typically begin to work with families during the mother's pregnancy, and continue until the "target" child for the program is 2 years old. There are a number of rationales for such timing. Parents tend to be particularly receptive to an extra measure of support and guidance during this period, while conversely, a lack of support during this time of major adjustments can lead to personal and family crisis (Belsky, Robins, & Gamble, 1984; Osofsky & Osofsky, 1984). Potentially dysfunctional parent–child interaction patterns may not yet be established or deeply rooted during this period of family life. And, of course, children are particularly vulnerable to inadequate environmental conditions and parenting during their earliest years (Ricciuti, 1977; Sameroff & Chandler, 1975).

The direct service and support to parents in the Child Survival/Fair Start programs are provided by lay workers from the target community. For example, in the program for migrant farmworkers the home visitors are either former farmworkers or members of farmworker families. The lay workers are trained and supervised by a professional—a nurse practitioner, child development specialist, or social worker—whose main role is to nurture the lay workers' skills and self-concepts, and when necessary to bolster their credibility within the local professional community. In all projects the lay workers receive a stipend or small salary.

Table 1. Program Characteristics

Program Name	Fair Start Program	Parent Child Program*	M.I.H.O.W. Project	R.A.P.I.H. Project	Haitian Perinatal Project
Location	Dade County, Florida	Austin, Texas	Appalachia	Eutaw, Alabama	Broward County, Florida
Sponsoring Agency	Community health clinic	Independent agency	Various agencies	Community health center	Medical center
Target Population	Mexican and Mexican-American migrant and seasonal farmworkers recruited in pregnancy	Low-income Mexican and Mexican-American families with infants	Rural black and white families in Appalachia mostly young, recruited during pregnancy	Young rural black families, recruited during pregnancy	Haitian entrants and refugees, recruited in pregnancy
Community Served	2 farmworker camps	2 urban barrios	6 isolated communities in Appalachia	3 west Alabama counties	2 sites: an urban area, a rural farmworker camp
Duration of Program	pregnancy through 12 months	September to June during 10 month period during infancy	pregnancy through 2 years	pregnancy through 2 years	pregnancy through 18 months
Schedule of Contacts	12 home visits planned 5 in prenatal period 3 in postpartum period 4 during first year	24 or more home visits scheduled weekly during program year	ca. 20 home visits, scheduled monthly up to 12 months, bi-monthly to 24 months	ca. 35 home visits bi-weekly up to 6 mos. monthly till 12 mos. every 6 weeks during infant's second year	ca. 36 home visits, bi-weekly up to 12 mos. monthly until infant is 18 months old
Service Providers	4 home visitors, from farmworker families, two working full-time two part-time	6 home visitors from barrio communities, all working full-time	1 professional in each community, assisted by several natural helpers who she trains and supervises	10 home visitors from the counties served, all working part-time	4 full-time home visitors all are Haitian, but with longer residence in the U.S. and more education than the refugees they serve
Program Emphasis	prenatal care, self-care in pregnancy, breastfeeding, family planning, infant illness, health care, developmental milestones; social service assistance	early child assessment, stimulation, parent–child interaction, nutrition and health education, community involvement, social service referrals	prenatal care, self-care during pregnancy, childbirth preparation, breastfeeding, mother–infant activities, appropriate expectations, general support	use of medical services, self-care during pregnancy, infant feeding, appropriate expectations, mother–infant activities, personal goals and plans	prenatal care, self-care during pregnancy, home safety, infant feeding, child development, mother–infant activities and infant stimulation

*1984–85 program year

The lay workers typically start on a modest scale. The idea is for them to establish credibility as a natural, albeit deliberate, support system in the minds of the young families targeted for support. A gradual start also allows time for these family support workers to "invent" their new role, with its elements of both professional intervention and informal social support. Client loads typically build to 10 to 15 per part-time worker, 20 to 25 per full-time worker.

The bulk of the work with families in the ongoing Child Survival/Fair Start programs is conducted through regular (e.g., bi-weekly to monthly) home visits. During these visits the home visitor catches up with the expectant or new mother on significant events since the last visit, she checks on follow-through with appointments, she discusses health or child development topics that are relevant to the stage in pregnancy or age of the infant, she demonstrates and asks the mother to try out infant care and stimulation activities, and she reminds the mother of coming appointments. Throughout, the home visitor makes herself available to listen to the mother's concerns, questions, and concrete problems and she helps forge strategies to address such problems.

Home visits represent a reaching out to a young family and do not, on the surface, require the family to actively seek help and support. They place the helping interaction in a relatively less threatening environment than is found in most agencies. They give the home visitor a fuller appreciation of factors in the family context that influence childrearing, and they lend realism and relevance to the home visitor's demonstration and modelling of parent–child interaction and caregiving. Most important, they provide the sustained contact that allows a mutual relationship to develop.

A significant amount of work is done by home visitors and supervisors between visits, focusing on case-related review, planning, and problem solving. For example, program staff typically spend a good deal of time helping families gain access to medical and social services and enroll in Medicaid, WIC, or for Food Stamps. Program staff also spend hours on the phone or in visits to community agencies, attempting to resolve crises such as eviction from housing, running out of food or money, dealing with life-threatening illnesses, and so forth.

In a number of programs, home visiting has been complemented by home visits with clusters of parents, or by meetings of parent groups in a community center. Contacting peers and moving out of the home into the community is rewarding for many of the isolated families served by CS/FS. Moreover, in some communities, the program has provided a vehicle for building a sense of community cohesiveness and identity. The family workers are local residents and the program is usually seen as belonging to the community. It serves as a reminder that community members can band together to address common needs.

Following is an in-depth look at influences on the program development process of one of the Child Survival/Fair Start projects. Consideration of that program's experiences leads into a discussion of how the strengths and limitations of local family workers have contributed to the evolution of the different CS/FS programs. We then turn to a cross-project examination of how family, community, and sponsoring agency characteristics generally shape program priorities and activities.

A CLOSER LOOK AT ONE PROGRAM'S DEVELOPMENT: THE RURAL ALABAMA PREGNANCY AND INFANT HEALTH PROGRAM

The Rural Alabama Pregnancy and Infant Health (RAPIH) Program offers home visits to young black mothers in several of the poorest counties of rural west Alabama. Here, the visiting is done by lay community women, trained and supervised by a professional whose background is in human development. The program is sponsored by West Alabama Health Services (WAHS), a system of community health centers that is widely respected and well-integrated into the communities it serves.

The RAPIH program's development illustrates the negotiation among competing forces that was noted earlier as characteristic of program development. In this case, the original understanding of client needs and the program's approach to delivering services were modified by ''feedback'' from clients, picked up by the program supervisor who was well placed to hear their concerns. It was further modified as the program's leadership came to see a lack of congruence between the role designed for lay home visitors, the needs of the young women, and the helping styles that come naturally to community members. As a result of the negotiation process, changes were made in the program's philosophy, in the topics stressed in home visits, in the types of home visitors who were selected, and in the way they were trained.

The process of program modification was complicated, ironically, by the fact that the program was being developed and implemented in an innovative health agency with deep community roots. The program was designed by a team of specialists in maternal and child health care who had created a successful community health program in depressed western Alabama during a time of growing fiscal constraint. This team had a strong sense that their past success was based on their understanding of community needs, and they had no reason to expect that this new initiative would be difficult to mount. During the first year of implementation, however, the program supervisor had to struggle with problems that arose in the field. Over time, she and her employers came to believe that everyone still had a lot to learn about young mothers' support needs and about using lay helpers to meet those needs. A closer look at their experiences shows how one program changed to better fit its context.

West Alabama Health Services initiated the RAPIH program in 1983 as a promising new way to carry out the agency's preventive community health mandate. The agency already provided a range of support services (transportation, social work services, prenatal education classes), believing that they play an important role in maintaining health. Many young pregnant women, however, did not make active use of these services; they enrolled late for prenatal care, missed appointments, spoke little to the health care providers, and often failed to follow recommendations. The RAPIH program was designed to reach out to those young women, using community women as home visitors in an updated version of the tradition of using granny midwives for maternity care. (One of the visitors was in fact a well-known granny midwife).

The program initiators developed what appeared to be a strong plan for recruiting home visitors, training the visitors, and working with the young women. They had a relatively clear vision of who should be served (teenagers in their first pregnancy), what the young women needed (basic health and nutrition information), and how the home visits would meet that need (the teens would be taught, in an individualized fashion, by authoritative community women). The program would complement other health center activities by reinforcing messages delivered in the clinic-based education classes. Most fundamentally, the program developers were confident that they "knew their population"—which young women were at greatest risk of problems, the kind of support they needed and wanted, and how they would respond to the home visiting program.

In a decision that was to prove crucial to the program's evolution, the program initiators hired as supervisor a ·woman whose training was in human development. This background gave her a broader understanding of learning processes and developmental needs than was reflected in the straightforward, didactic program proposed by the health professionals. But she was new to the agency and had no prior experience with home-visiting or health programs, so she accepted the early plans and worked hard to implement them.

The first major step toward implementation came with the selection and training of the first group of home visitors. Fitting the vision that the program would use local leaders to work with young women in their homes, the home visitor candidates were typically "pillars of the community," well-respected, older women, whose own childrearing experiences took place 15 to 30 years ago. Their role was defined as one of teaching. Accordingly, the first cycle of preservice training for the visitors focused on lectures conveying detailed information on a broad range of health, nutrition, and child development topics so that the advice given to the young women would be current and correct.

As the supervisor participated in the training and went along on practice home visits, she discovered that the information-based training had created several difficulties. The home visitors were intimidated by this flood of new information, many became insecure and lost touch with the natural skills that led the staff to select them in the first place. For some visitors, that insecurity led to rigidity, giving an overly didactic character to their interactions with the young women they visited. In general, the early months of home visits reflected the tone and quality of the preservice training, as the home visitors lectured the pregnant teenagers as they had been lectured to.

The women selected as home visitors were not finding it easy to develop relationships with their young clients. The stiff, authoritative teaching style of some of the visitors was met with silence (and occasional resistance) on the part of many of the girls they visited. The open, personal exchange that the program developers had envisioned appeared to be the exception rather than the rule.

It was also proving difficult to recruit participants and to keep young women interested in the program, and there were more "not-at-homes" than would seem to be normal. When the supervisor asked the young women why they were disinterested, they complained about repetitiveness, pointing out that the home visitors were repeating the information stressed in the clinic's prenatal education classes. "Why do I have to have a person coming in talking about this when we already heard it in prenatal class?" In fact, the home visits were designed to reinforce and individualize the clinic's prenatal education messages, building in that unpopular redundancy. The environment was providing feedback to program staff.

This feedback was heard because both the supervisor and home visitors worked out in the community, gaining firsthand experience of the young women's life situations and concerns. Most prior contact with young pregnant women took place in the clinic and was circumscribed by their shyness and hesitation to discuss personal issues. The clinic's prenatal education program was not a setting where young women were comfortable sharing their feelings and questions. In contrast, the supervisor met the program's clients on their own turf, and, in her relaxed conversations with them, she learned a great deal about the interests, worries, and needs of the women the program intended to serve.

It began to appear that one reason why the program was not more popular was because it stressed health education without addressing the young women's developmental needs. Many were dealing with the stress and uncertainty of early pregnancy and parenthood on their own, lacking emotional support and role models even though they were living with their parents or sisters. The extended kinship ties that are traditional to rural black culture do not always provide emotional support or guidance in working through personal problems. As the supervisor noted: "Black women in general have been socialized since childhood to act as if everything is fine, that they can bear and handle all kinds of situations." As a result of that pride, many natural opportunities for sharing and support are lost.

Responding to the problems recruiting and retaining participants, the program initiators and supervisor held a crucial series of meetings late in the first year of implementation to begin reformulating the program. The supervisor would modify the home visiting program based on her growing knowledge of the young women to be served and of the dynamics of the home visitor–client relationship. The home visiting model would be modified to be more responsive to the expectations, fears, and developmental needs of the young women, stressing the provision of emotional support through the personal relationship that could be fostered between home visitor and client.

The existing home visitors, however, had been strongly influenced by the sponsoring agency's predominant style and saw themselves as teachers. Not all were prepared to create the more supportive, personal relationships envisioned in the modified program. To win the trust of their clients, the home visitors would have to be sensitive to emotional needs, flexible enough to create a relaxed personal relationship, and comfortable forging a niche for themselves in the family context (managing the powerful dynamics of the grandmother–mother–infant relationship in this setting, where the grandmother often assumes the care of her unwed daughter's first child). Thus, the revised view of the needs of the program clients led to emphasis on a different type of program activities (support, not teaching), and that change in turn crystallized a perceived need for different qualifications and training for the home visitors.

The supervisor was able to put her ideas into practice at the close of the first year, when the program expanded from one county to three and a new group of home visitors were selected and trained. Several of the original visitors left the program, and those who remained were retrained along with the new recruits. Criteria for visitor selection in this round shifted away from age and social status toward personal qualities including flexibility, sensitivity, and the candidate's sense of herself as a woman. The supervisor asked storeowners, beauticians, and program clients whom pregnant teens turned to for advice and support. She wound up with a group of younger home visitor candidates with varying life experiences, many of whom had been single parents or teen mothers themselves.

The training program was modified significantly, as well. Rather than thrust information at the trainees, the supervisor encouraged them to share their own past experiences and beliefs, and she related those to program messages and goals. While medical and nutritional information was still presented, emphasis was placed on understanding the developmental tasks facing infants and young mothers. The training stressed process issues such as where to find information, how to convey it effectively, how to build a relationship, and how to find a role within the family context. While the earlier training undermined the confidence of the home visitors, this experience was designed to bolster their self-esteem and support their independence.

In the revised program, the home visitors work at developing a comfortable relationship with the young women—not necessarily a peer relationship, but one marked by a measure of intimacy and reciprocity. The home visitors are given considerable latitude to choose ways of working with individual clients, picking topics and activities for home visits. Health issues—especially diet, exercise and smoking during pregnancy—are still stressed during home visits, but now these issues are discussed within a framework of encouraging the expectant or new mother to assume more responsibility for her life. The successful home visitor serves as role model, advisor, and friend to her young clients.

The RAPIH program model is still being negotiated, in its third year of implementation. The program no longer limits services to first-time teen pregnancies, but serves any mother whose first child was born during her teens, stretching to respond to the different needs of those mothers. A later round of inservice training sessions stressed the information that was to be conveyed on home visits, information that was deemphasized as the model became more relationship-focused. But the central program development issue in this case—that of a medical orientation learning to respond flexibly to the life situations and personal needs of its "patients"—has been largely resolved.

The success of the home visitors at gaining the cooperation of withdrawn and often resistant young mothers has won the respect of the agency leadership. Though the process was not painless, those who developed the original plans allowed the supervisor to alter the program's emphasis and approach, and her insights are now being used to modify other health programs as well. This system of community health centers has demonstrated its capacity to mold to the population being served and yet maintain its own identity and sense of purpose.

Building on the RAPIH program case study, in the remainder of the chapter we look across the CS/FS home visiting programs at three sets of influences that are especially powerful factors driving the program development process: the characteristics of lay workers, the needs and resources of target families and the communities where they live, and key aspects of the sponsoring agency and local political climate.

CHARACTERISTICS OF LAY WORKERS: EFFECTS ON THE IMPLEMENTED PROGRAM

As shown by the case study of the Alabama RAPIH program, the reality of the implemented home visiting program is inevitably influenced by the strengths and weaknesses of individual home visitors. In this section we examine how family worker characteristics shape program development, considering how programs strive to capitalize on lay workers' strengths and compensate for their weaknesses. We will look at three central program development tasks: discovering the characteristics of women who make the best home visitors under different local conditions, designing training and supervisory strategies that fit the home visitors' learning styles, and working out a realistic role for home visitors to play in the lives of the families they serve.

Considerable effort by the program supervisors has gone into learning the characteristics of women who make the best home visitors. A key feature of the Child Survival/Fair Start programs is their emphasis on training members of the target community to teach and support their peers, neighbors, and friends. In practice, the resemblance between home visitors and the families they work with has varied from project to project. That variation, in turn, influences the character of the program by leading to different interpersonal dynamics between visitors and families, and by shaping the role that program staff can play in the larger community.

For example, the Maternal Infant Health Outreach Worker (MIHOW) program operates several small-scale programs in sparsely populated, economically depressed Appalachian counties. Many of the home visitors in this model are recent program participants who are undeniably peers of the families they visit. In these isolated, traditional communities, this close social identification between visitors and families facilitates the process of introducing new ideas and models of parenting. The program creates a network of nonprofessional helpers, building on traditions of self-help and fitting naturally into the community fabric.

In contrast, the home visitors in the project serving Haitian families in southern Florida share a language and national heritage with the women they visit, but little else. The visitors are relatively advantaged Haitians who came to the United States years ago; they are educated and well integrated into American society. The program's target families are impoverished recent entrants. The shared cultural heritage creates a bond between the visitors and families, but it is not a peer relationship. These home visitors tend to relate to families as friendly authority figures, and their social status enhances their credibility and influence with the women they visit. In this project, having articulate, assertive visitors has been important, since they also act as spokespersons and advocates for the disenfranchised Haitian community and must command the attention of American professionals and political leaders.

Close connections between lay workers and the families they visit can pose problems for day-to-day program operations, especially in intimate Mexican-American communities. For example, in the Florida migrant project the home visitors lived in the same migrant labor camps as participating families, and sometimes found themselves "players in the same family and community dramas." Occasionally, family feuds forced individual visitors to stop working with certain clients. Their social and spatial closeness to the families meant they could empathize and were usually nearby, but it sometimes limited their ability to help with sensitive problems. The Austin, Texas, project had initially used Mexican-American women from the barrio neighborhoods as home visitors, but moved toward reliance on Hispanic women from other areas who had prior professional experience. Though they were socially more distant from the program families, they were no less caring. In addition, the program's administrators found they were better able to handle organizational demands and to keep from being overwhelmed by the multiple stresses of the families' lives.

The use of community women as family workers has had significant implications for home visitor training and supervision. It has been frequently noted in the human service literature that lay helpers should not be viewed as simply watered-down professional helpers (Pearl & Reissman, 1965). Professional helping is characterized by a carefully circumscribed relationship, focused on achieving a specified set of goals. It draws from an abstract body of knowledge, selectively applied to a concrete situation (Richan, 1979). In contrast, lay helping, while still goal-oriented, tends to be characterized by an ability to reach out and build a trusting, relatively unbounded relationship with families who might otherwise be unserved. The training and supervision challenge in programs like Child Survival/Fair Start is to augment the lay worker's natural interpersonal skills, substantive knowledge, and occasional goal orientation, without undermining natural strengths brought to the parenting role.

Introducing the home visitors to state-of-the-art health, parenting, and child development information has been a challenge for most of the CS/FS projects. Many of the lay workers have poor literacy skills, overlaid by unpleasant school experiences that make it difficult for them to respond to a school-like training program. As the Alabama case study illustrated, the flood of technical information can undermine the experience-based sense of mastery and successful coping that made these women a natural source of information and support to other community members. One after another, the CS/FS program developers have had to simplify the concepts and messages the home visitors are asked to master and convey to families, recognizing that the lay workers are not trained teachers and that the poor, stressed mothers are not students.

Preservice training and ongoing supervision for the lay helper merge into a long-term educational process. Early on, most projects learned to discuss the trainees' own beliefs, probing where they acquired those beliefs, and how comfortable they would feel sharing new information that might conflict with traditional views. "Discipline" has been one sensitive topic in many of the CS/FS communities where physical punishment is used with even very young children. The home visitors, reared in the same cultural tradition as the clients, often would not be willing to tell parents not to spank or switch their toddlers. Supervisors try to side-step the issue by asking the home visitors to suggest alternative ways of managing behavior that can avert the need for more severe (yet culturally accepted) forms of punishment.

Other program messages that sometimes conflict with the beliefs of lay workers include encouragement of breastfeeding and family planning in rural black communities, and of active parent–child play among both Haitian and Mexican-American migrant groups. In some cases, those topics are dropped from the curriculum, but most often, supervisors work hard to "win over" the home visitors to the views supported by the program.

In each project, with the help of team meetings and one-to-one supervision, the home visitors have to work out the meaning of their new social role. At its most general level, the role assumed by the home visitors in each program—the relative emphasis on social support, education, and service brokerage—shows the influence of the contextual factors discussed throughout this chapter. The visitors' concept of their role is also influenced by the supervisor's professional background, since they often respect and hope to emulate her. Individual workers tend to emphasize the aspects of their role that they find personally most fulfilling—for some, that means teaching, or being able to help in a crisis, or playing big sister to a troubled teenager. Even more specifically, with each family the home visitor develops a helping role that is acceptable to that family and responsive to its needs and concerns, and yet focussed enough to get the program's agenda implemented. In the next section of this chapter, we turn to the target families to examine how their needs and characteristics influence program development.

COMMUNITY CONTEXTS AND FAMILY SUPPORT NEEDS: THEIR INFLUENCE ON LOCAL PATTERNS OF PROGRAM DEVELOPMENT

At the outset of this chapter we noted that high risk young families and communities in the United States differ in a number of ways relevant to the design of family support programs like Child Survival/Fair Start. Local populations differ in beliefs and behavior with respect to health, nutrition, and childrearing; they also differ in life-cycle stage and developmental needs, use of social support, and patterns of help-seeking. Communities differ in the availability of formal supports and services, and in the sensitivity of formal helping institutions to cultural and linguistic differences. How do such differences influence program development?

Programs like Child Survival/Fair Start typically strive to introduce alternatives that will augment families' current modes of childrearing, caring, coping, help-seeking, and resource utilization. For the home visitor to help expand a young mother's repertoire in these areas requires both interpersonal skills and a variety of kinds of knowledge. Supervisors and home visitors must combine knowledge of accepted principles of healthy childrearing and coping with knowledge of the childrearing and coping strategies that prevail in the families they are serving. They must also learn what resources are offered by local institutions, how to gain access to those resources, and how the target families are typically treated by service providers. The goal is to identify the specific obstacles that contribute to health and childrearing problems for the CS/FS families. Here we will focus on how the developmental stage of the mother, cultural traditions and minority status, and aspects of the community context influence program operations.

Developmental Stage

Teenage parents constitute a significant target population for many of the CS/FS projects, and project experiences working with this age group illustrate some of the commonalties and differences confronted by community-based family support programs. Adolescent pregnancy and parenthood activates different social support and sanctioning responses among the different local populations served by CS/FS. For example, other things being equal, a Mexican-American teen from a migrant farmworker family is likely to set up a new household with the baby's father (often moving in with her mother-in-law), while a rural southern black teen will usually keep living in her mother's home. Motherhood will therefore mean very different things to the two young women. Yet overriding such variations are consistent challenges to working with this population that stem from the developmental issues common to adolescents in most cultures.

The CS/FS projects have found that, at the program's outset, pregnant adolescents are often more interested participants than are older women who have borne and raised several children. The pregnancy provokes anxiety, and the teens do not know what to expect of delivery or of their baby. However, though teenage clients may be more attentive during pregnancy than experienced mothers, the home visitors who work with adolescents find that they must make advice and suggestions concrete and immediate. For example, it may not be enough to remind a pregnant teen of her prenatal appointment in two weeks. It may be necessary to plan specifically with her how she will get to the appointment, and then check a day or two ahead of time on those plans. Dependency relationships can develop inadvertently when adolescent clients do not generalize suggestions to new situations, relying instead on the visitor to intervene again and again.

Especially in rural areas, pregnant and parenting teens are often reserved to the point of silence, making the establishment of a friendship a slow, patient process (O'Leary, Shore, & Wieder, 1984). Whether it shows respect or conceals resistance, the teenager's silence can leave the home visitor unsure how to tackle important topics. For example, if the adolescent resists breast feeding, it may be hard to discover why—modesty, fear of losing her figure, pride about using "modern" techniques (formula), interest in assuring that other caregivers should also be able to feed the baby? It may be impossible to delve into these personal matters until a trusting relationship develops between the home visitor and the adolescent.

The role of the home visitor with an adolescent client often strikes a delicate balance between advisor and friend. Adolescents generally do not want another mother—they usually already have one with whom the pregnancy has led to at least a measure of friction. In fact, a not infrequent role for home visitors working with teen parents is to help renew patterns of communication and intimacy between the teen and her mother that were disrupted when the teen became pregnant. After the birth, the roles of the teen and her mother can become confused when the two share infant care (Furstenburg, 1981). Though they cherish the baby, the adolescents often do not identify themselves as mothers (Thompson, 1986), and many lose interest in a parenting program after the baby is several months old. Mothering often seems a less salient role to the adolescent mother than being a teenager, and most of the CS/FS programs find they must "piggyback" the parenting agenda on to the adolescent's own agenda as a teenager.

Work with adolescents on issues of parenting poses similar challenges to program staff serving different cultural groups, in both large and small communities. However, developmental stage is only one of several characteristics of the target population that shape program activities and approaches. Aspects of culture and community characteristics also leave their mark on family support programs.

Cultural Traditions and Minority Status

The strong cultural traditions and the socially marginal status of families in immigrant groups have been key influences on several of the Child Survival/Fair Start programs. For example, many immigrant families seem to operate comfortably in two worlds when it comes to illness and medical care. Mexican and Mexican-American families in the South Florida migrant project accept and even value Western medical care at the same time as they continue to ascribe traditional causes to specific illnesses and employ traditional cures. Yet some families do not know how to use Western care appropriately, and others are put off by institutional barriers.

The CS/FS projects have learned that beliefs and behavior, even when they can be said to be harmful, are often adaptive responses to perceived environmental risks. The lives of migrant farmworkers are defined by mobility, unpredictability, and disruption. To compensate for these stresses, families struggle to maintain whatever stability they can, and traditionalism in beliefs and behavior may provide one form of continuity that the migrant family can carry along from place to place. The extended family often offers a more stable and reliable source of help and advice than formal helping agencies.

How do these traditions affect the home visiting program? To take one example, a Mexican mother might ascribe a fever in her infant to the exposure of that child to a neighbor's stares (''mal ojo''). In this case she would tend to use traditional therapies, only bringing the child in for medical care as a later resort. The home visitor's work in this situation is not to convince the mother that a neighbor's stare cannot cause fever, but to discuss other possible causes, help the mother learn to use a thermometer, take steps to reduce the fever, and suggest that temperatures above a certain level require medical attention.

On the other side of that challenge, success in encouraging families to use medical care in a timely and appropriate manner is influenced by the basic availability of care and by the response of providers when a family does come in for care. The reluctance of the Mexican mother to use Western medical explanation and treatment may have been exacerbated by negative experiences in the past when she did present her children for care—communication problems, long waits that translate into lost income, excessive paperwork required to prove eligibility, or implied criticism of the mother by medical staff.

To address those institutional problems, the home visitors in the project serving Mexican-American migrants have worked with clinic staff to find ways of reducing red tape and waiting times, and sometimes have accompanied the family to the clinic to assure that referrals led to a constructive response on the part of clinic staff. Family help-seeking patterns and institutional responses to those patterns together form the context for the home visitor's work.

Another arena in which home visitors' work is strongly affected by families' deeply rooted beliefs is infant care and stimulation. For example, the Haitian Perinatal Intervention Project serves mothers who have recently immigrated from Haiti, who are strongly attached to their infants and eager for their children to be healthy and successful in school. At the same time, there is little tradition in Haitian culture of playing and interacting verbally with infants (Nachman, Widmayer, Archer, Moon, & Almeroth, 1984). The dictum that "children should be seen but not heard" is firmly held.

The Haitian project's home visitors approach the issue of infant stimulation by encouraging the mothers to spend a certain amount of time every day on specific, simple play activities. The activities build as much as possible on traditional Haitian forms of maternal—infant interaction, particularly singing to infants. The visitors explain to the mothers that play and stimulation will help their children succeed in American schools. This straightforward, concrete explanation often convinces the mothers to try American-style patterns of interaction, yet it does not directly challenge traditional Haitian child-rearing values. This is one example of a program trying to communicate respect for traditional practices while introducing new alternatives.

While the home visits in the Haitian project focus on mother—infant interaction, staff cannot ignore the stresses faced by many Haitian entrants: delicate legal status with constant fear of deportation, insecure work compounded by inadequate child care, depression over separation from family left behind in Haiti, lack of English, and crowded, unsafe housing conditions. In the United States, the Haitian entrant has few rights and fewer advocates. The project has had to work out boundaries to guide staff responses to the families' seemingly limitless needs for crisis assistance, referrals, translation, and advocacy, to keep these activities from consuming the project's limited resources. It is difficult to strike a balance between efforts to address parenting issues with the families and efforts to force local institutions to respond at least minimally to the needs of the Haitian families.

Community Context

The lives of Haitian entrant and Mexican migrant families involve enormous stress, cultural differences in childrearing, and pressing material needs. Other problems confront such long-time United States citizens as the poor Appalachian families served by the Maternal Infant Health Outreach Worker (MIHOW) project. For generations, these families have faced patterns of economic development that extract natural resources but do not develop human resources, dealing with geographic isolation, worsening economic conditions, and an absolute lack of services. They have learned not to get their hopes up. This resignation can translate into passivity and depression, and low expectations that children will be healthy or find success in life.

Operating in this context, the MIHOW project designed small local programs that would work on an intimate scale, focusing their energies on developing local capacities for self-help and mutual support. Agencies are few and far between in the small, isolated counties that were to be served. Thus, a satellite program model was developed, anchored by a few core staff at Vanderbilt University. With training, a curriculum, and general support from Vanderbilt, a local community leader in each of six Appalachian counties was helped to build an organization around herself. This professional started out making home visits to families and discovered through her own experiences the way the MIHOW program needed to work locally.

Through her community work, this leader identified local women with little education or work experience whose creativity and interpersonal skills were going unused, and trained them to work with her as natural helpers. For a small stipend, these natural helpers make monthly visits to pregnant women and new mothers throughout the county, revitalizing old traditions of mutual help and sisterhood. Over time, the program organizer has focused a growing proportion of her energies on the personal and professional development of these women, who are now the main service providers. The human resource development that is a by-product of most CS/FS programs was a deliberate, central element of the MIHOW model.

This local professional and her staff have also used the specific substantive concerns of the program—the focus on healthy pregnancies and babies, as well as women's development—in two complementary ways. One is to help women see that their actions can have an effect on their own health and their children's well-being, and by extension on other aspects of their lives. The second is as a means of building local networks that could eventually be mobilized around other community development concerns. This approach to community development is not uncommon in Appalachia and the mid-South, and fits the historic lack of community structures to address economic and social inequalities.

Community contexts shape programs in various ways, and the evolution of the CEDEN program within the denser urban environment of Austin also mirrors the problems and resources of its community context. Here, while crime is not so threatening as to prevent staff from walking in the Mexican-American barrio neighborhoods (as is the case in some large cities), the problems that confront the program families are distinctly urban in character, often involving drug or alcohol abuse and domestic violence. Families initially may be mistrustful when approached by program staff, because they have had disappointing experiences with other human service programs. In an urban area, a new program will seldom be able to start with a blank slate.

The urban context brings with it a rich service environment populated by a range of institutions, agencies, and special programs. Their services are not all easily accessible, supportive, or sensitive to the needs of families, but they do exist. Consequently, considerable program energies go to clarifying family needs and providing referrals to help them access relevant services from other agencies. In the CEDEN program's early years, the home visitors became overloaded with demands for crisis assistance, and a social worker and student interns were recruited to handle referrals and mobilize resources to address unmet family needs. Staff members cultivate friendly ties with gatekeepers and responsive individuals throughout the Austin human service network, using those ties to leverage services for the barrio families.

It would be possible to exaggerate the effects of differences in population and community attributes on the work of the local Child Survival/Fair Start projects. Inadequate housing and hunger at the end of the month can be found in all the communities served by Child Survival/Fair Start. The effects of poverty, isolation, and stress on health, childrearing, and family coping challenge all the programs. Indeed, differences between families within a single program can be greater than those between the different populations. Yet the populations and communities do not feel alike when one spends any time with them, and as a result, these community-based programs have developed along distinct lines.

THE INFLUENCE OF SPONSORING AGENCY CHARACTERISTICS ON PROGRAM DEVELOPMENT

Thus far we have examined how family and community attributes and family worker characteristics interact with basic program goals to shape program development. Family support programs like Child Survival/Fair Start also develop within a specific institutional context, and they inevitably bear the mark of their sponsoring agency. In this final substantive section of the chapter, we examine how sponsoring agency characteristics influence the program development process, facilitating or complicating daily operations, coloring the public image of the program, and determining prospects for long-term institutionalization.

The Child Survival/Fair Start programs are located in a wide range of agencies, including community health clinics, the developmental evaluation unit of a large hospital, a child care center, a Planned Parenthood clinic, and an independent research and development organization. The issues addressed by the CS/FS home-visiting programs are germane to many disciplines, and so the programs fit comfortably under the auspices of several major helping systems. The relationships that exist between the programs and their sponsoring agencies do, nonetheless, differ. In one case, the home visiting program is the core service around which the agency is organized; in another case, the link between program and agency is primarily one of convenience. More often, CS/FS program purposes and strategy complement the basic services of the agency, by extending the agency's reach, serving families longer, or working with them in different ways.

The extent to which the program can draw on and link with other agency resources, without losing its identity as a separate innovative component, varies. For example, the Haitian program is administered by the regional developmental evaluation unit based in a major hospital. This unit is responsible for following, evaluating, and providing developmental services to high risk infants who have "graduated" from neonatal intensive care in a large area of southern Florida. Many of these babies are Haitian. The home visiting program has added an independent preventive component to the clinic's work, where other staff are preoccupied with the medical and developmental consequences of obstetric problems and lack of prenatal care. In turn, the program has been able to draw on the evaluation unit's resources—free formula, skilled testers, and the expertise of an interdisciplinary professional team. Both parties profit from their association.

Sometimes, staff or task integration with the sponsoring agency can undermine the program's independence. The Fair Start program serving migrants in Florida is operated by the clinic that provides nearly all health care to migrants in the area. Here, the home visitors were trained and are supervised by a nurse. An orientation toward health, health education, and linkage to health services permeates the program to such an extent that parenting and child development goals receive relatively little attention. In the eyes of clinic staff, the home visitors follow in the footsteps of the lay "family health workers" who once served as all-purpose aides and outreach workers in the clinic. It has been a struggle to clarify that the home visitors have a more defined role than their forebears, and they are not available to fill in whenever needs arise in the clinic.

Nonetheless, health services are important in the risk-filled lives of the migrants, and since the Fair Start program is sponsored by the clinic it has been easier for the home visitors to help families access services than it would otherwise be. Pressure brought by the program has led to some changes in clinic policies (speeding eligibility decisions and reducing some waiting times), and the visitors and supervisor run interference within the clinic to ensure that the families get proper care. When serious medical problems arise, the home visitors intercede on behalf of families with staff at the hospital in Miami. In that huge medical bureaucracy, the home visitors are received more positively when they explain that they, too, are affiliated with the health care system. Close linkage between the program and sponsoring agency brings a mixed bag of advantages and disadvantages.

When the program is seen as sharing the agency's philosophy but extending its mission in new ways, co-existence sometimes comes easier. Internal presentation of the program as an innovation increases the respect agency staff have for the program's independence, and its "differentness" can be seen as desirable. The Alabama program described earlier falls in this category. The program draws on the clinic's resources and serves its clients, but it has explored new ways of working with young mothers, emphasizing personal development and emotional support rather than authoritative instruction. The open endorsement of the new program by agency administrators was an important factor in winning acceptance by other clinic staff.

Financial stability and style of managing resources contribute much to the climate in which the program defines and pursues its goals. Agencies that are struggling under serious financial pressures understandably do not provide a supportive environment for an innovative program. Tight budgets limit the resources available to the program (from pens and paper clips to access to supervision from professionals on staff). They can also increase internal pressures to divert program budget and staff time away from intended activities to cover core agency functions.

Prospects for institutionalizing the program within the set of agency services depend upon many of the same agency characteristics. Of course, only agencies with reasonable fiscal security will be able to assume funding responsibility for an additional program. The agency's decision to adopt an innovative program also depends somewhat on the point the agency has reached in its own life cycle. A young agency may have the creative energy needed to incorporate new program ideas, but prefer to focus development energies on the agency's core services. At the other pole, in some mature agencies, existing approaches and philosophies are too entrenched to permit experimentation. A stable, sound agency with a conscious orientation toward innovation usually offers the most fertile environment for both developing and sustaining new program ideas.

The nature of links between program and agency, discussed above in the context of program development and implementation, is important to institutionalization as well. When the new program is seen as sharing the agency's philosophy and furthering its goals, it is far more likely to be absorbed (in one form or another) than when the link between agency and program was only one of convenience.

Even under optimal circumstances, however, institutionalization often brings with it considerable modification of program elements. Home visitors may be kept on staff but given responsibility for visiting elderly patients as well as new mothers, or the intervention period may be shortened so more people can be served with the same resources. Faithful adoption of all the key program elements shows that the program developers succeeded in "selling" the program's philosophy and strategy to agency leaders.

Looking at the broader community context, the program derives its credibility and inherits a niche in the community service structure from its sponsoring agency, and the agency's image is likely (at least initially) to color the public perception of the program. If the sponsoring agency is a well-respected member of the local human service network, the program will usually enjoy a positive reception by other professionals and even families. For example, one of the MIHOW projects in an Appalachian county is run by a clinic staffed by dedicated professionals who have demonstrated their commitment to the area and have a track record of providing innovative reliable health care services. There, the supervisor could begin her work with a ready-made network of good contacts with other local service providers.

Other programs have had to establish a place of their own in the community, carefully defining their role in a way that complemented the services of other agencies to avoid bitter turf battles. As an independent organization that is a relative newcomer in Austin, CEDEN has approached this problem by addressing an unmet need (providing parent education to barrio families), actively exchanging referrals with other agencies, joining interagency councils and networks of human service providers, and establishing a strong advisory board that represents many sectors of the community. The effort expended in building these relationships has been repaid by CEDEN's acceptance by the community, local funders, and other agencies.

In most contexts, collegial contacts with professionals in other agencies are established only gradually, as the program matures and becomes known in the community. Such professional relationships are often launched when workers from several organizations learn they are all working with one troubled family, and they meet to coordinate their efforts. In the migrant program, several impromptu case management conferences involving the home visitor, clinic nurse, caseworker, mental health counselor, and child care center director led to a series of meetings (more regular but still informal) to discuss ways of improving interagency cooperation and client access to all types of services.

Finally, the Child Survival/Fair Start programs also play an advocacy role in the community that complements the one-to-one support offered to families on home visits. The emphasis given to advocacy and political issues differs considerably across programs. Typically, the fact that the programs are working with the most disenfranchised families in their communities means that someone is watching and documenting the services those families actually receive from major helping institutions. The Haitian project has found that because it is gathering data on the Haitian women's receipt of prenatal care, one public health department has been motivated to sharply increase its efforts to provide prenatal care to all Haitians (not knowing which women are being followed by the project).

The process of discovering the key political issues confronting the target families, and then developing a way to address those issues without losing sight of the program goals and without compromising or embarrassing the sponsoring agency, has been a delicate task in the highly charged political atmosphere of some communities. Program resources could easily be dissipated in broad-scale advocacy for more accessible formal services and adequate economic opportunity. Child Survival/Fair Start's particular purposes are to help families cope with the invariably harmful, but community-specific effects of poverty in young families' lives.

CONCLUSIONS

Family support programs occupy a peculiar place in the social fabric. They have roots in both informal social support and formal professional service. These dual roots lead to a unique perspective on social problem solving. To paraphrase Pilisuk and Parks (1986, pp. 166-7), family support programs view human problems as rips in the tapestry of social life, and their purpose is to renew the torn fabric. Although practice in family support programs focuses on concrete problem-solving, their strength lies mainly in the less tangible act of strengthening the cloth.

The program development process, then, reflects the fact that the social fabric is torn in different ways in different communities. Each program initiative faces anew the challenge of learning how to provide new sources of support to families without supplanting or tearing down existing ones. At the community level, the parallel challenge is to open up procedures and patterns of service delivery to new sources of influence, specifically the feedback from the most disenfranchised members of the community.

REFERENCES

Andrews, S., Blumenthal, J., Johnson, D., Kahn, A., Ferguson, C., Lasater, T., Malone, P., & Wallace, D. (1984). The skills of mothering: A study of Parent Child Development Centers. *Monographs of the Society for Research in Child Development, 47* (6, Serial No. 198).

Belsky, J., Robins, E., & Gamble, W. (1984). The determinants of parental competence: Toward a contextual theory. In M. Lewis (Ed.), *Beyond the dyad* (pp. 251–279). New York: Plenum Press.

Dokecki, P., Hargrove, E., & Sandler, H. (1983). An overview of the Parent Child Development Center Social Experiment. In R. Haskins & D. Adams (Eds.), *Parent education and public policy* (pp. 80–111). Norwood, New Jersey: Ablex Publishing Corp.

Furstenburg, F. (1981). Implicating the family: Teenage parenthood and kinship involvement. In T. Ooms (Ed.), *Teenage pregnancy in a family context: Implications for policy* (pp. 131–164). Philadelphia, PA: Temple University Press.

Nachman, S., Widmayer, S., Archer, J., Moon, K., & Almeroth, N. (1984, November) *Infant feeding practices among Haitian refugees in South Florida.* Paper presented at the American Anthropology Association meeting, Denver, Colorado.

O'Leary, K., Shore, M., & Wieder, S. (1984). Contacting pregnant adolescents: Are we missing cues? *Social Casework: The Journal of Contemporary Social Work, 65*(5), 297–306.

Osofsky, J., & Osofsky, H. (1984). Psychological and developmental perspectives on expectant and new parenthood. In R. Parke (Ed.), *Review of child development research: Vol. 7. The family* (pp. 372–397). Chicago, IL: University of Chicago Press.

Pearl, A., & Reissman, F. (1965). *New careers for the poor.* New York: The Free Press.

Pilisuk, M., & Parks, S. (1986). *The healing web: Social networks and human survival.* Hanover, NH: Press of New England.

Ricciuti, H. (1977). Adverse social and biological influences on early development. In H. McGurk (Ed.), *Ecological factors in human development* (pp. 157–172). Amsterdam, Netherlands: North-Holland Press.

Richan, W. (1979). Training of lay helpers. In F. Kaslow (Ed.), *Supervision, consultation, and staff training in the helping professions* (pp. 115–132). San Francisco, CA: Jossey Bass.

Sameroff, A., & Chandler, M. J. (1975). Reproductive risk and the continuum of caretaking casualty. In F. D. Horowitz, M. Hetherington, S. Scarr-Salapatek, & G. Seigel (Eds.), *Review of child development research* (Vol. 4, pp. 187–243). Chicago, IL: University of Chicago Press.

Smith, M. (1975). Evaluation findings in Head Start Planned Variation. In A. Rivlin & P. Timpane (Eds.), *Planned variation in education* (pp. 101–112). Washington, DC: The Brookings Institution.

Stebbins, L, St. Pierre, R., Proper, E., Anderson, R., & Cerva, T. (1977). *Education as experimentation: A planned variation model.* Cambridge, MA: Abt Associates.

Thompson, M. (1986). The influence of supportive relations on the psychological well-being of teenage mothers. *Social Forces, 64*(4), 1006–1024.

Travers, J., & Light, R. (Eds.). (1982). *Learning from experience: Evaluating early childhood demonstration programs.* Washington DC: National Academy Press.

Travers, J., Nauta, M., & Irwin, N. (1982). *The effects of a social program: Final report of the Child and Family Resource Program's infant-toddler component.* Cambridge, MA: Abt Associates.

Chapter 9
The Role of Research in an Innovative Preventive Initiative*

Judith S. Musick
Linda Barbera-Stein
Ounce of Prevention Fund

INTRODUCTION

The utilization of research is a process carried out by social actors in interaction with one another. If and how research is used are empirical questions. In reviews of empirical studies on the utilization of research (Pelz, 1978; Beyer & Trice, 1982), three types of use were identified: instrumental, conceptual and symbolic. Instrumental use involves acting on research results in specific, direct ways, as is the case when technological research and innovation are used to change conditions of production (Perrow, 1970). Conceptual use involves using research results for general enlightenment where results influence actions in relatively general, indirect ways; e.g., a therapeutic ideology gives "shape" to treatment practices (Strauss, Schatzman, Bucher, Ehrlick, & Sabshin, 1964). Symbolic use involves utilizing research results to legitimate and sustain predetermined positions, as in the production of official statistics to ensure continued employment and support budget requests (Kitsuse & Cicourel, 1963).

Actors may choose any or none of these uses of research. Indeed, not all actors have knowledge of research findings, because not all social roles involve expectations of knowledge and use of research findings. Further, organizational structures vary in their capacity to facilitate the production and use of research. Kingdon (1984), for example, described the use of research in political contexts. The actors doing research and bearing knowledge of research findings in political contexts were in ancillary staff positions and distanced from political hierarchies. Political officials were those actors who set policy agendas but typically without the use of research. Research was used, however, to specify alternatives for public policy once the agenda was set. It was used conceptually to give shape to alternatives and symbolically to support policy positions. The actors making use of research in these ways were "hidden participants": academics, researchers, consultants, career bureaucrats, congressional staffers, and analysts who work for interest groups.

* The preparation of this paper was supported in part by a grant from the Rockefeller Foundation.

In contrast to the use of research findings in political contexts, Perrow (1970) described an electronics firm where management struggled with organizational design to maximize the instrumental use of research in problems of production. As personnel struggled to rationalize and routinize the firm's production, the actors doing research and bearing knowledge of research were positioned centrally in the firm's hierarchy. Consequently, if and how research is utilized depends upon the actor, what the actor does and is expected to do, and the organizational context in which the actor participates.

This chapter examines the utilization of research in the creation, shaping, and ongoing development and delivery of social services by the Ounce of Prevention Fund (OPF). OPF began in 1982 as an innovative statewide initiative in the primary prevention of child abuse and neglect. In its first year, it developed, monitored, and evaluated programs at six demonstration sites located in the State of Illinois. OPF currently administers community-based family support programs at 40 sites throughout Illinois. Its mission has been broadened to include the enhancement of family and child development among populations at risk for a complex of social problems associated with teenage pregnancy and/or resulting in child abuse and neglect.

The utilization of research on behalf of OPF programs can be understood by focusing on the actors involved in creating the initiative, shaping its programs and developing its services. Who were the actors? What concepts or ideologies did they share or argue and in what contexts? How is the production and utilization of research facilitated or obstructed by factors both internal and external to its organization?

The answers given here to these question are from the perspective of the current and founding director of OPF, Judith Musick. This paper documents her account of the role of research in the history and current nature of OPF.

THE NONUSE OF RESEARCH: SETTING THE AGENDA AND CREATING THE INITIATIVE

The political context.   In 1974, the Child Abuse Prevention and Treatment Act was created, and the prevention of child abuse became part of political agendas on the state and federal levels. In Illinois, there was increasing public awareness of the problem of child abuse. Reports of child abuse were on the rise, while budgets for social and welfare services were being trimmed.

At the time, solutions for the problem were not cost effective nor seemingly socially effective in light of an ever-increasing number of child abuse reports. These solutions were treatment oriented, reliant upon costly professional services, and administered by an unwieldy network of complex state and county bureaucracies involved in children and family services, corrections, mental health, and juvenile justice.

New approaches were in order, and their cost and social effectiveness were important political considerations. However, new approaches were not forthcoming until 1982, when a private philanthropist introduced a new approach to a state child welfare director. A meeting between these two persons (discussed below) coupled the problem of preventing child abuse, already set on the state's political agenda, with a new solution that was potentially effective though still empirically unproven.

The actors.   OPF was the creation of two forward-thinking decision makers. One, Gregory L. Coler, was a state child welfare agency director looking for and open to new ways to attack the seemingly intractable problem of child abuse. The other, Irving B. Harris, was a businessman with a long-standing philanthropic commitment to children.

In 1976, Harris had played a key role in helping Bernice Weissbourd found Family Focus, a pioneering model of community-based family support programming. There were two main themes in Weissbourd's rationale for the model: first, that the preschool or Head Start years were often too late; and second, that programs needed to be sensitive to the values of particular cultures and communities. Social and developmental problems resulting from difficulties in parenting thus could be prevented, but only if one could reach at-risk parents as early as possible and provide them with community-based programs to support them in their child-rearing roles. Presentations of the rationale generally were consistent with findings from research and clinical literatures (e.g., Garbarino & Associates, 1981). However, the scientific underpinnings of the model were cited post hoc to the articulation of the model itself. (See Weissbourd, 1987, on the history of family support programs.)

Over the years, Harris continued his involvement as a major funder, Board Chairman, and enthusiastic proponent of the Family Focus model. He was an articulate and committed spokesperson of a relatively new social service ideology, espoused by a small community of service providers in the Chicago area. The ideology emphasized the need for community-based centers with educational and social support components for families with young children.

In late 1982, Harris approached Coler, then Director of the Illinois Department of Children and Family Services, requesting funds to set up a new Family Focus program in Aurora, Illinois, where Harris had a company. The proposed program would, according to Harris, provide preventive parent support services to the highly stressed young Mexican families who lived and worked in the Aurora area. Coler, an administrator with a reputation for innovation, was intrigued by the notion of preventing child abuse and other serious parenting problems by actively promoting healthier family functioning. He offered a state child abuse grant of $400,000 to fund several such programs as demonstration models if Harris would provide matching private funds. This Harris agreed to do, and so a public-private partnership was created and named the Ounce of Prevention Fund.

Research on the community-based family support model had not been used to justify the need for OPF programs. Rather, it was more in the nature of testimonials and individual success stories from Family Focus, convincingly put forward by a private philanthropist with a long history of funding high-quality projects related to children and families. Further, these success stories of a new and creative way of addressing an old and serious problem made good sense to key figures in state government, especially Coler. The old fashioned, upbeat, nonpathological, grassroots, education-and-support orientation of the family support model (and of prevention in general) was very appealing to these decision makers. It does not act to foster dependency as do treatment oriented programs for at-risk families, and can be conceived as a form of self-help, which indeed it is. Given the political context at the time, this ethos struck just the right cord at just the right moment in Illinois.

Strongly stated beliefs, then, were used to convince others of the potential effectiveness of community-based family support programs in preventing child abuse. The creation of the OPF initiative was not generally shaped nor specifically guided by research findings. Rather, the initiative was seen as an innovative solution to a problem that had already been set on political agendas.

CONCEPTUAL USES OF RESEARCH: SHAPING OPF PROGRAMS

While research played almost no role in inspiring the OPF initiative, it was used conceptually to help design and develop OPF programs: the what, who, where, and when of OPF's initial services.

The actors shaping OPF services were under the direction of Judith Musick, a researcher and clinician by professional training and experience. OPF staff used their own educational and professional backgrounds in early childhood development to design OPF's educational and social support services for parents in community-based settings. OPF staff drew on research illustrating the effects of early parenting problems on later child development (e.g., Ainsworth & Bell, 1974; Sroufe, 1979) as well as on studies of environmental and psychological stressors as they affect parents' capacities to adequately nurture their children (e.g., Bronfenbrenner, 1979). Additionally, use was made of findings on the ameliorative effects of social support on major family problems (e.g., Whittaker & Garbarino, 1983) and on the superiority of techniques which focused on parents and/or the family system, rather than on the child alone (e.g., Bronfenbrenner, 1979).

Research also was used by OPF staff to describe who would be at greatest risk for problems associated with parenting, where they could be found, and at what point in their parenting they could best be served. According to a variety of studies (e.g., Pavenstedt, 1967; Fraiberg, 1977), those families living in communities with high rates of child maltreatment and its correlates of poverty, unemployment, infant mortality/morbidity, and single and adolescent parenthood would be at greatest risk for problems associated with parenting. This knowledge was used in developing OPF's Request for Proposals (RFP) from potential service sites. Agencies and organizations responding to the RFP needed to locate their OPF programs in such communities. Further, research on the efficacy of reaching families as early as possible (e.g., Andrews, 1981; Andrews et al., 1982) was used to guide decisions about eligibility criteria for program participants. The call was for programs which would focus on new parents, engaging them if possible during the prenatal period.

Among the initial six demonstration sites, three were exclusively for adolescent parents and three for a mixed-age population of at-risk parents with young children. While the participants in the latter group were no longer teens, they were predominately young single parents. Many had also had their first child while still a teen.

SYMBOLIC USES OF RESEARCH: ADVOCATING OPF PROGRAMS

Concurrent with the conceptual use of research in designing and developing OPF programs was the symbolic use of research in advocating OPF programs. Research served as policy's handmaiden in raising public awareness about the importance of early preventive approaches.

Clinical and research staff spent a considerable portion of their time educating potential funders, agency administrators, and community leaders about the need for and efficacy of such services as home visitors, developmental child care and parent education, and support groups. In fact, the use of these examples of concrete, comprehensible program components was powerfully persuasive—much more so than an abstract discussion of "problems" and "need for services." Public education and advocacy efforts seldom directly cited specific investigators or research projects. Rather, in advocating community-based parent support services, general statements were made. Examples are: "Research at Cornell shows the need to work with the family and community if you want to improve a child's chances" (Bronfenbrenner, 1974), and "Studies from Johns Hopkins University indicate that there are serious problems with teens as parents" (Bierman & Streett, 1982). While it may be the practice of OPF staff to discuss the nuances of various scholarly clinical and research reports among themselves, by the time these diverse materials were used in public education or advocacy, they had been synthesized and condensed. Only the essence was used, for the sake of both economy and persuasiveness.

EXTERNAL POLITICAL AND ORGANIZATIONAL INFLUENCES ON OPF'S STRUCTURE AND USES OF RESEARCH

Once an organization is created with an identity of its own, an organizational environment is created as well (Perrow, 1970). Insofar as an organization must interact with its environment, it is open to influencing and being influenced by that environment (Meyer & Associates, 1978). The symbolic uses of research by OPF staff are cases in point. In relating to outside audiences and organizations, OPF staff consciously changed their manner of using research from a conceptual to a symbolic mode. Whereas they used research conceptually to enlighten and generally shape the initial OPF programs, they used research symbolically to legitimate and support existing OPF programs.

Before the first year of the OPF initiative had passed, there was a change in the political context of OPF which had a profound effect on the size of OPF's organizational structure and its target populations and programs, as well as its uses of research. Though research had not been used in the initial political negotiations effecting the creation of the OPF initiative, it was used by OPF staff, both conceptually and symbolically, in their response to a change in political agendas.

The Impact of a Changing Political Context. By 1982, teen pregnancy had reached crisis proportions in Illinois, as in other states across the country. Governor James Thompson responded by creating the Parents Too Soon initiative (PTS), a comprehensive statewide effort designed to reduce the incidence of teenage pregnancy, to reduce the health risks associated with adolescent pregnancy (especially infant mortality), and to improve teen parents' ability to cope with the responsibilities of parenthood. PTS monies were divided among three State agencies: the departments of Public Aid, Public Health, and Children and Family Services. An RFP was issued by the Department of Children and Family Services and OPF staff responded.

In OPF's response to the RFP, OPF's first year of experiences with teens and its track record with the Department of Children and Family Services were brought together with the burgeoning research on adolescent pregnancy and parenthood, to justify the decision for shifting OPF's target populations and programming. Studies on the high incidence of child abuse (e.g., Bolton, 1980) and subsequent pregnancies on poor-prenatal-care, and low-birthweight infants among teen parents (Moore & Burt, 1982; Zelnick, Kantner & Ford, 1981), made convincing arguments for large-scale preventive efforts with this population; so too did data on school drop-outs and chronic welfare dependency.

The Department of Children and Family Services selected OPF to administer its portion of PTS monies. Early in 1983, OPF launched 22 new community-based family support programs aimed exclusively at adolescent parents and their children. Then, in the following year, 12 new pregnancy preventive programs were added for school-aged children, preteens, and their families, bringing the total number of OPF programs to 40.

The new programs for parenting teens were structurally similar to the original six sites, since the populations served were identical in some cases and closely overlapping in others. The pregnancy prevention services were naturally somewhat different, although the family-oriented philosophy and community-based outreach approach were basically the same in both types of programs.

The decision to shift from serving a mixed population of somewhat older parents as well as teens to an almost exclusive focus on teens, definitely was affected by the shift in the availability of State funds from child abuse grants to PTS monies. While OPF staff rationalized the shift in target populations as making theoretical sense because of the high rates of child abuse, infant mortality, and developmental problems in populations of parenting teens, accusations of opportunism were not without some basis in reality.

Conceptual and symbolic uses of research.   In summary, research was used by OPF staff to shape and advocate OPF programs and also to respond to shifts in political agendas and funds. But the influence of research described so far was minor relative to that of political agendas which affected the creation of the OPF initiative in the first place and then profoundly impacted upon the size of OPF's organization, its target populations, and its programs. In relating to its political and organizational environment, the importance of OPF's use of research was diminished. However, within OPF's own organizational boundaries, the role of research was enhanced to include the production and instrumental use of research. The production and instrumental use of research are integral functions of OPF's organization and essential ingredients of its current nature.

INSTRUMENTAL USES OF RESEARCH: THE EMPIRICAL BASE OF OPF'S ADMINISTRATIVE AND CLINICAL SERVICES

OPF is a somewhat unusual social service organization in its dedication to building programs on a sound empirical base. Both clinicians and researchers contribute to OPF's empirical base.

Clinicians are organized into roles called *regional program manager* and *regional coordinator*. One manager and the two coordinators under her are responsible for the program development of sites in southern Illinois. The other manager and the four coordinators under her are responsible for the program development of sites in northern Illinois, including Chicago. Sites are divided among the coordinators so that the lines of authority and accountability are quite clear.

In monitoring sites and their programs, managers and coordinators regularly visit each of their sites. They conduct on-site observations of programs and participate in meetings and discussions with service providers and participants. Observations and insights are discussed at OPF meetings and recorded in structured quarterly reports which include quantitative as well as qualitative data. Sites also submit quarterly reports which include statistics and narratives pertaining to their programs, staff, and participants. Thus, the contributions of OPF's clinical staff to OPF's empirical base include clinical observations, informal interviews, and documentary data.

Currently, there are four permanent research positions at OPF. However, the actual size of OPF's research staff varies in response to the number and extensiveness of formal research investigations at any given time.

Permanent research staff are and have been responsible for the Parents Too Soon (PTS) Tracking System. The tracking system includes demographic data and updates on all OPF participants and their children, as well as data on services rendered to each participant. Currently, the system tracks approximately 5,000 participants and 8,000 children. Statistical reports, aggregating these data, are produced monthly and annually by OPF researchers. A sample of OPF participants currently is being matched to a sample from the National Longitudinal Survey of Youth (Center for Human Resource Research, 1986) in order to compare outcomes on a number of variables, including rates of repeat pregnancy and school and employment statuses. In addition, information from a new OPF program called the Developmental Screening Project is being added to the tracking system. These data will be used to investigate issues of child development and quality of parent–child interactions among OPF participants and their children.

In addition to the tracking system and the reports and studies based upon its data, OPF researchers have conducted several other research projects.

The Adoption Study.   Semistructured interviews with groups of teen mothers and service providers were conducted at five OPF sites to investigate views on adoption as an alternative resolution to pregnancy (Musick, Handler, & Wadill, 1984). Information was gathered on the teens' psychology of sexuality, male–female relationships, kin, childbearing, pregnancy, and future life goals. Information also was gathered on service providers' attitudes toward sexuality and what they discuss or fail to talk about in the course of providing services to teen mothers.

The Child Care Study.   This is a study of 101 teen mothers and their 2-year-old children. Interviews and observational scales were used with the mothers to document a variety of factors, including family history, health, social support networks, and division of labor regarding child care. Dimensions of the children's development were assessed using formal instruments such as the Bayley Scales of Infant Development (Bayley, 1969), the Preschool Language Scale (Zimmerman, Steiner, & Pond, 1979), and the Greenspan Rating Scale (Greenspan & Poisson, 1983). The HOME Inventory (Caldwell & Bradley, 1979) also was used to assess the quality of home environments and parent–child interactions (See Musick, Gershenson, Syc, Umeh, & Rosenberg, 1986.)

Sexual Abuse Survey.   This is a survey of the prevalence of sexual abuse among 445 teen mothers who were participants in OPF programs. Data were gathered on the age(s) at victimization, number of occurrences, relationship and age of perpetrator, and number of perpetrators. The survey data, in conjunction with journals kept by teen mothers and group leaders participating in Heart-to-Heart, a sexual abuse prevention program (discussed below), provide a close view of socialization into sexuality through sexual abuse and victimization.

Peer Power.   This is an evaluation of a pregnancy prevention program using random assignment and a pretest-posttest control group design. Observational, interview, and questionnaire data were collected from 60 7th and 8th grade females (control group, n = 30; experimental group, n = 30). (See Handler, 1987.) Data were gathered on knowledge and attitudes toward sexuality, sexual decision making, self-esteem, male–female relationships, sexual and other victimization, school functioning, and life goals. Like the data from Heart-to-Heart and the Sexual Abuse Survey, these data also document aspects of the adolescents' socialization experiences with sexual abuse and victimization.

Although the projects vary in the scientific rigor of their design and methods of data collection, they contribute to the richness, breath, and depth of OPF's empirical base. The sites themselves also add to the richness of OPF's empirical base. Sites are located in large urban centers, small towns, and rural areas; they serve black, white, and Hispanic families, ranging in socioeconomic status from extremely poor and welfare dependent to stable working class.

In conjunction with theory, OPF staff use this empirical base, with its contributions from both clinical and research personnel, to design and field test new preventive approaches and evaluate their effectiveness. Sites are engaged in research and programmatic changes as a condition of their funding. The production of a growing empirical base, and the instrumental use of clinical and research findings, to shape, refine and correct services are routine work activities at OPF. OPF's empirical base both documents OPF's work and measures its effectiveness.

OPF's organizational goal is nothing less than the achievement of significant positive changes in high-risk families and communities targeted by OPF programs. Successes and failures at achieving this goal are grounded in empirical data, a tough standard by which to assess accountability and judge effectiveness. However, falling short of the goal does not necessarily threaten OPF's viability. Rather, setbacks or failures are the impetus for growth—additional research and program development. The viability of OPF as an organization thus rests upon its being a self-correcting system of administrative and clinical services.

Professional Backgrounds of OPF Staff

Not surprisingly, such complex, multidimensional work could not be carried out by an organization staffed with the traditional mix of social work and child welfare administrators which characterizes most social service programs in the public and private sectors. Because of this, OPF staff are recruited very thoughtfully and selected with the goal of maintaining an interdisciplinary team capable of working with and speaking to a variety of audiences.

Core staff includes professionals from the fields of maternal–child health (public health); social work; early childhood development; developmental, counseling and educational psychology; child welfare; nursing; and public administration. This team of approximately 18 senior-level clinical and research staff provide ongoing training and technical assistance to the projects in the central office and to the sites in the field. The team is also responsible for developing research tools and conducting assessments of OPF programs and participants.

Training, research and program development are discussed at formal and informal meetings of core staff, with periodic input from University-based researchers who have special interests in one or more OPF projects. Discussions span diverse fields of knowledge: infant and early childhood development; parent–child and family relationships; social support; maternal–child health; adolescent development; child abuse and neglect; education; psychopathology/mental health; risk-taking behavior; and manpower development. Decisions about training, research, and program development thus are based on an integration of field observations and OPF evaluation data with current theory and research from a variety of disciplines.

The Integration of Research and Clinical Work

OPF's clinical and research components are highly interactive. Clinical observations inspire new services as well as new lines of research, while research findings are used to design, evaluate, and correct clinical services. The following examples illustrate the interaction between OPF's clinical and research components, as well as the self-correcting nature of OPF's work. The first two examples are from initial bodies of data which indicated discrepancies between OPF service goals and those of site directors and service providers, and resulting problems in the implementation of services.

PTS Tracking System.   Data from the tracking system were among the first to indicate problems in the implementation of service goals and delivery of OPF services. Some sites had significantly higher rates of low birth weight, prematurity, and repeat pregnancy than other sites. The demographic heterogeneity among populations of participants and communities might contribute to the differences in rates among the sites. However, demographic profiles cannot be manipulated by OPF staff. OPF staff questioned whether or not the values of service providers, commitment of an agency to OPF goals, and levels of implementation might be critical discriminating factors as well. These factors could be manipulated by OPF staff through changes in the training and technical assistance provided to sites and service providers. Data from the Adoption Study gave OPF staff further information as well as insights into how training and technical assistance to sites might be improved.

The Adoption Study.   In the first year of the initiative, OPF staff received a grant from the Administration for Children, Youth and Families to examine why so few adolescents consider adoption as an alternative resolution to pregnancy (Moore & Burt, 1982). Analysis of taped interviews indicated the reluctance of service providers to even broach the topic of adoption (Musick, Handler & Wadill, 1984) and the lack of motivation of teen girls to *not* become parents. These findings were used to revise and refine training and service programs.

In training sessions, service providers were guided by OPF staff in discus-

sions of controversial topics, such as adoption, in an effort to help them overcome their ambivalence about these topics and to clarify their values. They also
were encouraged to be forthright and authoritative in guiding teen mothers. The
service programs themselves were changed in form and content. Service providers were able to be somewhat more directive than they had been, and program
agendas specifically included such topics as adoption and sexuality for discussion with participants.

The impetus to change training and service programs came not only from relatively formal efforts at data collection, such as the PTS Tracking System and
Adoption Study, but also from an integration of observations and assessments
made by clinical staff as they regularly monitored programs. Whereas both the
PTS Tracking System and Adoption Study are examples of research influencing
program development, including changes in training and technical assistance, the
Developmental Screening Project illustrates the reverse process.

The Developmental Screening Project.   The provision of comprehensive
outreach and community-based services for adolescent parents was OPF's first
step in the delivery of prevention services. However, over the course of several
years of monitoring and observing such services, OPF staff became dissatisfied
with the results of their efforts to measurably improve developmental outcomes
for the *children* of teen parents. OPF staff reasoned that, if developmental outcomes for children were expected to improve, then services directly oriented toward positively affecting parenting practices were needed. Further, because of
the increased probability of risk for the infants of teen parents, early and concerted efforts also would have to be made to identify children in need of intervention services.

An effort such as this presents a challenge for prevention (as opposed to
small-scale intervention/treatment) programs, since they must provide a wide
range of services for a great many families within their communities and generally are staffed at the direct service level by either trained paraprofessionals from
the community or social work/counseling professionals. As OPF staff observed
the programs, they found that, although service providers may have had extensive experience with adults and adolescents, they had little education, training,
or work experience related to children. This lack of in-depth knowledge of child
development was a barrier to full implementation of services targeted *directly* to
parent–child relationships and to the early identification of any developmental
delays or handicapping conditions these children might have. While service providers could enroll a teen mother in a GED or employment readiness program or
help her to feel better about herself, they did little with the teen as a parent and
virtually ignored her child.

Beyond this, OPF staff became skeptical about a basic tenet of family support
programs: When a mother is doing well in her own life, it somehow automati-
cally makes her a better parent. Improved adult functioning was expected to improve her child's development. OPF staff did not find this to be the case. In fact,

many young women do quite well themselves (e.g., finished school and secured employment) while remaining inadequate parents (Brooks-Gunn & Furstenberg, 1986).

Therefore, in order to serve *children* better, OPF's training program was expanded to include a greater emphasis on positively influencing parenting and child outcomes than had heretofore been the case. These changes brought about only small improvements in the situation, until they were coupled with the implementation of a specially designed program of developmental screening.

The screening project, which was initially launched at three pilot sites, focused on the presence of potentially handicapping conditions and developmental delays, as well as early or precursor signs of social-emotional dysfunction and problems around the parent–child relationship (Bernstein, Percansky, & Hans, 1987). A component to address the parent–child relationship was included because of OPF staff's growing concern about teen parents' abilities to adequately nurture their children. Many of the interactional problems observed in somewhat older, troubled mothers by investigators such as Fraiberg, Adelson, and Shapiro (1980), Greenspan (1981), and Musick, Cohler, Stott, and Klehr (1987) can be found among adolescent mothers. OPF research and clinical staff had observed young mothers to be generally less responsive and less involved with their children than older mothers. They looked at and talked to their babies less often, held them less closely, had less reciprocal interaction, and preferred physical interaction as opposed to interaction involving verbal and visual stimulation. The new screening program was the first step in a major new initiative designed to improve these relationships. Staff now would have to be trained in child development in order to use the screening techniques, and use of the screening techniques would guide staff in focusing on parent–child interactions and relationships.

As explained above, data from the Developmental Screening Project is being added to the PTS Tracking System and likely will be the basis for new research investigations.

Child Care Study. The importance of the parenting role for child development also is evident in the analysis of data from the Child Care Study. For example, there was markedly greater competence among those toddlers whose mothers provided mediated learning experiences, such as looking at picture books and reading or interacting with objects, than among those who were not engaged in such joint activities. The differences are especially notable because they were independent of maternal I.Q. (Musick, Gershenson, Umeh, Syc, & Rosenberg, 1986).

Insights such as these, embedded in OPF's growing understanding of subpopulations at greatest risk, are being used in OPF teen parent programs and public education efforts. They are also an integral part of OPF's newest project, the Center for Successful Child Development, a comprehensive research and demonstration program for infants and parents residing in the Robert Taylor Homes housing project. Much of what has been learned over the past years is thus going towards the development of the next generation of service, training, and research programs.

Heart-to-Heart.   OPF began several years ago to take a close look at the problem of child sexual abuse. Program staff at sites across the state had been reporting disclosures of sexual abuse among their program participants. Staff at one site reported that every participant in one of its larger parent-education groups had disclosed experiences of sexual victimization. Clearly, teen parents were a very high risk group. These facts pointed to the need to offer a child sexual abuse prevention program for adolescent parents. OPF launched a full scale review of current resources and programs addressing the problem of child sexual abuse.

In surveying available resources, OPF staff discovered that most child sexual abuse prevention programs focused attention primarily on educating and raising the awareness of the potential child/victim, with almost no attention given to the parents' role and responsibility in protecting their children. Additionally, almost all programs are for older children and thus not developmentally appropriate for children from birth to age 3. Unfortunately, the youngest children are the most vulnerable of potential victims. Certainly it is valuable to teach older children about exploitative physical contact, but what happens to infants and preschoolers who are not yet capable of expressing themselves verbally? In addition, since most children are sexually abused by persons known to them, it becomes the *parents'* responsibility to protect their infants and small children from threatening and unsafe situations.

A review of existing resources found no programs for this population in urgent need of a program—adolescents who were pregnant or parenting, many of whom were survivors of sexual abuse. OPF's clinical observations indicated that the infants and young children of such young women are highly vulnerable because their teenage mothers: (a) may have experienced or still be experiencing abuse within their own homes and neighborhoods; (b) may not be developmentally capable of providing safe, nurturing, and appropriate child care; and (c) may casually expose their child to a number of persons who have only transient interest in the well-being of the child.

In order to protect very young children and their adolescent mothers from sexual abuse, OPF staff reasoned that mothers would need to be educated about the incidence, causes, and effects of child sexual abuse and provided with a supportive atmosphere in which to discuss and come to terms with their own abusive experiences. Once given this opportunity, parents then could be taught specific strategies for protecting their children. Communities also would be made aware of the problem of child sexual abuse and of the appropriate resources required to solve the problem on an individual and community-wide basis. Finally, there would have to be a component directed to males. Since OPF staff found no program which contained these components, they decided to create one. In 1986, OPF began work on a child sexual abuse prevention demonstration program for pregnant and parenting teens. *Heart-to-Heart,* as it was called, is an intensive

10-week program designed to include group support, education for mothers and public awareness components for community involvement.

During 1986, the Heart to Heart model was pilot tested at three demographically different sites. The effectiveness of materials and procedures was measured, and revisions undertaken. At the same time, a survey of the prevalence of sexual victimization among pregnant and parenting adolescents was conducted at 19 sites across the state. The findings from this study are very sobering. Of the 445 mothers taking part in the assessment, 61% had experienced sexual victimization and 65% of these victims had been abused by more than one perpetrator on multiple occasions (Gershenson & Musick, 1987). The Heart to Heart model currently is undergoing a second, more extensive field test in anticipation of replication at the other 37 sites. Later, after this second field test of the model, it will be available for dissemination to other organizations.

Data from Heart to Heart and Peer Power, as well as from interviews with hundreds of adolescents, pointed to the strongly coercive nature of much adolescent sexual behavior. Socialized early into the passive role of victim, a very high proportion of the young women in OPF programs find themselves in sexually abusive relationships with older males beginning in the early middle-school years. Evidence of the relationship between sexual victimization, early initiation of sexual activity, and teen pregnancy sheds new light on a complex problem. Unless prevention programs are prepared to grapple with this "touchy" issue, they may fail to reach a significant subpopulation of preteens and teens. Knowledge, values, and decision-making skills are clearly necessary and useful for some participants, but they are probably beside the point for these young women until they have gained some emotional distance on this painful aspect of their lives. Valuable insights afforded by such programs and research have enabled OPF staff to develop effective strategies for dealing with a neglected but serious problem.

Summary

OPF staff are bearers of professional knowledge, including research findings. Staff are organized into roles specifically involving the use of clinical and research methodologies of observation, documentation, and analysis. OPF's clinical and research components are highly interactive: programs inspire new research, and research leads to program development. On a routine basis, information is produced and used. Ideas are tested in the field, and the "field" for OPF is a heterogeneous sample of high-risk communities throughout the State of Illinois. OPF truly is an experimenting organization which makes instrumental use of research.

BARRIERS TO THE APPLICATION OF RESEARCH FINDINGS

It is heartening when research can be used to inform policy and programming, and discouraging when such worthwhile endeavors are thwarted. This is particularly true when research findings have the potential for affecting positive change for children and families. In the first sections of this chapter, the utilization of research by OPF staff was described. This section addresses the difficulties faced when evaluation or clinical research data point to hard truths for policy makers or program developers.

Looking at data gathered from programs and participants, OPF staff, in collaboration with several nationally known experts, saw evidence of a link between childhood sexual victimization, early initiation of sexual activity, and teen pregnancy. Interestingly, there was at first strong resistance to this notion in certain quarters. Conservative groups who viewed teen pregnancy prevention as needing to take place only within the family ignored the evidence and failed to understand that, for some young women, the family was the problem, not the solution. Decision makers are sometimes reluctant to acknowledge that not all families can be helped and that some community norms are not conducive to healthy sexual or personal development. At times, particularly in regard to what an adolescent parent is going to do about her future, program staff have to give up trying to engage her family and instead put their energies into helping her "decouple" from a toxic, growth-inhibiting family system. When this happens, a program must, to a certain degree, function as a transitional family or it cannot possibly hope to reach the young person.

OPF staff have found concepts such as these to be unpopular with some liberal as well as conservative thinkers, because the credo of family support stresses the obligation to work with the family. However, community norms which encourage exploitation of girls and discourage responsible decision making about family planning must be acknowledged as hindering forward movement for young females. Such acknowledgement does not imply that all families or all community values are negative influences, only that some are. OPF evaluations and clinical research reports document the difficulties encountered by many young people in our programs as they struggle to succeed and to "do it better" than, or differently from, their parents.

Other "hard truths" go against prevailing theory and practice in social service provision. For example, adolescents are not like adult therapeutic clients. They seek—indeed, they seem to crave—direction, straight talk, and explicitly stated values, even when they appear to rebel against them. Empathic listening is necessary, but it is insufficient in facilitating positive change in stressed and troubled young people. If a program's goal is for its participants to be better parents and more responsible decision makers, strong guidance and clear expectations will be needed. Teen parent programs need not be judgemental, but they cannot be value free.

Recent social welfare policy has emphasized the importance of jobs for teen parents in order to prevent a lifetime of welfare dependency and social incompetence (Quint, Polit, & Guy, 1986). OPF data give striking evidence of the naive and simplistic nature of this notion, particularly in regard to young teen parents or those with few skills who already have more than one child. The road to employment will be long and rough, and, all too often, the children will suffer (e.g., Musick, Gershenson, Umeh, Syc & Rosenberg, 1986). There can be no unidimensional solution to the multi-dimensional problem of dysfunctional patterns of living. Those who put their faith in employment as the answer have not yet been willing to accept this fact.

Perhaps the most troublesome obstacles to the application of research evidence have been those surrounding the use of paraprofessionals in home visitor, parent group facilitator, and other direct service roles. Troubled and chaotic families and communities are not the only barriers to lasting positive changes in young people. In many cases, the limitations of service staff can present formidable barriers as well. Young people in community-based programs must generally rely on service providers who, while caring and well-meaning, may nonetheless be severely limited by their own poorly or inadequately resolved problems with, e.g., sexuality, parenting, and autonomy. As the teens, they too may have unresolved issues around success, change, and separation from the norms and behaviors of their own families and friends. Paraprofessional staff often are able to help a teen mother stay in or return to school, but they often cannot help her be a better parent because to do so touches on fears about their own too-early parenting. Similarly, they may not be able to give consistent, straightforward guidance on sexual behavior and values because of personal conflicts arising from their own experiences with early and/or prolonged sexual victimization. Limitations such as these pose a very real challenge for program development. They affect every level of service provision, and severely limit program implementation.

Using the rich and varied material that comprises OPF's empirical base, OPF staff saw the magnitude of these limitations and attempted to restructure OPF's training and technical assistance system. While acknowledging the concern, senior level OPF staff felt conflicted about how to remedy the problem. Employing paraprofessional indigeneous staff is very appealing to program directors, policy makers and the general public because of its relatively low cost and congruence with a grassroots approach. The notion of community-based programs is central to prevention philosophy. It makes sense to attack social problems by engaging insiders in the battle to overcome the social and family problems of their communities. However, as OPF staff examined program difficulties, they came face to face with the lack of human as well as material resources in underclass communities (Wilson, 1985). OPF staff, therefore, were obliged to bring both program and policy decision makers the unwelcome news that, if they wanted to have a noticeable positive impact on family functioning and child development outcomes, they were going to have to spend a little more money and a lot more time in the training and supervision of their staff than had heretofore been the case. There was little doubt that even well-trained paraprofessionals were going to require considerable ongoing input from specialists. OPF staff could give program development assistance, but agency directors would need to be committed to the enterprise and willing to release staff for training. In like manner, policy makers and the general public would have to commit to longer range more realistic goals, and stop expecting and pressing for a "quick fix."

CONCLUSION

OPF's insistence on *realistic* prevention strategies has resulted in slow but steady shifts in the attitudes of Illinois decision makers. The presence of OPF and its role as a research-using and -producing organization has acted as a catalyst for a number of positive changes at the program, community, and state levels. OPF programs and research projects have been instrumental in raising awareness about teen pregnancy, child development, and parent support and have created a climate which fosters the growth of child- and family-oriented initiatives. Cities, even very conservative ones such as Peoria and Moline, have organized task forces involving a broad sector of their communities in creative efforts to prevent teen pregnancy. In 1986, Governor Thompson launched a statewide Infant Mortality Reduction Initiative (IMRI) and more recently called for even greater emphasis on the young child (Inaugural address by Governor James R. Thompson, January 12, 1987). The structure and proposed content of the IMRI community-based networks closely resembles that of OPF programs; the rationale for focusing on children, particularly at-risk infants and young children, is based in large part on the OPF experience.

The Developmental Screening Program and Center for Successful Child Development were both created out of a concern that teen parent programs were failing to address either parenting per se or the prevention of developmental problems in children. The research of others on the critical importance of the early years was integrated with OPF's own clinical and research data to make the case for these programs. This, in turn, was used by Irving Harris to encourage state and federal policy makers to make an investment in young children. The State also has funded a national symposium on the treatment and prevention of child sexual abuse. The symposium spotlights Heart-to-Heart as a promising prevention model with lessons to teach about breaking transgenerational cycles of psychosocial pathology.

OPF staff now are engaged in the task of using what they have learned to affect changes in federal, as well as state policy, and to educate the public about prevention. At the same time, they are undertaking a new generation of intervention studies based on the experiences of the last 5 years. These investigations will examine questions of family functioning in relation to successful program outcome, and effective versus ineffective strategies for fostering better parenting and reducing subsequent pregnancies. They also are interested in gathering longer-term outcome data on parents and children participating in the 40 PTS programs and the new Center for Successful Child Development. Like their predecessors, these studies grow out of OPF's continuing quest for meaningful answers to complex, serious problems. Hopefully, they too will add to the knowledge in this field and, in so doing, will make a contribution to the prevention of wasted lives and unfulfilled potential.

REFERENCES

Ainsworth, M., & Bell, S. (1974). Mother–infant interaction and the development of competence. In K. Connolly J. Bruner (Eds.), *The growth of competence*. New York: Academic Press.

Andrews, S. (1981). Mother–infant interaction and child development: Findings from an experimental study of parent-child programs. In M. Begab, H. Haywood, & H. Garber (Eds.), *Psychosocial influences in retarded performance: Strategies for improving competence*. Baltimore, MD: University Park Press.

Andrews, S., Blumenthal, J., Johnson, D., Kahn, A., Ferguson, C., Laseter, T., Malone, P., & Wallace, D. (1982). The skills of mothering: A study of parent child development centers. *Monographs of the Society for Research in Child Development, 47* (6, Serial No. 198).

Bayley, N. (1969). *Bayley Scales of Infant development: Manual*. New York: Psychological Corporation.

Bernstein, V., Percansky, C., & Hans, S. (1987, April). *Screening for social-emotional impairment in infants born to teenage mothers*. Paper presented at the biennual meeting of the Society for Research in Child Development, Baltimore.

Beyer, J., & Trice, H. (1982). The utilization process: A conceptual framework and synthesis of empirical findings. *Administrative Science Quarterly, 27*, 591-622.

Bierman, B., & Streett, R. (1982). Adolescent girls as mothers: Problems in parenting. In I. Stuart & C. Wells (Eds.), *Pregnancy in adolescence: needs, problems, and management* (pp. 407-426). New York: Van Nastrand Co.

Bolton, Jr., F. (1980). *The pregnant adolescent*. Beverly Hills, CA: Sage.

Bronfenbrenner, U. (1974). Is early education effective? *Columbia Teachers College Record, 76*, 279-303.

Bronfenbrenner, U. (1979). *The ecology of human development*. Cambridge, MA: Harvard University Press.

Brooks-Gunn, J., & Furstenberg, Jr., F. (1986). The children of adolescent mothers: Physical, academic, and psychological outcomes. *Developmental Review, 6*, 224-251.

Caldwell, B., & Bradley, R. (1979). *HOME observation for measurement of the environment*. Little Rock, AR: University of Arkansas at Little Rock, Center for Child Development and Education.

Center for Human Resource Research. (1986). *The national longitudinal surveys handbook*. Columbus, OH: Center for Human Resource Research, Ohio State University.

Fraiberg, S. (1977). *Every child's birthright: In defense of mothering*. New York: Basic Books.

Fraiberg, S., Adelson, E., & Shapiro, V. (1980). Ghosts in the nursery: A psychoanalytic approach to the problems of impaired mother-infant relationships. in S. Fraiberg (Ed.), *Clinical studies in infant mental health: The first year of life* (pp. 164-196). New York: Basic Books.

Garbarino, J., & Associates. (1981). *Children and families in the social environment*. New York: Aldine.

Gershenson, H., & Musick, J. (1987, April). *Three new studies on environmental risk for the children of teenage mothers*. Paper presented at the biennial meeting of the Society for Research in Child Development, Baltimore.

Greenspan, S. (1981). Psychopathology and adaptation in infancy and early childhood: Principles of clinical diagnosis and preventive intervention. *Clinical Infant Reports: Report I*. New York: International Universities Press.

Greenspan, S., & Poisson, S. (1983). *Greenspan-Lieberman Observation System for Assessment of Caregiver-Infant Interaction During Semi-structured play (GLOS)*. Rockville, MD: Division of Maternal and Child Health, HRSA, DHHS.

Handler, A. (1987). *An evaluation of a school-based adolescent pregnancy prevention program*. Unpublished doctoral dissertation, University of Illinois, Chicago, IL.

Kingdon, J. (1984). *Agendas, alternatives, and public policies*. Boston: Little, Brown.

Kitsuse, J., & Cicourel, A. (1963). A note on the use of official statistics. *Social Problems, 2*, 131-139.

Meyer, M., & Associates. (1978). *Environments and organizations*. San Francisco, CA: Jossey Bass.

Moore, K., & Burt, M. (1982). *Private crisis, public cost*. Washington, DC: Urban Institute Press.

Musick, J., Cohler, B., Stott, F., & Klehr, K. (1987). Maternal factors related to vulnerability and resiliency in young children at risk. In E. Anthony & B. Cohler (Eds.), *The invulnerable child* (pp. 229-252). New York: Guilford.

Musick, J., Gershenson, H. Umeh, B., Syc, S., & Rosenberg, D. (1986). *A statewide study of the effects of child care on the children of adolescent mothers*. Chicago: Ounce of Prevention Fund.

Musick, J., Handler, A., & Waddill, K. (1984). Teens and adoption: A pregnancy resolution alternative? *Children Today, 13*, 24-29.

Pavenstedt, E. (Ed.). (1967). *The drifters: Children of disorganized lower class families*. Boston: Little, Brown.

Pelz, D. (1978). Some expanded perspectives on use of social science in public policy. In M. Yinger & S. Cutler (Eds.), *Major social issues: a multidisciplinary view*. New York: Free Press.

Perrow, C. (1970). *Organizational analysis: A sociological view*. Belmont, CA: Wadsworth.

Quint, J., Polit, D., & Guy, C. (1986). *New chance: Laying the groundwork for a new demonstration to build human capital among low-income young mothers*. New York: Manpower Demonstration Research Corporation.

Sroufe, L. A. (1979). Socio-emotional development. In J. Osofsky (Ed.), *Handbook of infant development* (pp. 462-516). New York: Wiley.

Strauss, A., Schatzman, L., Bucher, R., Ehrlick, D., & Sabshin, M. (1964). *Psychiatric ideologies and institutions*. New York: Free Press.

Thompson, J. (1987). Inaugural address. State of Illinois, 1987.

Weissbourd, B. (1987). A brief history of family support programs. In S. L. Kagan, D. R. Powell, B. Weissbourd, & E. F. Zigler (Eds.), *America's family support programs: Perspectives and prospects* (pp. 38-56). New Haven, CT: Yale University Press.

Whittaker, J., & Garbarino, J. (1983). *Social support networks*. New York: Aldine.

Wilson, W. (1985, May). *Cycles of deprivation and the underclass debate*. Lecture delivered at the ninth annual Social Service Review, School of Social Service Administration, University of Chicago.

Zelnick, M., Kantner, J., & Ford, K. (1981). *Adolescent pathways to pregnancy*. Final report to the National Institute for Child Health and Human Development.

Zimmerman, I., Steiner, V., & Pond, R. (1979). *PLS: Preschool language scale: manual*. Columbus, OH: Charles Merrill.

Chapter 10
Challenges in the Design and Evaluation of Parent–Child Intervention Programs

Douglas R. Powell
Purdue University

The chapters in this volume contain abundant evidence of a potential shift in the paradigm that guides the design, implementation, and evaluation of programs for parents. The conventional program development model calls for predetermined and well-specified planned experiences to be delivered in uniform fashion to participants. As described in Chapter 1 and illustrated in subsequent chapters, inherent weaknesses of this top-down, professionally driven approach have led to emerging directions in matching programs to parents, in the nature of program–parent relations, and in programmatic attention to the social context of parenthood. The directions hold promise of improving the method and effectiveness of educational and support programs for parents. At the same time, new problems have surfaced in existing efforts to address the limitations of traditional strategies of parent education. Whether a paradigm shift is realized in parent programs depends largely on adequate resolution of the new problems and issues.

The aim of this final chapter is to provide a point of departure for future work in the development and evaluation of programs for parents of young children considered to be at development risk. It draws upon chapters in this volume to identify key challenges in the design and evaluation of parent–oriented early intervention programs. In many ways the chapter is a continuation of Chapter 1. The three emerging directions described in Chapter 1 are used as an organizing framework for pointing to unresolved and unanswered problems in parent program design and research.

Matching Programs and Parents

Matching programs and parents: What dimensions? Without doubt, there is movement in the parent education field to match program structure and content to the needs and characteristics of parents. This theme is found in nearly every chapter in this volume. To operationalize the idea, a conceptual framework is necessary: At present, we are en route without a road map. Ideally, program designers need a theoretically driven and research-based chart of the types of intervention approaches that are likely to be effective with different populations. The appearance of such a chart is a long way off. Its development would be aided considerably by a conceptual guide that delineates the dimensions or variables that need to be considered in decisions about person–program match. To date, most discussions of critical variables have dealt with program structure (group-versus home-based) and parenting information and skill needs (e.g., Dokecki, Roberts, & Moroney, 1979).

One candidate nominated for consideration in decisions about program–parent match by chapters in this volume is the congruence of perceived needs of parents among parents and program providers. That is, the "goodness of fit" between parent and program may be partly a function of the level of agreement among parent and program worker about the definition of, and programmatic response to, parenting needs. This phenomenon can be thought of as a shared world view. It is evident in Dunst and Trivette's (Chapter 7) principle that program services should be congruent with the parent's perception of what is needed. It also is seen in Cochran's (Chapters 2 a nd 4) argument that program substance should be defined by the participants. In addition, Halpern and Larner (Chapter 8) indirectly point to the importance of shared world views in their premise that program design ultimately is shaped by what key actors (providers, parents, sponsoring agencies) think parents need. Some issues in operationalizing this dimension of program–parent match are noted in a subsequent section of this chapter. The point here is that program–parent agreement about the nature of parents' needs warrants consideration in decisions about matching parent and program.

Research reported in this volume points to child gender, family structure, and race as participant characteristics in need of further investigation relative to program design. The finding that the school functioning of girls but not boys appeared to benefit from the Syracuse Family Development Research Program (Lally, Mangione, & Honig, Chapter 5) contributes to a growing research literature on interactions between gender and effects of early childhood intervention programs (e.g., Miller & Bizzell, 1983). More needs to be known about the nature and antecedents of interactions between program and child gender. Cochran's (Chapter 2) research suggests that family structure and race may mediate program effects. Again, future work needs to determine what specific attributes of these variables are operating in relation to program participation and outcome.

While the existing data on aptitude–treatment interactions in parent programs are too equivocal to permit a specification of program design implications, the findings increase the field's expectations about necessary analyses for research on program participation and effects. Future investigations are likely to be deemed simplistic and incomplete if there is no serious consideration of potential interactions between program effects and participant characteristics.

Evaluation designs.   The individualization of program services to parents' needs presents major methodological hurdles to program evaluators (Powell, 1987). Uniformity in the delivery of the treatment variable is a central element of the experimental design. While there are research designs to accommodate some variation in the treatment condition (e.g., treatment partitioning; see Seitz, 1987), the considerable range in content, duration, and frequency of services inherent in the individualized approach leaves the evaluator with a choice between individual case studies or a global treatment–control group comparison that defies specification of the treatment variable. The former may illuminate program life for particular families but is unlikely to provide convincing evidence of a program's effectiveness. The latter design, which ignores variation in the treatment variable, lacks precision and power in the explanation of program effects; it leaves unanswered the key question of what was or was not operating in the intervention program to cause or not cause effects. A major challenge is to augment conventional evaluation designs to accommodate the varied realities of program life from the participant perspective.

Reaching the hard-to-reach.   Recruiting and sustaining the involvement of parents living in exceptionally stressful circumstances is a persistent problem in social intervention programs. There are data in the present volume (Lally, Mangione, & Honig, Chapter 5) and elsewhere (e.g., Slaughter, 1983; Seitz, Rosenbaum, & Apfel, 1985) to indicate early intervention programs involving parents living in poverty can have positive effects on child and parent behavior. There also are data, however, to suggest that subsets of a population to be served do not respond to the program in the intended manner. For example, the Family Matters program, while not targeted exclusively for a low-income population, had lower utilization rates among parents from lower-income families (Mindick, Chapter 3). Also, the home-based program for rural, poor adolescent mothers organized by Unger and Wandersman (Chapter 6) did not sustain the participation of mothers who were highly mobile and had limited or no ties to their families. The concern generated by data of this type is a familiar one: Are intervention programs serving those who may need the program the most?

A major challenge is to determine the conditions under which education and support programs can be useful to parents experiencing high levels of environmental stress. As discussed in Chapter 1, one strategy is to offer program services that help parents reduce the negative effects of environmental stress. While this approach has merit, it can lead to a new set of program issues and does not necessarily contribute to positive change in the child (see "Balancing Child, Parent, and Family Needs" below). It also cannot be carried out with limited financial resources. Contributions to this volume suggest that advances in our understanding of how programs might serve the hard-to-reach require, among other things, recognition of variations in the nature and effects of poverty (Halpern & Larner, Chapter 8) and in the characteristics of nonusers of programs (Unger & Wandersman, Chapter 6); and program sensitivity to and support of the parents' existing sources of informal and formal help (Dunst & Trivette, Chapter 7; Halpern & Larner, Chapter 8).

Organizational structure and decision-making.   Mindick's (Chapter 3) analysis of the decision-making structure of the Family Matters program points to a critical unanswered question in the field: What types of internal arrangement of staff roles, communication patterns, and decision-making structures enable a program to learn about and respond to characteristics of its client pool? Mindick raises questions about the utility of egalitarian staff relations for social intervention programs that have a short lifespan and lack a well-trained, homogeneous staff from the outset. Minimal hierarchical arrangements can deter prompt decision making and inhibit needed staff supervision. On the other hand, there is a perspective in the organizational literature—stemming from a classic study of organization–environment relations (Burns & Stalker, 1961)—that calls for informal and flexible systems of internal communication and change in organizations operating in new or changing environments.

Conceptual and empirical work is needed to answer the question of how intervention programs can best organize themselves to learn about and respond to potential and actual participants. The literature on organization–environment relations provides a useful framework for addressing this challenge. Work reported in this volume is illustrative of needed directions in organizational research and experimentation with program mechanisms for gathering information on participant needs and program responsiveness. In particular, the field needs examination of the use of program-generated research as a feedback on organizational functioning (Musick & Barbera-Stein, Chapter 9), the conditions that lead to change in the design and practices of ongoing programs (Halpern & Larner, Chapter 8), and relations between organizational decision making structure and organizational effectiveness (Mindick, Chapter 3).

Realignment of Parent-Professional Relations

Targeted programs and the nondeficit model.   As described in Chapter 1, criticism of the deficit model was a major precursor of the movement toward more co-equal parent–staff relations in parent programs. However, there is a basic incongruity between the nondeficit model and the practice of targeting programs for parents of children considered to be at risk. The term *intervention* connotes a dysfunctional situation in need of treatment. When particular populations are viewed as "needier" than others, what assumptions are operating about the resourcefulness of parents? Is it feasible to carry out a nondeficit program for parents who have been labeled "high risk"? (Weiss, 1987). The Family Matters program (Cochran, Chapters 2 and 4) is a striking example of a strong "no" response to this question. In this program, a range of neighborhoods and parents were intentionally recruited to participate; so-called family inadequacies or deficiencies were not used as a demonstration of program need. The prevailing social service ideology and practice of targeting special populations for programs provides a context that is orthogonal if not antagonistic to the assumptions of a nondeficit approach. Most members of the medical, psychological, and social work professions view families as less than capable caregivers (Moroney, 1980). Professional training programs and the pathology-oriented ethos of human service institutions are powerful socialization agents in instilling the medical model of professional–client relations. The Family Matters experiment and similar nondeficit programs are anomalies in the system.

An obvious resolution of this incongruity is to alter societal values and practices that contribute to the targeted program approach. Indeed, a key public policy issue is whether our society can adapt a human service orientation that assumes most if not all parents could benefit from informal and formal support systems for child rearing (Kagan, Powell, Weissbourd, & Zigler, 1987; Kamerman & Kahn, 1976), or maintain the current residual welfare state wherein the poor are seen as incapable of providing for themselves (Titmuss, 1968, 1974). This is a complicated policy issue in need of careful exploration (see Moroney, 1987). Another partial resolution of the nondeficit program/ targeted population incongruity is to alter the rationale for aiming programs at given populations. For instance, Laosa (1979) has proposed a sociocultural paradigm to explain retarded educational and economic development of black, Hispanic and similarly placed children. In this paradigm, social competence involves functional adaptations to more than one environment. No society or subculture is superior to others; a child's success in two different environments (e.g., home and school) may depend on the overlap of characteristics of the two settings. Laosa's perspective contrasts with the cultural deficit and genetic-inheritance paradigms typically advanced to account for the lower social position and school failure of ethnic minorities (Laosa, 1984).

In sum, if the nondeficit model is to have a central position in parent programs, current prevailing theories that give rise to the practice of targeting programs for specific populations will need to be abandoned or significantly modified. The dominant social service ideology is not a healthy context for the survival of nondeficit approaches.

Staff roles and competencies.   In addition to a resolution of the incongruity between targeted services and the nondeficit model, there are critical needs and dilemmas that must be addressed if a realignment of parent–professional relations is to be permanent and widespread in parent education programs. A major challenge is to define in clear and detailed operational terms the competencies and behaviors that are indigenous to the collaborator or facilitator roles increasingly advocated for professionals in working with families. What repertoire of responses is needed for different presenting situations of parents? By what process do parents and program staff collaboratively move toward an agreement about the shared world view—that is, the content and method of program services? Experimentation is needed with alternative modes of operation, including negotiation processes. At present, much of the program literature describing the desired realignment delineates what is inappropriate (e.g., dictate to parents) rather than what is appropriate practice. The principles set forth by Dunst and Trivette (Chapter 7), and the experiences of home visitors in the Family Matters program (Mindick, Chapter 3; Cochran, Chapter 4), provide useful guides for future work.

Another challenge is to maintain a practice of co-equal parent–professional relations in a field where there is considerable push to improve workers' professional status. The move toward increased professional status is understandable and needed. There is a problem, though, if such efforts adopt the dominant view of professional status, viz., freedom from lay control, jurisdiction over diagnosis and prescription, and general superiority over the client (Joffe, 1977). Needed in the field is an image of professionalism that incorporates elements of the parent–professional realignment described in Chapter 1 (see also Cochran, Chapter 2; Dunst & Trivette, Chapter 7) while providing a basis for improved salaries and working conditions.

Processes and conditions of empowerment. Advances in the use of empowerment approaches to working with parents depend on conceptual refinement of the construct and further research on the process by which parents come to feel empowered in their child-rearing role. Chapters in this volume point to promising domains for future inquiry. Cochran's research (Chapter 2) suggests the importance of self-perceptions and network ties in the empowerment process. Dunst and Trivette (Chapter 7) offer a conceptual framework that emphasizes the ways in which help is provided. At the same time, the exchange between Mindick (Chapter 3) and Cochran (Chapter 4) on the definition of empowerment is at least one indication that more work needs to be done.

Whether the collaborative parent–professional relations implied in most definitions of the empowerment concept are feasible or appropriate with some population groups needs thoughtful consideration. In reflecting on the extensive experience of the Ounce of Prevention Fund programs for adolescent mothers, Musick and Barbera-Stein (Chapter 9) observe that teenage mothers want structure and firm direction from program staff. In a similar vein, recommendations for conducting psychotherapy with ethnic-minority clients imply that therapists should be structured, authoritarian, and surface-problem orientated (see Sue & Zane, 1987). We need further research on the responses of particular population groups to program workers operating in a nondidactic, collaborative mode. For some populations, the imposition of co-equal relations may be a form of inconsistent world views of what parents need: parents may want a highly didactic professional mode, while the program worker may see a need for the parent to experience a proactive relationship within the program. Staff adherence to a collaborative role may need to be phased in over time, or perhaps not pursued at all. At this point, however, the empirical data base for such decisions is weak. A challenge is to determine the conditions under which collaborative ties between professionals and parents are acceptable and useful to the population to be served.

Social Context of Parenthood

Balancing child, parent, and family needs. As described in Chapter 1, the increased programmatic focus on the social context of family functioning stems from the premise that (a) parental competence is improved when stresses external to the family are reduced or eliminated; and/or (b) it is difficult for parents to attend to the information and suggestions of a parent education program when serious environmental pressures are unresolved. Dunst and Trivette (Chapter 7) offer a detailed rationale for this concept in general and for the latter idea in particular with their argument that parents of handicapped children give low priority to professionally prescribed regimens when basic needs (e.g., shelter, health care) go unmet. Similarly, Unger and Wandersman (Chapter 6) speculate that supportive family ties provide a teenage mother with enough resources so she need not attend to basic stressors on a constant basis. In their study, active program participants had more supportive family ties than inactive program participants. The findings coincide with results of other research involving non-teenage samples (see Powell, 1984; Kessen, Fein, Clarke-Stewart, & Starr, 1975).

The problem with program efforts to reduce environmental stress in parents' lives is that child and parenting issues may get lost in attempts to tackle pressing and multiple stressors. Musick and Barbera-Stein (Chapter 9) report experiences of this nature in Ounce of Prevention Fund programs for teenage mothers. Moreover, the evaluation results of the Child and Family Resource Program may be interpreted as suggesting that family circumstances but not child functioning were improved by the program because home visitors focused almost exclusively on family needs; parenting and child development issues were discussed infrequently (Travers, Irwin, & Nauta, 1982). The assumption that improved conditions for family life (e.g., better housing) or parent functioning (e.g., job training) lead directly to positive child outcomes may be faulty, at least in the case of families in high risk circumstances (Musick & Barbera-Stein, Chapter 9).

Thus, a major challenge is to balance the needs of child, parent, and family in an intervention that has broad content parameters. Demands for crisis assistance may overload program workers, as in the case of the CEDEN program described by Halpern and Larner (Chapter 8). An observational study of one group-based intervention found that even when child and parenting topics were a program focus, parents' interests and needs pushed the content toward larger contextual issues (Powell & Eisenstadt, 1988). Parents' developmental needs may overshadow their interests in a program that gives primary attention to the child (see Halpern & Larner, Chapter 8). To attend to the needs of one party at the exclusion or diminishment of another may prove to be ineffective, however.

Strategies for improving parent–environment relations. Systematic consideration of the social context of parenthood is a relatively new programmatic interest in the parent education field. Some might argue that program attention to environmental influences on parents is not within the domain of parent education. Clearly, it stretches the content boundaries of a field historically focused on the ages, stages, and management of children.

The field needs further development of and experimentation with different models of parent programs that attempt to strengthen parents' relations with the larger social environment. Chapters in this volume provide examples of an empowerment model where direct work with parents is the means by which parent–environment relations are to be improved. The Family, Infant and Pre-school Program (Dunst & Trivette, Chapter 7) gives considerable attention to parents' informal social network ties as an environmental buffer and resource. So did the Family Matters program (Cochran, Chapter 2), although both Family Matters and the Family Development Research Program (Lally, Mangione, & Honig, Chapter 5) also focused on community organizing and formal institutions such as schools. It is interesting to contemplate whether greater program effects could be achieved with an alternative model where there is direct work with both parent *and* community institution(s). One wonders, for instance, whether human service institutions in Syracuse, New York—where both the Family Matters and Family Development Research Program operated at different times—would demonstrate greater responsiveness to families today if the two programs had attempted to have *direct* impact on institutions as well as on parents.

CONCLUDING COMMENT

This brief exploration of future challenges in the design and evaluation of parent–child intervention programs underscores the fragility of emerging direc-tions in the field. The fate of the trends hinges on public policy decisions as well as further advances in conceptual, empirical, and program development work re-garding parent education. Contributions to this volume attest to the progress made to date in understanding appropriate and inappropriate uses of parent edu-cation in early childhood intervention. The chapters give promise of significantly improved strategies for working with parents. The superordinate challenge is to build upon past accomplishments while reframing the concept of parent educa-tion.

REFERENCES

Burns, T., & Stalker, G. M. (1961). *The management of innovation.* London: Tavistock.

Dokecki, P., Roberts, F., & Moroney, R. (1979, August). *Families and professional psychology: Policy implications for training and service.* Paper presented at the annual meeting of the American Psychological Association, New York.

Joffe, C. E. (1977). *Friendly intruders: Childcare professionals and family life.* Berkeley, CA: University of California Press.

Kagan, S. L., Powell, D. R., Weissbourd, B., & Zigler, E. F. (1987). Past accomplishments: Future challenges. In S. L. Kagan, D. R. Powell, B. Weissbourd, & E. F. Zigler (Eds.), *America's family support programs: Perspectives and prospects* (pp. 365-380). New Haven, CT: Yale University Press.

Kamerman, S., & Kahn, A. (1976). *Social services in the United States.* Philadelphia, PA: Temple University Press.

Kessen, W., Fein, G., Clarke-Stewart, A., & Starr, S. (1975). *Variations in home-based infant edu-cation: Language, play and social development.* Final report to the Office of Child Develop-ment, U.S. Department of Health, Education and Welfare. New Haven, CT: Yale University.

Laosa, L. M. (1979). Social competence in childhood: Toward a developmental, socioculturally relativistic paradigm. In M. W. Kent & J. E. Rolf (Eds.), *Primary prevention of psychopathology* (Vol. 3): *Social competence in children.* Hanover, NH: University Press of New England.

Laosa, L. (1984). Social policies toward children of diverse ethnic, racial, and language groups in the United States. In H. W. Stevenson & A. E. Siegel (Eds.), *Child development research and social policy* (pp. 1-109). Chicago, IL: University of Chicago Press.

Miller, L. B., & Bizzell, R. P. (1983). Long-term effects of four preschool programs: 6th, 7th, and 8th grades. *Child Development, 54,* 727-741.

Moroney, R. M. (1980). *Families, social services and social policy.* Washington, DC: U.S. Government Printing Office.

Moroney, R. M. (1987). Social support systems: Families and social policy. In S. L. Kagan, D. R. Powell, B. Weissbourd, & E. F. Zigler (Eds.), *America's family support programs: Perspectives and prospects* (pp. 21-37). New Haven, CT: Yale University Press.

Powell, D. R. (1984). Social network and demographic predictors of length of participation in a parent education program. *Journal of Community Psychology. 12,* 13-20.

Powell, D. R. (1987). Methodological and conceptual problems in research. In S. L. Kagan, D. R. Powell, B. Weissbourd, & E. Zigler (Eds.), *America's family support programs: Perspectives and prospects* (pp. 311-328). New Haven, CT: Yale University Press.

Powell, D. R., & Eisenstadt, J. W. (1988). Informal and formal conversations in parent discussion groups: An observational study. *Family Relations, 37,* 166-170.

Seitz, V. (1987). Outcome evaluation of family support programs: Research design alternatives to true experiments. In S. L. Kagan, D. R. Powell, B. Weissbourd, & E. Zigler (Eds.), *America's family support programs: Perspectives and prospects* (pp. 329-344). New Haven, CT: Yale University Press.

Seitz, V., Rosenbaum, L., & Apfel, N. (1985). Long-term effects of family support intervention: A ten-year followup. *Child Development, 56,* 376-391.

Slaughter, D. T. (1983). Early intervention and its effects on maternal and child development. *Monographs of the Society for Research in Child Development, 48,* (4, Serial No. 202).

Sue, S., & Zane, N. (1987). The role of culture and cultural techniques in psychotherapy: A critique and reformation. *American Psychologist, 42,* 37-45.

Titmuss, R. M. (1968). *Commitment to welfare.* London: Allen & Unwin.

Titmuss, R. M. (1974). *Social policy: An introduction.* New York: Pantheon Books.

Travers, J., Nauta, M., & Irwin, N. (1982). *The effects of a social program: Final report of the Child and Family Resource Program's Infant-Toddler Component.* Cambridge, MA: Abt Associates.

Weiss, H. (1987). Family support and education in early childhood programs. In S. L. Kagan, D. R. Powell, B. Weissbourd, & E. Zigler (Eds.), *America's family support programs: Perspectives and prospects* (pp. 133-160). New Haven, CT: Yale University Press.

Author Index

Subject Index